DESKTOP PUBLISHING SOURCEBOOK

FONTS and CLIP-ART

For the IBM™ PC and Compatibles

Jami Lynne Borman

Prima Publishing & Communications
P.O. Box 1260IBM
Rocklin, CA 95677
(916) 624-5718

Editing, Typography, and Production by Instruction Writers
Jacket Design by Wolfe Design Group

Prima Publishing & Communications
Rocklin, CA

Library of Congress Cataloging-in-Publication Data

Borman, Jami Lynne.
Desktop publishing sourcebook : fonts and clip-art for the IBM-PC and compatibles / Jami Lynne Borman.
p. cm.
ISBN 1-55958-031-3
1. Desktop publishing. 2. IBM Personal Computer--Programming. 3. Type and type-founding--Data processing. 4. Copy art--Data processing. I. Title.
Z286.D47B62 1990
686.2'2544536--dc20
90-36215
CIP

90 91 92 93 RRD 10 9 8 7 6 5 4 3 2 1

Printed in the United States of America

How To Order
Quantity discounts are available from the publisher, Prima Publishing & Communications, P.O. Box 1260IBM, Rocklin, CA 95677; telephone (916) 624-5718. On your letterhead include information concerning the intended use of the books and the number of books you wish to purchase.

U.S. Bookstores and Libraries: Please submit all orders to St. Martin's Press, 175 Fifth Avenue, New York, NY 10010; telephone (212) 674-5151.

Dedication

For all of us who refused to believe that powerful, effective desktop publishing can't be done on a PC.

Acknowledgements

My many thanks to the following writers and artists for their contribution in preparing this manuscript: Gene Bjerke, Scott Borman-Allen, Carole Garner, Edward Offutt, Thomas M. Schach, and C. Claire Smith.

I would also like to thank the companies represented in this book for their contribution of time, technical assistance, and evaluation software.

Thanks to all of you at St. Martin's Press, Prima Publishing, Bookman Productions, and Waterside Productions for your input and enthusiastic support of this project. And especially to Ben Dominitz who helped make my idea for this book a reality.

Foreword

The Number One problem desktop publishers face when choosing appropriate typefaces and clip-art is not one of selection but of accessibility.

The problem is not that numerous typefaces— or fonts— and clip-art illustrations aren't available, the problem is *finding them when you need them!* But, help is available: Jami Borman's *Desktop Publishing Sourcebook: Fonts and Clip-Art for the IBM PC and Compatibles* to the rescue!

In this handy volume, Jami Borman has assembled representative samples of type and clip-art from leading software publishers — both large and small. Leafing through the *Desktop Publishing Sourcebook* is like having the world's largest computer store at your disposal — only there's scant hope that even the world's largest computer store would offer as many alternatives!

Desktop Publishing Sourcebook is a major improvement over the catalogs offered by individual typeface publishers. This is because typefaces are organized by characteristics. This broadens your options, allowing you to choose by design, rather than by publisher. Since upper and lowercase alphabet samples are reproduced in the same size, you can easily compare word density and line lengths.

Likewise, the clip-art section allows you to easily compare both image appropriateness and quality from numerous vendors. By analyzing the illustration quality offered by the various clip-art publishers, you can avoid making an expensive mistake by "buying blind." Before you buy, you can make sure that the image quality is appropriate for your publication.

Jami Borman has done more than simply catalog available typefaces and clip-art in *Desktop Publishing Sourcebook*, however. Jami has included a great deal of practical advice. This advice can help you choose the right typeface and make the most of it when it arrives. The *Desktop Publishing Sourcebook* also contains discussions of the various clip-art file formats, information about re-sizing images and warnings about possible copyright limitations.

If you're new to desktop publishing, you'll appreciate *Desktop Publishing Sourcebook*'s combination of helpful information and useful reference materials. If you're a more experienced desktop publisher, you'll find the *Desktop Publishing Sourcebook* will help you review the basics and quickly locate the particular typeface or illustration needed to complete your project.

Roger C. Parker
Author of *Looking Good in Print: A Guide to Basic Design for Desktop Publishing*

Contents

1 Introduction

2 Working With Fonts

3 PostScript Fonts

4 LaserJet Fonts

5 Font Companies

6 Working With Graphics

7 Graphic Companies

8 Appendix

9 Index

1 Introduction

Welcome to ***Desktop Publishing Sourcebook*** *(Blue Book, for short)* for IBM PCs and compatibles. If you're an experienced desktop publisher (or even if you're not) you'll find this book indispensable. No need to drive for hours or read through mountains of brochures to find what you need. The *Blue Book* brings the store to you.

Throughout these pages you'll find hundreds of font and clip-art (graphic) samples from dozens of manufacturers. We've even included two chapters which cover font and graphic basics. Learning the basics will help make your font and graphic purchases go more smoothly. (See Chapter 2, *Working With Fonts* and Chapter 6, *Working With Graphics*.)

What's Here

The *Blue Book* is divided into eight chapters and an index.

Chapter 1 Introduction

The *Introduction* (this chapter) gives you an overview of the *Blue Book*. It explains how to use the book effectively; purchase fonts and clip-art; and select fonts that are compatible with your laser printer.

Chapter 2 Working With Fonts

Working With Fonts covers the font basics such as font terminology, how to refer to fonts, and how to manage fonts.

Chapter 3 PostScript Fonts

Chapter 3 is the first of two chapters in which fonts are displayed. *PostScript Fonts* has hundreds of font samples that are available for PostScript printers. If your printer has both PostScript and LaserJet capabilities, you'll want to refer to both this chapter and Chapter 4 *LaserJet Fonts.*

Chapter 4 LaserJet Fonts

Chapter 4 is the second chapter in which fonts are displayed. *LaserJet Fonts* has hundreds of font samples that are available for your Hewlett Packard LaserJet Series II, LaserJet III, or printer that emulates the Hewlett Packard LaserJet printers (printers that use *PCL,* which stands for Printer Control Language). If your printer also has PostScript capabilities, you'll want to refer to this chapter and Chapter 3 *PostScript Fonts.*

Chapter 5 Font Companies

This chapter provides a short profile on each font company and lists the company's font product line.

Chapter 6 Working With Graphics

Working With Graphics covers graphic basics such as different graphic formats, scaling images correctly, and staying within the copyright law.

Chapter 7 Graphic Companies

This chapter provides a short profile on each graphic company and shows you samples from each clip-art collection that the company offers.[1]

---

[1] *Archive Arts* only provided the author with two complete clip-art packages. For this reason, only two of their packages are shown.

Chapter 8 Appendix

The *Appendix* lists various foreign language and symbol fonts that are available.

How This Book Can Help You

The *Blue Book* shows you so many fonts and graphics that it's hard to spend much time with the book without getting your creative juices flowing.

But the main goal of the *Blue Book* is to help you quickly put your fingers on the information you need. It tells you the *who*, the *what*, and the *what else* of fonts and graphics.

The Who

The *Who*, of course, are the companies who make fonts and graphics. Suppose that you want to know...

Which fonts work with your printer.

The *Blue Book* has two chapters of font samples for the two most popular font formats (PostScript and LaserJet).

If your printer has Postscript capabilities, check Chapter 3 *PostScript Fonts*.

If your printer has LaserJet capabilities, check Chapter 4 *LaserJet Fonts*.

If your printer has both Postscript and LaserJet capabilities, be sure to check both chapters: Chapter 3 *PostScript Fonts* and Chapter 4 *LaserJet Fonts*.

Which company carries a font that you like.

Lookup the font alphabetically in the index.

How to contact a font or graphic company.

Check the company's listing in Chapter 5, *Font Companies* or Chapter 7, *Graphic Companies*. Here you'll find a short profile about each company and their products as well as the company's address, phone number, and FAX number.

Which companies make a specific foreign language or symbol font.

In the *Appendix*, you'll find two alphabetical listings: one for foreign language fonts and another for symbol fonts. Each foreign language and symbol font is accompanied by the names of the companies which offer the font. At the end of the *Appendix*, each company's name, address, and phone number is listed.

The What

The *What* refers to the fonts and graphics themselves. Suppose you want to...

Learn some font basics.

Read Chapter 2, *Working With Fonts*. This chapter has information on how to use, manage, and refer to fonts.

Learn more about graphics.

Open the book to Chapter 6, *Working With Graphics*. Here you'll learn about graphic formats, how to scale a graphic image while keeping it in proportion, and how to use graphics without violating the copyright law.

See hundreds of font samples.

Refer to Chapters 3 and 4. There you'll find hundreds of font samples in alphabetical order, each displayed in 14pt type (when available).

Each sample includes the entire upper and lower case alphabet[2], the numbers 0-9, and several popular symbols. The companies that carry the font follow each font sample.

See hundreds of clip-art samples.
Open the *Blue Book* to Chapter 7, *Graphic Companies.* Here you'll find sample clip-art from the collections offered by each graphic company. You can also read about each company and its product line.

Know which font package includes the font you've selected.
Chapter 5, *Font Companies,* displays each company's product line of English-language fonts organized by font package. (Most font packages include a *font family*--three or four weights of the same font style.) You can find a font by browsing through the package listings or looking up the font name in the *Index.*

What foreign language fonts and symbol fonts are available.
In the *Appendix* you'll discover a list of foreign language fonts and a list of symbol fonts. Each font is followed by the name of the companies which offer it.

The What Else

Some products are also available for the Macintosh.
If your office uses both IBMs and Macs, you may want to purchase identical fonts or graphics for both systems.

In Chapter 5 *(Font Companies)* and Chapter 7 *(Graphic Companies)* you'll find a key in the upper right-hand corner of the first page of each company's listing. This key tells you whether the company's products are only available for the IBM, or are also available for the Macintosh.

---

[2] Some display fonts do not include lower case letters, numbers, and/or symbols.

When the key indicates that products are available for the Mac, it doesn't necessarily mean that *all* of the company's products are available for the Mac. Be sure to read the short section of text that follows the company listing to determine which part of the product line is available for Macintosh computers.

For a broader selection of Mac fonts and graphics, see ***Desktop Publishing Sourcebook, Fonts and Clip-Art For the Macintosh*** by Jami Lynne Borman (Prima Publishing).

What You See Is How It Looks.

All of the text and samples for the *Blue Book* were produced using 300 *dpi* (*d*ots *p*er *i*nch) laser printers. Why didn't we use a typesetter (1000+ dpi)? Because most businesses are using 300 dpi laser printers to produce their final copy.

Since most of our readers are printing at 300 dpi, we elected to show the font and graphic samples at the same resolution as most office laser printers. Of course, if you are using a typesetter, your output will look even better than the samples in this book.

Take advantage of the *Blue Book's* cross-referencing.

When you see a font in one of the font chapters (Chapters 3 and 4) that you'd like to purchase, look at the names of the font companies that appear below it. These are the companies that offer the font.

Next, flip to Chapter 5 *(Font Companies)* to locate one of the companies that was listed below the font name. Browse through the pages that follow the company listing to identify which font package includes the font you like. Alternatively, you can look-up the font name in the *Index*.

Purchasing fonts and clip-art.

Many of the fonts and graphics displayed on these pages *cannot* be found at your local software store. Fortunately, most font and graphic companies will sell you their products directly or at least point you to a store that carries them.

Upon request, *some* companies will also sell a font or graphic individually--although the per item price is not as competitive as the package price. If you prefer to purchase an individual font or graphic instead of the entire package, just contact the company and ask.

Printers and the PC

The *resolution* (print quality) of a laser printer is measured in dots per linear inch, commonly referred to as *dpi*. The higher the dpi, the sharper the printed image. Typeset quality begins around 1000 dpi.

Most business use laser printers, rather than dot matrix or daisy-wheel printers, because of their superior print quality. Laser printers typically have a resolution of 300 dpi (90,000 dots per square inch)--a significantly higher number than dot matrix printers. Even as you read this, laser printer products are being introduced to the market with resolutions of 600 dpi (360,000 dots per square inch) and higher.

The resolution of daisy-wheel printers is not measured in dpi. A daisy-wheel printer is similar to a typewriter in that each letter is printed when a key strikes the paper. For this reason, daisy-wheel printers cannot use the fonts and graphics that are displayed in this book.

How Does PostScript Work?

PostScript is a page description language licensed by Adobe Systems, Inc. PostScript instructions are sent to the printer by your computer which describes the shape of every PostScript character or graphic to be printed. The printer, upon receiving these instructions, converts each object into a dot pattern. The dot patterns are then fused to your paper using *toner*, an ink-like chemical.

PostScript Printers

PostScript laser printers typically have a number of popular fonts built-in, 300 dpi resolution, and a processor (a brain) which converts the PostScript instructions (sent by your computer) into the dots that make up the printed image. This processor is what typically makes PostScript laser printers more expensive than LaserJet or LaserJet-compatible printers. Not all PostScript printers use the Abode-licensed language. Printers which do not use Adobe PostScript are sometime referred to as *PostScript-compatible* printers.

PostScript printers handle fonts very differently than LaserJet printers. When you purchase a PostScript font you are actually purchasing a *font outline* that can be scaled to any size you want.

When you select a font in your document, you are telling your word processing or page layout program which size font you want to use. Later, when you print your document, your printer scales the fonts *on the fly*. In other words, your printer scales the fonts to the sizes you selected, as needed.

PostScript fonts have two advantages and one disadvantage when compared to LaserJet fonts. The first advantage is that one font outline gives you every font size possible. The second advantage is that since a font outline is used rather that individual fonts for each and every point size, PostScript fonts take up significantly less space on your hard disk and memory in your computer. The disadvantage is that pages that are printed using PostScript outlines take longer to print than pages which are printed with LaserJet fonts that have been downloaded to your printer.

PostScript printers have an edge over LaserJets when it comes to graphics. Graphics for PostScript printers typically come in a format called *Encapsulated PostScript* (commonly referred to as *EPS*). Similar to PostScript fonts, EPS graphics may be scaled to any size you wish without affecting the quality of your image. PostScript printers can also print the graphic formats that are available for LaserJet printers.

LaserJet Printers

LaserJet printers are typically less expensive than their PostScript cousins. They vary in features, typically have 300 dpi resolution, and sport a limited number of high-quality fonts. They frequently include expansion slots that allow you to increase the printer's memory, upgrade the resolution, and/or add PostScript capabilities.

LaserJet printers require that you have fonts in each size that you want to use. Most companies offer LaserJet fonts in specific sizes. Other companies offer *scalable* fonts for the LaserJet. With scalable fonts you get font generation software that lets you create fonts in any size. Unlike PostScript outlines, however, scalable fonts are *not* created on the fly. Specific fonts sizes must be selected and created before using the fonts in your document.

Getting Included

If your company produces original fonts or clip-art and would like to be included in the next edition of the *Blue Book*, please contact the author at the address shown below.

Getting In Touch

The author would like to receive your comments on how future editions of the *Blue Book* can be improved. You may write to her (no phone calls please) care of

Instruction Writers
P.O. Box 2218
Montgomery Village, Maryland 20886

About The Author

Jami Lynne Borman is Director of Software Support for Instruction Writers, a company in Gaithersburg, Maryland which writes user manuals for computer software and other products. Ms. Borman's other books include

Desktop Publishing Sourcebook Fonts and Clip-Art For the Macintosh (Prima Publishing)

WordPerfect 5 Desktop Publishing Ideas & Techniques (COMPUTE! Books)

WordPerfect Business Macros (Scott Foresman).

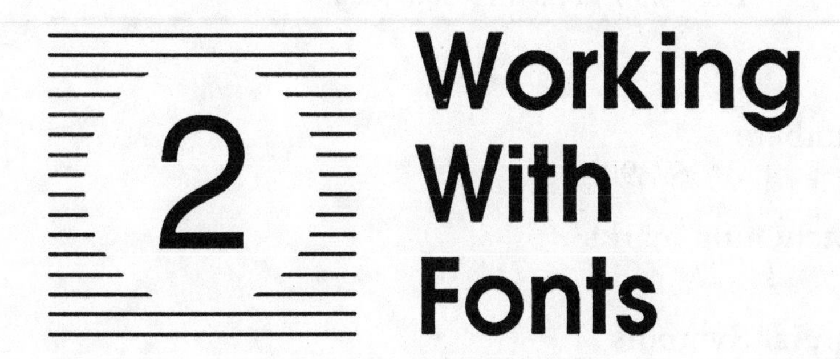

Making a decision about which fonts to buy can be as complex and technical as selecting the right computer. This chapter will help you make your font purchases go more smoothly.

If you are just beginning to work with fonts (or have never worked with them before), you need to learn some basics. If you have worked with fonts before, you may want to skip the basics and begin with *Making A Font Purchase* (page 17).

Font Basics

What Is A Font?

A font is a collection of characters (called a character set) of the same size and type style. Every character set[1] includes at minimum the characters shown below.

- **Upper Case Alphabet**
  ABCDEFGHIJKLMNOPQRSTUVWXYZ
- **Lower Case Alphabet**
  abcdefghijklmnopqrstuvwxyz

---

[1] Some special purpose fonts (e.g., dingbats, display fonts) may not include all the characters in a typical character set.

- **Numbers**
  1234567890
- **Punctuation marks**
  !,.?;:'"
- **Popular Symbols**
  <>/[]{}=+-_()*&^%$#@~'\ |

Many character sets also include bullets, arrows, foreign language accents, the copyright symbol, the line draw characters, and other useful symbols.

Talking About Fonts

Every font is identified by its *style, weight* and *size.* For example,

Times Roman	**Bold**	**12pt**
ITC Bookman	Light	10pt
Hevetica Narrow	*Oblique*	*14pt*

Font Style

The font style is the *look* of the font--the characteristics that make it visually unique. Every font is referred to by its style name. For example,

Times Roman
Helvetica
Palatino
New Century Schoolbook
Avant Garde

Many style names have the name of the type foundry (the company that designed the font) as a prefix. The two most common prefixes are *CG* (Compugraphic Corporation) and *ITC* (International Typeface Corporation).

Font Size

Font size is measured in points (pts). The size most often used for text is 10-12 pts. Point size is a vertical measurement; horizontal measurement is not taken into consideration. At first, you may find it difficult to use an unfamiliar measurement; but soon it will feel very natural to refer to a font in points.

8pt
10pt
11pt
12pt
14pt
16pt
18pt
20pt
24pt
30pt
36pt
45pt
72pt

When measuring the point size of a font, the measurement is taken from the top of an ascender (b, f, h, k, l, t) to the bottom of a descender (g, j, p, q, y). Since few characters have both an ascender and a descender, an individual character typically does not measure the full point size. As a matter of fact, the same letter in different font styles can have different vertical measurements, even when both letters are the same point size.

A font's x-height refers to the size of a character, ignoring its ascender and/or descender. X-height also refers to the size of a font's characters that have no ascender or descender (a, c, e, m, n, o, r, s, u, v, x, z).

X-HEIGHT

xylophone xylophone

Avant Garde 20pt **Times Roman 20pt**

Font Weight

Weight refers to the heft and/or slant of a font. Most fonts are available in the weights

Medium (or Roman or Book)
Bold
Italics (or Oblique)
Bold Italics

Some decorative fonts (e.g., *Zapf Chancery® Medium Italic*) are only available in one weight. A few fonts (e.g. Helvetica) are available in a variety of weights.

Letter Spacing

Most fonts are proportionally spaced. This means that the amount of horizontal space that each letter occupies on the line varies. For example, an *m* takes up more line space than an *i* or a *j*.

Some fonts are fixed-pitch. Fixed-pitch fonts are similar to typewriter type in that each letter occupies the same amount of line space. Fixed-pitch fonts are typically measured in characters per inch (c.p.i.). Most printers come with at least one fixed-pitch font built-in (typically courier).

Courier Sample

```
Who are you who lives behind my mirror?
You follow my every move.  Are you
imitating me?  Perhaps, I'm imitating
you.
```

Times Roman Sample

Who are you who lives behind my mirror? You follow my every move. Are you imitating me? Perhaps, I'm imitating you.

Kerning is a type of letter spacing between specific letter pairs (e.g., *th* and *fi*). The space between the letters is reduced to improve their readability and aesthetic appearance. Kerning is not very visible in fonts smaller than 16 points. Most word processing and page layout programs let you turn the kerning off and on. Other programs let you control which letter pairs are kerned and how close together the letters are placed.

Line Spacing

Many word processing and other programs allow you to vary the amount of space between your lines of text. This space is called leading (rhymes with wedding). Font styles which have long ascenders or descenders need more leading than fonts that don't. In publishing, the font size and leading is described as a fraction. For example, *10/12* (which is read "10 on 12") indicates 10pt type with 2pt leading.

Unlike fonts, lines have a horizontal as well as a vertical measurement. This measurement is expressed in picas.

12pt = 1 pica
72pt = 1 inch
6 picas = 1 inch

Although many programs do not use the terms *leading* and *pica*, you should be familiar with them if you plan to have your documents typeset at the printer.

Font Groups

There is much discussion on the emotional effect that one type style has over another. The type styles you select for your document or presentation material will have an effect on how your message is perceived. Fonts help convey certain *feelings*.

Fonts are not divided into classifications based on their emotional effect, but they are typically divided into three groups: Serif, Sans Serif, and Display.

Serif Fonts

Typefaces in the *serif* group category have additional strokes (often called feet) at the bottom of each letter. Serif type styles are typically considered businesslike, formal, and authoritative. Sample serif fonts include

Courier
Bookman
Palatino
Times Roman

Many people feel that serif type styles are more readable than sans serif type styles for large bodies of text--particularly when the text is printed in 12pt type or smaller.

Sans Serif Fonts

Type styles in the *sans serif* group do not have serifs. As a matter of fact, *sans* means *without* in French. Sans serif fonts have very clean lines and are typically considered friendly, casual, and familiar. Sample sans serif fonts include

Avant Garde
Helvetica
Micro

Display Fonts

Display (or decorative) type styles can be either serif or sans serif. Type styles in this group are used to create a dramatic effect in headings, logos, and product names. They are rarely used in long passages of text since they are typically difficult to read. Sample display fonts include

Gregorian
Kells
Paladin
Zapf Chancery Medium Italic

Making A Font Purchase

All of the fonts displayed in this book are soft fonts. Soft fonts come on diskettes, are copied into your computer, and are then *downloaded* (sent) to your printer. All laser printers made today can accept soft fonts of one type or another.

Soft Font Formats

Today, in the IBM-compatible world, there are two main font standards: PostScript and LaserJet II/III (printers that use PCL). (*PCL* is the language found in Hewlett Packard (HP) printers and those that emulate the HP printers.)

Before you select fonts for your printer, you must determine whether your printer can accept PostScript fonts, LaserJet fonts, or both. PostScript fonts and LaserJet fonts are not compatible--hence, they are not interchangeable.

If you have a printer that accepts both PostScript and LaserJet fonts, you need to decide which fonts you want to have in the PostScript version and which fonts you want to have in the LaserJet version. Not all fonts are available in both formats; nor may you mix formats within the same document. For a more extensive discussion of PostScript and LaserJet printers, see Chapter 1, *Introduction*.

Printer Memory

Before you purchase fonts, you need to make sure that you have enough memory in your printer to handle the fonts. If you are purchasing PostScript fonts, this is less of an issue than when you are purchasing LaserJet fonts. PostScript outlines take significantly less printer memory than most of the individual fonts required by LaserJet printers.

Many printers come standard with 500K of memory. This amount of memory is typically insufficient for desktop publishing. At least 2000K (2 megabytes) of memory is recommended if you want to create complex page layouts.

Font Management Software

Word processing and page layout programs (application programs) need a printer driver that explains how to use the fonts that you've purchased. Font management software is often included with your font purchase and helps you create the needed printer driver.

Since the printer drivers used by each application program are unique, make sure that the font company's font management software can create a printer driver for *your* word processing and/or page layout program.

Some font management software also lets you download the fonts to your printer. This is a necessity if your application program does not include a feature that downloads your fonts for you. Even if your application program has a download feature, downloading your fonts before entering your application significantly decreases the time it takes to print your document.

Screen Fonts

Some fonts come with both screen fonts and printer fonts. The screen font is used to display your font on the screen so you may see the font as you manipulate your text. Programs that do not show your text in *WYSIWYG* format (*What You See Is What You Get*) do not use screen fonts. If you plan to use your fonts in a WYSIWYG program, be sure that the fonts you want to purchase have both screen fonts and printer fonts available.

3 PostScript Fonts

There is no shortage of the selection of fonts that are available for your PostScript printer. This chapter includes over 550 English-language font styles that are available exclusively for printers with PostScript capabilities. These pages include fonts from

Adobe® Systems, Inc.
Bitstream®, Inc.
Casady & Greene, Inc.

Each font is displayed in 14-point type and includes the name of the font; the upper case and lower case alphabets; the numbers 0-9; and several symbols. Some fonts (such as those used for display) do not include all these characters. The fonts are listed in alphabetical order by font name, except when

- The font style is not the first part of the font name. For example, *Stempel Garamond* appears with the *Garamond* styles.
- The font name has a prefix such as *Adobe, Bitstream,* CG or *ITC*.

Below each font you'll find the company or companies that offer the font for sale. For more information about each font company and its product line, see Chapter 5, *Font Companies*.

Aachen Bold

ABCDEFGHIJKLMNOPQRSTUVWXYZ
abcdefghijklmnopqrstuvwxyz
1234567890?!$%&

Adobe Systems, Inc.

ABILENE

ABCDEFGHIJKLMNOPQRSTUVWXYZ
ABCDEFGHIJKLMNOPQRSTUVWXYZ
1234567890?!$%&

Casady & Greene, Inc.

Akzidenz Grotesk Roman

ABCDEFGHIJKLMNOPQRSTUVWXYZ
abcdefghijklmnopqrstuvwxyz
1234567890?!$%&

Adobe Systems, Inc.

Akzidenz Grotesk Bold

ABCDEFGHIJKLMNOPQRSTUVWXYZ
abcdefghijklmnopqrstuvwxyz
1234567890?!$%&

Adobe Systems, Inc.

Akzidenz Grotesk® Black

ABCDEFGHIJKLMNOPQRSTUVWXYZ
abcdefghijklmnopqrstuvwxyz
1234567890?!$%&

Adobe Systems, Inc.

Akzidenz Grotesk Light

ABCDEFGHIJKLMNOPQRSTUVWXYZ
abcdefghijklmnopqrstuvwxyz
1234567890?!$%&

Adobe Systems, Inc.

Alexandria

ABCDEFGHIJKLMNOPQRSTUVWXYZ
abcdefghijklmnopqrstuvwxyz
1234567890?!$%&

Casady & Greene, Inc.

Alexandria Italic

ABCDEFGHIJKLMNOPQRSTUVWXYZ
abcdefghijklmnopqrstuvwxyz
1234567890?!$%&

Casady & Greene, Inc.

Alexandria Bold

ABCDEFGHIJKLMNOPQRSTUVWXYZ
abcdefghijklmnopqrstuvwxyz
1234567890?!$%&

Casady & Greene, Inc.

Alexandria Bold Italic

ABCDEFGHIJKLMNOPQRSTUVWXYZ
abcdefghijklmnopqrstuvwxyz
1234567890?!$%&

Casady & Greene, Inc.

ITC American Typewriter®

ABCDEFGHIJKLMNOPQRSTUVWXYZ
abcdefghijklmnopqrstuvwxyz
1234567890?!$%&

Adobe Systems, Inc. / Bitstream, Inc.

American Typewriter Bold

ABCDEFGHIJKLMNOPQRSTUVWXYZ
abcdefghijklmnopqrstuvwxyz
1234567890?!$%&

Adobe Systems, Inc. / Bitstream, Inc.

Americana®

ABCDEFGHIJKLMNOPQRSTUVWXYZ
abcdefghijklmnopqrstuvwxyz
1234567890?!$%&

Adobe Systems, Inc.

Americana Italic

ABCDEFGHIJKLMNOPQRSTUVWXYZ
abcdefghijklmnopqrstuvwxyz
1234567890?!$%&

Adobe Systems, Inc.

Americana Bold

ABCDEFGHIJKLMNOPQRSTUVWXYZ
abcdefghijklmnopqrstuvwxyz
1234567890?!$%&

Adobe Systems, Inc.

Americana Extra Bold
ABCDEFGHIJKLMNOPQRSTUVWXYZ
abcdefghijklmnopqrstuvwxyz
1234567890?!$%&
Adobe Systems, Inc.

Antique Olive™
ABCDEFGHIJKLMNOPQRSTUVWXYZ
abcdefghijklmnopqrstuvwxyz
1234567890?!$%&
Adobe Systems, Inc.

Antique Olive Italic
ABCDEFGHIJKLMNOPQRSTUVWXYZ
abcdefghijklmnopqrstuvwxyz
1234567890?!$%&
Adobe Systems, Inc.

Antique Olive Bold
ABCDEFGHIJKLMNOPQRSTUVWXYZ
abcdefghijklmnopqrstuvwxyz
1234567890?!$%&
Adobe Systems, Inc.

Antique Olive Black
ABCDEFGHIJKLMNOPQRSTUVWXYZ
abcdefghijklmnopqrstuvwxyz
1234567890?!$%&
Adobe Systems, Inc.

Antique Olive Light

ABCDEFGHIJKLMNOPQRSTUVWXYZ
abcdefghijklmnopqrstuvwxyz
1234567890?!$%&

Adobe Systems, Inc.

Arnold Bocklin

ABCDEFGHIJKLMNOPQRSTUVWXYZ
abcdefghijklmnopqrstuvwxyz
1234567890?!$%&

Adobe Systems, Inc.

ITC Avant Garde Gothic® Book

ABCDEFGHIJKLMNOPQRSTUVWXYZ
abcdefghijklmnopqrstuvwxyz
1234567890?!$%&

Adobe Systems, Inc. / Bitstream, Inc.

ITC Avant Garde Gothic Book Oblique

ABCDEFGHIJKLMNOPQRSTUVWXYZ
abcdefghijklmnopqrstuvwxyz
1234567890?!$%&

Adobe Systems, Inc.

ITC Avant Garde Gothic Demi

ABCDEFGHIJKLMNOPQRSTUVWXYZ
abcdefghijklmnopqrstuvwxyz
1234567890?!$%&

Adobe Systems, Inc. / Bitstream, Inc.

ITC Avant Garde Gothic Demi Oblique

ABCDEFGHIJKLMNOPQRSTUVWXYZ

abcdefghijklmnopqrstuvwxyz

1234567890?!$%&

Adobe Systems, Inc.

Avenir™ 35 Light

ABCDEFGHIJKLMNOPQRSTUVWXYZ

abcdefghijklmnopqrstuvwxyz

1234567890?!$%&

Adobe Systems, Inc.

Avenir 35 Light Oblique

ABCDEFGHIJKLMNOPQRSTUVWXYZ

abcdefghijklmnopqrstuvwxyz

1234567890?!$%&

Adobe Systems, Inc.

Avenir 45 Book

ABCDEFGHIJKLMNOPQRSTUVWXYZ

abcdefghijklmnopqrstuvwxyz

1234567890?!$%&

Adobe Systems, Inc.

Avenir 45 Book Oblique

ABCDEFGHIJKLMNOPQRSTUVWXYZ

abcdefghijklmnopqrstuvwxyz

1234567890?!$%&

Adobe Systems, Inc.

Avenir 55 Roman

ABCDEFGHIJKLMNOPQRSTUVWXYZ
abcdefghijklmnopqrstuvwxyz
1234567890?!$%&
Adobe Systems, Inc.

Avenir 55 Oblique

ABCDEFGHIJKLMNOPQRSTUVWXYZ
abcdefghijklmnopqrstuvwxyz
1234567890?!$%&
Adobe Systems, Inc.

Avenir 65 Medium

ABCDEFGHIJKLMNOPQRSTUVWXYZ
abcdefghijklmnopqrstuvwxyz
1234567890?!$%&
Adobe Systems, Inc.

Avenir 65 Medium Oblique

ABCDEFGHIJKLMNOPQRSTUVWXYZ
abcdefghijklmnopqrstuvwxyz
1234567890?!$%&
Adobe Systems, Inc.

Avenir 85 Heavy

ABCDEFGHIJKLMNOPQRSTUVWXYZ
abcdefghijklmnopqrstuvwxyz
1234567890?!$%&
Adobe Systems, Inc.

Avenir 85 Heavy Oblique

ABCDEFGHIJKLMNOPQRSTUVWXYZ

abcdefghijklmnopqrstuvwxyz

1234567890?!$%&

Adobe Systems, Inc.

Avenir 95 Black

ABCDEFGHIJKLMNOPQRSTUVWXYZ

abcdefghijklmnopqrstuvwxyz

1234567890?!$%&

Adobe Systems, Inc.

Avenir 95 Black Oblique

ABCDEFGHIJKLMNOPQRSTUVWXYZ

abcdefghijklmnopqrstuvwxyz

1234567890?!$%&

Adobe Systems, Inc.

Bauer Bodoni Roman

ABCDEFGHIJKLMNOPQRSTUVWXYZ

abcdefghijklmnopqrstuvwxyz

1234567890?!$%&

Adobe Systems, Inc.

Bauer Bodoni Italic

ABCDEFGHIJKLMNOPQRSTUVWXYZ

abcdefghijklmnopqrstuvwxyz

1234567890?!$%&

Adobe Systems, Inc.

Bauer Bodoni® Bold

ABCDEFGHIJKLMNOPQRSTUVWXYZ
abcdefghijklmnopqrstuvwxyz
1234567890?!$%&
Adobe Systems, Inc.

Bauer Bodoni Bold Italic

ABCDEFGHIJKLMNOPQRSTUVWXYZ
abcdefghijklmnopqrstuvwxyz
1234567890?!$%&
Adobe Systems, Inc.

ITC Bauhaus Medium

ABCDEFGHIJKLMNOPQRSTUVWXYZ
abcdefghijklmnopqrstuvwxyz
1234567890?!$%&
Adobe Systems, Inc.

ITC Bauhaus™ Bold

ABCDEFGHIJKLMNOPQRSTUVWXYZ
abcdefghijklmnopqrstuvwxyz
1234567890?!$%&
Adobe Systems, Inc.

ITC Bauhaus Demi

ABCDEFGHIJKLMNOPQRSTUVWXYZ
abcdefghijklmnopqrstuvwxyz
1234567890?!$%&
Adobe Systems, Inc.

ITC Bauhaus Heavy

ABCDEFGHIJKLMNOPQRSTUVWXYZ
abcdefghijklmnopqrstuvwxyz
1234567890?!$%&
Adobe Systems, Inc.

ITC Bauhaus Light

ABCDEFGHIJKLMNOPQRSTUVWXYZ
abcdefghijklmnopqrstuvwxyz
1234567890?!$%&
Adobe Systems, Inc.

Belwe Medium

ABCDEFGHIJKLMNOPQRSTUVWXYZ
abcdefghijklmnopqrstuvwxyz
1234567890?!$%&
Adobe Systems, Inc.

Belwe Bold

ABCDEFGHIJKLMNOPQRSTUVWXYZ
abcdefghijklmnopqrstuvwxyz
1234567890?!$%&
Adobe Systems, Inc.

Belwe Light

ABCDEFGHIJKLMNOPQRSTUVWXYZ
abcdefghijklmnopqrstuvwxyz
1234567890?!$%&
Adobe Systems, Inc.

Belwe Condensed

ABCDEFGHIJKLMNOPQRSTUVWXYZ
abcdefghijklmnopqrstuvwxyz
1234567890?!$%&

Adobe Systems, Inc.

ITC Benguiat®

ABCDEFGHIJKLMNOPQRSTUVWXYZ
abcdefghijklmnopqrstuvwxyz
1234567890?!$%&

Adobe Systems, Inc. / Bitstream, Inc.

ITC Benguiat Book Italic

ABCDEFGHIJKLMNOPQRSTUVWXYZ
abcdefghijklmnopqrstuvwxyz
1234567890?!$%&

Bitstream, Inc.

ITC Benguiat Bold

ABCDEFGHIJKLMNOPQRSTUVWXYZ
abcdefghijklmnopqrstuvwxyz
1234567890?!$%&

Adobe Systems, Inc. / Bitstream, Inc.

ITC Benguiat Bold Italic

ABCDEFGHIJKLMNOPQRSTUVWXYZ
abcdefghijklmnopqrstuvwxyz
1234567890?!$%&

Bitstream, Inc.

Bodoni

ABCDEFGHIJKLMNOPQRSTUVWXYZ
abcdefghijklmnopqrstuvwxyz
1234567890?!$%&

Adobe Systems, Inc.

Bodoni

ABCDEFGHIJKLMNOPQRSTUVWXYZ
abcdefghijklmnopqrstuvwxyz
1234567890?!$%&

Casady & Greene, Inc.

Bodoni Book

ABCDEFGHIJKLMNOPQRSTUVWXYZ
abcdefghijklmnopqrstuvwxyz
1234567890?!$%&

Bitstream, Inc.

Bodoni Italic

ABCDEFGHIJKLMNOPQRSTUVWXYZ
abcdefghijklmnopqrstuvwxyz
1234567890?!$%&

Adobe Systems, Inc.

Bodoni Italic

ABCDEFGHIJKLMNOPQRSTUVWXYZ
abcdefghijklmnopqrstuvwxyz
1234567890?!$%&

Casady & Greene, Inc.

Bodoni Book Italic

ABCDEFGHIJKLMNOPQRSTUVWXYZ

abcdefghijklmnopqrstuvwxyz

1234567890?!$%&

Bitstream, Inc.

Bodoni Bold

ABCDEFGHIJKLMNOPQRSTUVWXYZ

abcdefghijklmnopqrstuvwxyz

1234567890?!$%&

Adobe Systems, Inc.

Bodoni Bold

ABCDEFGHIJKLMNOPQRSTUVWXYZ

abcdefghijklmnopqrstuvwxyz

1234567890?!$%&

Bitstream, Inc.

Bodoni Bold

ABCDEFGHIJKLMNOPQRSTUVWXYZ

abcdefghijklmnopqrstuvwxyz

1234567890?!$%&

Casady & Greene, Inc.

Bodoni Ultra

ABCDEFGHIJKLMNOPQRSTUVWXYZ

abcdefghijklmnopqrstuvwxyz

1234567890?!$%&

Casady & Greene, Inc.

Bodoni Poster

ABCDEFGHIJKLMNOPQRSTUVWXYZ
abcdefghijklmnopqrstuvwxyz
1234567890?!$%&

Adobe Systems, Inc.

Bodoni Bold Italic

ABCDEFGHIJKLMNOPQRSTUVWXYZ
abcdefghijklmnopqrstuvwxyz
1234567890?!$%&

Adobe Systems, Inc.

Bodoni Bold Italic

ABCDEFGHIJKLMNOPQRSTUVWXYZ
abcdefghijklmnopqrstuvwxyz
1234567890?!$%&

Bitstream, Inc.

Bodoni Bold Italic

ABCDEFGHIJKLMNOPQRSTUVWXYZ
abcdefghijklmnopqrstuvwxyz
1234567890?!$%&

Casady & Greene, Inc.

Bodoni Ultra Italic

ABCDEFGHIJKLMNOPQRSTUVWXYZ
abcdefghijklmnopqrstuvwxyz
1234567890?!$%&

Casady & Greene, Inc.

Bodoni Ultra Condensed

ABCDEFGHIJKLMNOPQRSTUVWXYZ

abcdefghijklmnopqrstuvwxyz

1234567890?!$%&

Casady & Greene, Inc.

Bodoni Ultra Condensed Italic

ABCDEFGHIJKLMNOPQRSTUVWXYZ

abcdefghijklmnopqrstuvwxyz

1234567890?!$%&

Casady & Greene, Inc.

ITC Bolt Bold

ABCDEFGHIJKLMNOPQRSTUVWXYZ

abcdefghijklmnopqrstuvwxyz

1234567890?!$%&

Bitstream, Inc.

ITC Bookman® Demi

ABCDEFGHIJKLMNOPQRSTUVWXYZ

abcdefghijklmnopqrstuvwxyz

1234567890?!$%&

Adobe Systems, Inc. / Bitstream, Inc.

ITC Bookman Demi Italic

ABCDEFGHIJKLMNOPQRSTUVWXYZ

abcdefghijklmnopqrstuvwxyz

1234567890?!$%&

Adobe Systems, Inc. / Bitstream, Inc.

ITC Bookman Light

ABCDEFGHIJKLMNOPQRSTUVWXYZ
abcdefghijklmnopqrstuvwxyz
1234567890?!$%&
Adobe Systems, Inc. / Bitstream, Inc.

ITC Bookman Light Italic

ABCDEFGHIJKLMNOPQRSTUVWXYZ
abcdefghijklmnopqrstuvwxyz
1234567890?!$%&
Adobe Systems, Inc. / Bitstream, Inc.

Broadway

ABCDEFGHIJKLMNOPQRSTUVWXYZ
abcdefghijklmnopqrstuvwxyz
1234567890?!$%&
Bitstream, Inc.

Brush Script

ABCDEFGHIJKLMNOPQRSTUVWXYZ
abcdefghijklmnopqrstuvwxyz
1234567890?!$%&
Adobe Systems, Inc.

Calligraphy

ABCDEFGHIJKLMNOPQRSTUVWXYZ
abcdefghijklmnopqrstuvwxyz
1234567890?!$%&
Casady & Greene, Inc.

Campanile

ABCDEFGHIJKLMNOPQRSTUVWXYZ

abcdefghijklmnopqrstuvwxyz

1234567890?!$%&

Casady & Greene, Inc.

Candida Roman

ABCDEFGHIJKLMNOPQRSTUVWXYZ

abcdefghijklmnopqrstuvwxyz

1234567890?!$%&

Adobe Systems, Inc.

Candida Italic

ABCDEFGHIJKLMNOPQRSTUVWXYZ

abcdefghijklmnopqrstuvwxyz

1234567890?!$%&

Adobe Systems, Inc.

Candida® Bold

ABCDEFGHIJKLMNOPQRSTUVWXYZ

abcdefghijklmnopqrstuvwxyz

1234567890?!$%&

Adobe Systems, Inc.

Caslon 3 Roman

ABCDEFGHIJKLMNOPQRSTUVWXYZ

abcdefghijklmnopqrstuvwxyz

1234567890?!$%&

Adobe Systems, Inc.

Caslon 3 Italic

ABCDEFGHIJKLMNOPQRSTUVWXYZ

abcdefghijklmnopqrstuvwxyz

1234567890?!$%&

Adobe Systems, Inc.

Caslon 540 Roman

ABCDEFGHIJKLMNOPQRSTUVWXYZ

abcdefghijklmnopqrstuvwxyz

1234567890?!$%&

Adobe Systems, Inc.

Caslon 540 Italic

ABCDEFGHIJKLMNOPQRSTUVWXYZ

abcdefghijklmnopqrstuvwxyz

1234567890?!$%&

Adobe Systems, Inc.

Caslon Open Face

ABCDEFGHIJKLMNOPQRSTUVWXYZ

abcdefghijklmnopqrstuvwxyz

1234567890?!$%&

Adobe Systems, Inc.

Century Expanded

ABCDEFGHIJKLMNOPQRSTUVWXYZ

abcdefghijklmnopqrstuvwxyz

1234567890?!$%&

Adobe Systems, Inc.

Century Expanded Italic

ABCDEFGHIJKLMNOPQRSTUVWXYZ

abcdefghijklmnopqrstuvwxyz

1234567890?!$%&

Adobe Systems, Inc.

Century Old Style

ABCDEFGHIJKLMNOPQRSTUVWXYZ

abcdefghijklmnopqrstuvwxyz

1234567890?!$%&

Adobe Systems, Inc.

Century Old Style Italic

ABCDEFGHIJKLMNOPQRSTUVWXYZ

abcdefghijklmnopqrstuvwxyz

1234567890?!$%&

Adobe Systems, Inc.

Century Old Style Bold

ABCDEFGHIJKLMNOPQRSTUVWXYZ

abcdefghijklmnopqrstuvwxyz

1234567890?!$%&

Adobe Systems, Inc.

ITC Cheltenham Book

ABCDEFGHIJKLMNOPQRSTUVWXYZ

abcdefghijklmnopqrstuvwxyz

1234567890?!$%&

Adobe Systems, Inc.

ITC Cheltenham Book Italic

ABCDEFGHIJKLMNOPQRSTUVWXYZ

abcdefghijklmnopqrstuvwxyz

1234567890?!$%&

Adobe Systems, Inc.

ITC Cheltenham® Bold

ABCDEFGHIJKLMNOPQRSTUVWXYZ

abcdefghijklmnopqrstuvwxyz

1234567890?!$%&

Adobe Systems, Inc.

ITC Cheltenham Bold Italic

ABCDEFGHIJKLMNOPQRSTUVWXYZ

abcdefghijklmnopqrstuvwxyz

1234567890?!$%&

Adobe Systems, Inc.

Clarendon™

ABCDEFGHIJKLMNOPQRSTUVWXYZ

abcdefghijklmnopqrstuvwxyz

1234567890?!$%&

Adobe Systems, Inc.

Clarendon Bold

ABCDEFGHIJKLMNOPQRSTUVWXYZ

abcdefghijklmnopqrstuvwxyz

1234567890?!$%&

Adobe Systems, Inc.

Clarendon Light

ABCDEFGHIJKLMNOPQRSTUVWXYZ
abcdefghijklmnopqrstuvwxyz
1234567890?!$%&
Adobe Systems, Inc.

ITC Clearface Regular

ABCDEFGHIJKLMNOPQRSTUVWXYZ
abcdefghijklmnopqrstuvwxyz
1234567890?!$%&
Adobe Systems, Inc. / Bitstream, Inc.

ITC Clearface Regular Italic

ABCDEFGHIJKLMNOPQRSTUVWXYZ
abcdefghijklmnopqrstuvwxyz
1234567890?!$%&
Adobe Systems, Inc. / Bitstream, Inc.

ITC Clearface Bold

ABCDEFGHIJKLMNOPQRSTUVWXYZ
abcdefghijklmnopqrstuvwxyz
1234567890?!$%&
Adobe Systems, Inc.

ITC Clearface® Black

ABCDEFGHIJKLMNOPQRSTUVWXYZ
abcdefghijklmnopqrstuvwxyz
1234567890?!$%&
Adobe Systems, Inc.

ITC Clearface Heavy

ABCDEFGHIJKLMNOPQRSTUVWXYZ

abcdefghijklmnopqrstuvwxyz

1234567890?!$%&

Adobe Systems, Inc. / Bitstream, Inc.

ITC Clearface Bold Italic

ABCDEFGHIJKLMNOPQRSTUVWXYZ

abcdefghijklmnopqrstuvwxyz

1234567890?!$%&

Adobe Systems, Inc.

ITC Clearface Black Italic

ABCDEFGHIJKLMNOPQRSTUVWXYZ

abcdefghijklmnopqrstuvwxyz

1234567890?!$%&

Adobe Systems, Inc.

ITC Clearface Heavy Italic

ABCDEFGHIJKLMNOPQRSTUVWXYZ

abcdefghijklmnopqrstuvwxyz

1234567890?!$%&

Adobe Systems, Inc. / Bitstream, Inc.

Cloister Black

ABCDEFGHIJKLMNOPQRSTUVWXYZ

abcdefghijklmnopqrstuvwxyz

1234567890?!$%&

Bitstream, Inc.

Cochin™

ABCDEFGHIJKLMNOPQRSTUVWXYZ
abcdefghijklmnopqrstuvwxyz
1234567890?!$%&
Adobe Systems, Inc.

Cochin Italic

ABCDEFGHIJKLMNOPQRSTUVWXYZ
abcdefghijklmnopqrstuvwxyz
1234567890?!$%&
Adobe Systems, Inc.

Cochin Bold

ABCDEFGHIJKLMNOPQRSTUVWXYZ
abcdefghijklmnopqrstuvwxyz
1234567890?!$%&
Adobe Systems, Inc.

Cochin Bold Italic

ABCDEFGHIJKLMNOPQRSTUVWXYZ
abcdefghijklmnopqrstuvwxyz
1234567890?!$%&
Adobe Systems, Inc.

COLLEGIATE

ABCDEFGHIJKLMNOPQRSTUVWXYZ
ABCDEFGHIJKLMNOPQRSTUVWXYZ
1234567890?!$%&
Casady & Greene, Inc.

COLLEGIATE BLACK

ABCDEFGHIJKLMNOPQRSTUVWXYZ

ABCDEFGHIJKLMNOPQRSTUVWXYZ

1234567890?!$%&

Casady & Greene, Inc.

COLLEGIATE OUTLINE

ABCDEFGHIJKLMNOPQRSTUVWXYZ

ABCDEFGHIJKLMNOPQRSTUVWXYZ

1234567890?!$%&

Casady & Greene, Inc.

Concorde®

ABCDEFGHIJKLMNOPQRSTUVWXYZ

abcdefghijklmnopqrstuvwxyz

1234567890?!$%&

Adobe Systems, Inc.

Concorde Italic

ABCDEFGHIJKLMNOPQRSTUVWXYZ

abcdefghijklmnopqrstuvwxyz

1234567890?!$%&

Adobe Systems, Inc.

Concorde Bold

ABCDEFGHIJKLMNOPQRSTUVWXYZ

abcdefghijklmnopqrstuvwxyz

1234567890?!$%&

Adobe Systems, Inc.

Concorde Bold Italic

ABCDEFGHIJKLMNOPQRSTUVWXYZ

abcdefghijklmnopqrstuvwxyz

1234567890?!$%&

Adobe Systems, Inc.

Cooper Black

ABCDEFGHIJKLMNOPQRSTUVWXYZ

abcdefghijklmnopqrstuvwxyz

1234567890?!$%&

Adobe Systems, Inc.

Bitstream Cooper Black

ABCDEFGHIJKLMNOPQRSTUVWXYZ

abcdefghijklmnopqrstuvwxyz

1234567890?!$%&

Bitstream, Inc.

Cooper Black Italic

ABCDEFGHIJKLMNOPQRSTUVWXYZ

abcdefghijklmnopqrstuvwxyz

1234567890?!$%&

Adobe Systems, Inc.

Corona™

ABCDEFGHIJKLMNOPQRSTUVWXYZ

abcdefghijklmnopqrstuvwxyz

1234567890?!$%&

Adobe Systems, Inc.

Corona Italic

ABCDEFGHIJKLMNOPQRSTUVWXYZ

abcdefghijklmnopqrstuvwxyz

1234567890?!$%&

Adobe Systems, Inc.

Corona Bold

ABCDEFGHIJKLMNOPQRSTUVWXYZ

abcdefghijklmnopqrstuvwxyz

1234567890?!$%&

Adobe Systems, Inc.

Coventry Script

ABCDEFGHIJKLMNOPQRSTUVWXYZ

abcdefghijklmnopqrstuvwxyz

1234567890?!$%&

Casady & Greene, Inc.

DESPERADO

ABCDEFGHIJKLMNOPQRSTUVWXYZ

ABCDEFGHIJKLMNOPQRSTUVWXYZ

1234567890?!$%&

Casady & Greene, Inc.

Dom Casual

ABCDEFGHIJKLMNOPQRSTUVWXYZ

abcdefghijklmnopqrstuvwxyz

1234567890?!$%&

Adobe Systems, Inc.

Dom Casual

ABCDEFGHIJKLMNOPQRSTUVWXYZ
abcdefghijklmnopqrstuvwxyz
1234567890?!$%&
Bitstream, Inc.

Dom Casual Bold

ABCDEFGHIJKLMNOPQRSTUVWXYZ
abcdefghijklmnopqrstuvwxyz
1234567890?!$%&
Adobe Systems, Inc.

Dorovar

ABCDEFGHIJKLMNOPQRSTUVWXYZ
abcdefghijklmnopqrstuvwxyz
1234567890?!$%&
Casady & Greene, Inc.

Dorovar Italic

ABCDEFGHIJKLMNOPQRSTUVWXYZ
abcdefghijklmnopqrstuvwxyz
1234567890?!$%&
Casady & Greene, Inc.

DRY GULCH

ABCDEFGHIJKLMNOPQRSTUVWXYZ
ABCDEFGHIJKLMNOPQRSTUVWXYZ
1234567890?!$%&
Casady & Greene, Inc.

Dutch Roman

ABCDEFGHIJKLMNOPQRSTUVWXYZ

abcdefghijklmnopqrstuvwxyz

1234567890?!$%&

Bitstream, Inc.

Dutch Italic

ABCDEFGHIJKLMNOPQRSTUVWXYZ

abcdefghijklmnopqrstuvwxyz

1234567890?!$%&

Bitstream, Inc.

Dutch Bold

ABCDEFGHIJKLMNOPQRSTUVWXYZ

abcdefghijklmnopqrstuvwxyz

1234567890?!$%&

Bitstream, Inc.

Dutch Bold Italic

ABCDEFGHIJKLMNOPQRSTUVWXYZ

abcdefghijklmnopqrstuvwxyz

1234567890?!$%&

Bitstream, Inc.

ITC Eras Medium

ABCDEFGHIJKLMNOPQRSTUVWXYZ

abcdefghijklmnopqrstuvwxyz

1234567890?!$%&

Adobe Systems, Inc.

ITC Eras Book

ABCDEFGHIJKLMNOPQRSTUVWXYZ
abcdefghijklmnopqrstuvwxyz
1234567890?!$%&
Adobe Systems, Inc.

ITC Eras® Bold

ABCDEFGHIJKLMNOPQRSTUVWXYZ
abcdefghijklmnopqrstuvwxyz
1234567890?!$%&
Adobe Systems, Inc.

ITC Eras Demi

ABCDEFGHIJKLMNOPQRSTUVWXYZ
abcdefghijklmnopqrstuvwxyz
1234567890?!$%&
Adobe Systems, Inc.

ITC Eras Ultra

ABCDEFGHIJKLMNOPQRSTUVWXYZ
abcdefghijklmnopqrstuvwxyz
1234567890?!$%&
Adobe Systems, Inc.

ITC Eras Light

ABCDEFGHIJKLMNOPQRSTUVWXYZ
abcdefghijklmnopqrstuvwxyz
1234567890?!$%&
Adobe Systems, Inc.

Eurostile®

ABCDEFGHIJKLMNOPQRSTUVWXYZ
abcdefghijklmnopqrstuvwxyz
1234567890?!$%&
Adobe Systems, Inc.

Eurostile Oblique

ABCDEFGHIJKLMNOPQRSTUVWXYZ
abcdefghijklmnopqrstuvwxyz
1234567890?!$%&
Adobe Systems, Inc.

Eurostile Bold

ABCDEFGHIJKLMNOPQRSTUVWXYZ
abcdefghijklmnopqrstuvwxyz
1234567890?!$%&
Adobe Systems, Inc.

Eurostile Demi

ABCDEFGHIJKLMNOPQRSTUVWXYZ
abcdefghijklmnopqrstuvwxyz
1234567890?!$%&
Adobe Systems, Inc.

Eurostile Bold Oblique

ABCDEFGHIJKLMNOPQRSTUVWXYZ
abcdefghijklmnopqrstuvwxyz
1234567890?!$%&
Adobe Systems, Inc.

Eurostile Demi Oblique

ABCDEFGHIJKLMNOPQRSTUVWXYZ

abcdefghijklmnopqrstuvwxyz

1234567890?!$%&

Adobe Systems, Inc.

Excelsior™

ABCDEFGHIJKLMNOPQRSTUVWXYZ

abcdefghijklmnopqrstuvwxyz

1234567890?!$%&

Adobe Systems, Inc.

Excelsior Italic

ABCDEFGHIJKLMNOPQRSTUVWXYZ

abcdefghijklmnopqrstuvwxyz

1234567890?!$%&

Adobe Systems, Inc.

Excelsior Bold

ABCDEFGHIJKLMNOPQRSTUVWXYZ

abcdefghijklmnopqrstuvwxyz

1234567890?!$%&

Adobe Systems, Inc.

Fette Fraktur

ABCDEFGHIJKLMNOPQRSTUVWXYZ

abcdefghijklmnopqrstuvwxyz

1234567890?!$%&

Adobe Systems, Inc.

Folio Medium

ABCDEFGHIJKLMNOPQRSTUVWXYZ
abcdefghijklmnopqrstuvwxyz
1234567890?!$%&
Adobe Systems, Inc.

Folio® Bold

ABCDEFGHIJKLMNOPQRSTUVWXYZ
abcdefghijklmnopqrstuvwxyz
1234567890?!$%&
Adobe Systems, Inc.

Folio Extra Bold

ABCDEFGHIJKLMNOPQRSTUVWXYZ
abcdefghijklmnopqrstuvwxyz
1234567890?!$%&
Adobe Systems, Inc.

Folio Light

ABCDEFGHIJKLMNOPQRSTUVWXYZ
abcdefghijklmnopqrstuvwxyz
1234567890?!$%&
Adobe Systems, Inc.

Folio Bold Condensed

ABCDEFGHIJKLMNOPQRSTUVWXYZ
abcdefghijklmnopqrstuvwxyz
1234567890?!$%&
Adobe Systems, Inc.

Franklin Gothic Roman

ABCDEFGHIJKLMNOPQRSTUVWXYZ
abcdefghijklmnopqrstuvwxyz
1234567890?!$%&

Bitstream, Inc.

Franklin Gothic Italic

ABCDEFGHIJKLMNOPQRSTUVWXYZ
abcdefghijklmnopqrstuvwxyz
1234567890?!$%&

Bitstream, Inc.

Franklin Gothic Condensed

ABCDEFGHIJKLMNOPQRSTUVWXYZ
abcdefghijklmnopqrstuvwxyz
1234567890?!$%&

Adobe Systems, Inc.

Franklin Gothic Extra Condensed

ABCDEFGHIJKLMNOPQRSTUVWXYZ
abcdefghijklmnopqrstuvwxyz
1234567890?!$%&

Adobe Systems, Inc.

Frankin Gothic Extra Condensed

ABCDEFGHIJKLMNOPQRSTUVWXYZ
abcdefghijklmnopqrstuvwxyz
1234567890?!$%&

Bitstream, Inc.

Franklin Gothic No. 2 Roman

ABCDEFGHIJKLMNOPQRSTUVWXYZ

abcdefghijklmnopqrstuvwxyz

1234567890?!$%&

Adobe Systems, Inc.

ITC Franklin Gothic® Book

ABCDEFGHIJKLMNOPQRSTUVWXYZ

abcdefghijklmnopqrstuvwxyz

1234567890?!$%&

Adobe Systems, Inc.

ITC Franklin Gothic Book Oblique

ABCDEFGHIJKLMNOPQRSTUVWXYZ

abcdefghijklmnopqrstuvwxyz

1234567890?!$%&

Adobe Systems, Inc.

ITC Franklin Gothic Demi

ABCDEFGHIJKLMNOPQRSTUVWXYZ

abcdefghijklmnopqrstuvwxyz

1234567890?!$%&

Adobe Systems, Inc.

ITC Franklin Gothic Heavy

ABCDEFGHIJKLMNOPQRSTUVWXYZ

abcdefghijklmnopqrstuvwxyz

1234567890?!$%&

Adobe Systems, Inc.

ITC Franklin Gothic Demi Oblique

ABCDEFGHIJKLMNOPQRSTUVWXYZ

abcdefghijklmnopqrstuvwxyz

1234567890?!$%&

Adobe Systems, Inc.

ITC Franklin Gothic Heavy Oblique

ABCDEFGHIJKLMNOPQRSTUVWXYZ

abcdefghijklmnopqrstuvwxyz

1234567890?!$%&

Adobe Systems, Inc.

Freestyle Script

ABCDEFGHIJKLMNOPQRSTUVWXYZ

abcdefghijklmnopqrstuvwxyz

1234567890?!$%&

Adobe Systems, Inc.

ITC Friz Quadrata®

ABCDEFGHIJKLMNOPQRSTUVWXYZ

abcdefghijklmnopqrstuvwxyz

1234567890?!$%&

Adobe Systems, Inc.

ITC Friz Quadrata Bold

ABCDEFGHIJKLMNOPQRSTUVWXYZ

abcdefghijklmnopqrstuvwxyz

1234567890?!$%&

Adobe Systems, Inc.

Frutiger™ 45 Light
ABCDEFGHIJKLMNOPQRSTUVWXYZ
abcdefghijklmnopqrstuvwxyz
1234567890?!$%&
Adobe Systems, Inc.

Frutiger 46 Light Italic
ABCDEFGHIJKLMNOPQRSTUVWXYZ
abcdefghijklmnopqrstuvwxyz
1234567890?!$%&
Adobe Systems, Inc.

Frutiger 55
ABCDEFGHIJKLMNOPQRSTUVWXYZ
abcdefghijklmnopqrstuvwxyz
1234567890?!$%&
Adobe Systems, Inc.

Frutiger 56 Italic
ABCDEFGHIJKLMNOPQRSTUVWXYZ
abcdefghijklmnopqrstuvwxyz
1234567890?!$%&
Adobe Systems, Inc.

Frutiger 65 Bold
ABCDEFGHIJKLMNOPQRSTUVWXYZ
abcdefghijklmnopqrstuvwxyz
1234567890?!$%&
Adobe Systems, Inc.

Frutiger 66 Bold Italic

ABCDEFGHIJKLMNOPQRSTUVWXYZ
abcdefghijklmnopqrstuvwxyz
1234567890?!$%&

Adobe Systems, Inc.

Frutiger 75 Black

ABCDEFGHIJKLMNOPQRSTUVWXYZ
abcdefghijklmnopqrstuvwxyz
1234567890?!$%&

Adobe Systems, Inc.

Frutiger 76 Black Italic

ABCDEFGHIJKLMNOPQRSTUVWXYZ
abcdefghijklmnopqrstuvwxyz
1234567890?!$%&

Adobe Systems, Inc.

Frutiger 95 Ultra Black

ABCDEFGHIJKLMNOPQRSTUVWXYZ
abcdefghijklmnopqrstuvwxyz
1234567890?!$%&

Adobe Systems, Inc.

Futura

ABCDEFGHIJKLMNOPQRSTUVWXYZ
abcdefghijklmnopqrstuvwxyz
1234567890?!$%&

Adobe Systems, Inc.

Futura Book

ABCDEFGHIJKLMNOPQRSTUVWXYZ
abcdefghijklmnopqrstuvwxyz
1234567890?!$%&
Adobe Systems, Inc.

Futura Oblique

ABCDEFGHIJKLMNOPQRSTUVWXYZ
abcdefghijklmnopqrstuvwxyz
1234567890?!$%&
Adobe Systems, Inc.

Futura Book Oblique

ABCDEFGHIJKLMNOPQRSTUVWXYZ
abcdefghijklmnopqrstuvwxyz
1234567890?!$%&
Adobe Systems, Inc.

Futura® Bold

ABCDEFGHIJKLMNOPQRSTUVWXYZ
abcdefghijklmnopqrstuvwxyz
1234567890?!$%&
Adobe Systems, Inc.

Futura Extra Bold

ABCDEFGHIJKLMNOPQRSTUVWXYZ
abcdefghijklmnopqrstuvwxyz
1234567890?!$%&
Adobe Systems, Inc.

Futura Black

ABCDEFGHIJKLMNOPQRSTUVWXYZ

abcdefghijklmnopqrstuvwxyz

1234567890?!$%&

Bitstream, Inc.

Futura Heavy

ABCDEFGHIJKLMNOPQRSTUVWXYZ

abcdefghijklmnopqrstuvwxyz

1234567890?!$%&

Adobe Systems, Inc.

Futura Bold Oblique

ABCDEFGHIJKLMNOPQRSTUVWXYZ

abcdefghijklmnopqrstuvwxyz

1234567890?!$%&

Adobe Systems, Inc.

Futura Extra Bold Oblique

ABCDEFGHIJKLMNOPQRSTUVWXYZ

abcdefghijklmnopqrstuvwxyz

1234567890?!$%&

Adobe Systems, Inc.

Futura Heavy Oblique

ABCDEFGHIJKLMNOPQRSTUVWXYZ

abcdefghijklmnopqrstuvwxyz

1234567890?!$%&

Adobe Systems, Inc.

Futura Light

ABCDEFGHIJKLMNOPQRSTUVWXYZ
abcdefghijklmnopqrstuvwxyz
1234567890?!$%&

Adobe Systems, Inc.

Futura Light Oblique

ABCDEFGHIJKLMNOPQRSTUVWXYZ
abcdefghijklmnopqrstuvwxyz
1234567890?!$%&

Adobe Systems, Inc.

Futura Condensed

ABCDEFGHIJKLMNOPQRSTUVWXYZ
abcdefghijklmnopqrstuvwxyz
1234567890?!$%&

Adobe Systems, Inc.

Futura Condensed Oblique

ABCDEFGHIJKLMNOPQRSTUVWXYZ
abcdefghijklmnopqrstuvwxyz
1234567890?!$%&

Adobe Systems, Inc.

Futura Condensed Bold

ABCDEFGHIJKLMNOPQRSTUVWXYZ
abcdefghijklmnopqrstuvwxyz
1234567890?!$%&

Adobe Systems, Inc.

Futura Condensed Extra Bold

ABCDEFGHIJKLMNOPQRSTUVWXYZ
abcdefghijklmnopqrstuvwxyz
1234567890?!$%&
Adobe Systems, Inc.

Futura Condensed Bold Oblique

ABCDEFGHIJKLMNOPQRSTUVWXYZ
abcdefghijklmnopqrstuvwxyz
1234567890?!$%&
Adobe Systems, Inc.

Futura Condensed Extra Bold Oblique

ABCDEFGHIJKLMNOPQRSTUVWXYZ
abcdefghijklmnopqrstuvwxyz
1234567890?!$%&
Adobe Systems, Inc.

Futura Condensed Light

ABCDEFGHIJKLMNOPQRSTUVWXYZ
abcdefghijklmnopqrstuvwxyz
1234567890?!$%&
Adobe Systems, Inc.

Futura Condensed Light Oblique

ABCDEFGHIJKLMNOPQRSTUVWXYZ
abcdefghijklmnopqrstuvwxyz
1234567890?!$%&
Adobe Systems, Inc.

Galileo Roman

ABCDEFGHIJKLMNOPQRSTUVWXYZ
abcdefghijklmnopqrstuvwxyz
1234567890?!$%&
Casady & Greene, Inc.

Galileo Italic

ABCDEFGHIJKLMNOPQRSTUVWXYZ
abcdefghijklmnopqrstuvwxyz
1234567890?!$%&
Casady & Greene, Inc.

Galileo Bold

ABCDEFGHIJKLMNOPQRSTUVWXYZ
abcdefghijklmnopqrstuvwxyz
1234567890?!$%&
Casady & Greene, Inc.

Galileo Bold Italic

ABCDEFGHIJKLMNOPQRSTUVWXYZ
abcdefghijklmnopqrstuvwxyz
1234567890?!$%&
Casady & Greene, Inc.

ITC Galliard Roman

ABCDEFGHIJKLMNOPQRSTUVWXYZ
abcdefghijklmnopqrstuvwxyz
1234567890?!$%&
Adobe Systems, Inc. / Bitstream, Inc.

ITC Galliard Italic

ABCDEFGHIJKLMNOPQRSTUVWXYZ

abcdefghijklmnopqrstuvwxyz

1234567890?!$%&

Adobe Systems, Inc. / Bitstream, Inc.

ITC Galliard® Bold

ABCDEFGHIJKLMNOPQRSTUVWXYZ

abcdefghijklmnopqrstuvwxyz

1234567890?!$%&

Adobe Systems, Inc. / Bitstream, Inc.

ITC Galliard Bold Italic

ABCDEFGHIJKLMNOPQRSTUVWXYZ

abcdefghijklmnopqrstuvwxyz

1234567890?!$%&

Adobe Systems, Inc. / Bitstream, Inc.

ADOBE GARAMOND EXPERT COLLECTION

ABCDEFGHIJKLMNOPQRSTUVWXYZ

ABCDEFGHIJKLMNOPQRSTUVWXYZ

Adobe Systems, Inc.

Adobe Garamond Regular

ABCDEFGHIJKLMNOPQRSTUVWXYZ

abcdefghijklmnopqrstuvwxyz

1234567890?!$%&

Adobe Systems, Inc.

Adobe Garamond Italic

ABCDEFGHIJKLMNOPQRSTUVWXYZ

abcdefghijklmnopqrstuvwxyz

1234567890?!$%&

Adobe Systems, Inc.

Adobe Garamond™ Bold

ABCDEFGHIJKLMNOPQRSTUVWXYZ

abcdefghijklmnopqrstuvwxyz

1234567890?!$%&

Adobe Systems, Inc.

Adobe Garamond Semibold

ABCDEFGHIJKLMNOPQRSTUVWXYZ

abcdefghijklmnopqrstuvwxyz

1234567890?!$%&

Adobe Systems, Inc.

Adobe Garamond Bold Italic

ABCDEFGHIJKLMNOPQRSTUVWXYZ

abcdefghijklmnopqrstuvwxyz

1234567890?!$%&

Adobe Systems, Inc.

Adobe Garamond Semibold Italic

ABCDEFGHIJKLMNOPQRSTUVWXYZ

abcdefghijklmnopqrstuvwxyz

1234567890?!$%&

Adobe Systems, Inc.

Garamond 3™

ABCDEFGHIJKLMNOPQRSTUVWXYZ
abcdefghijklmnopqrstuvwxyz
1234567890?!$%&
Adobe Systems, Inc.

Garamond 3 Italic

ABCDEFGHIJKLMNOPQRSTUVWXYZ
abcdefghijklmnopqrstuvwxyz
1234567890?!$%&
Adobe Systems, Inc.

Garamond 3 Bold

ABCDEFGHIJKLMNOPQRSTUVWXYZ
abcdefghijklmnopqrstuvwxyz
1234567890?!$%&
Adobe Systems, Inc.

Garamond 3 Bold Italic

ABCDEFGHIJKLMNOPQRSTUVWXYZ
abcdefghijklmnopqrstuvwxyz
1234567890?!$%&
Adobe Systems, Inc.

Garamond Antiqua

ABCDEFGHIJKLMNOPQRSTUVWXYZ
abcdefghijklmnopqrstuvwxyz
1234567890?!$%&
Adobe Systems, Inc.

Garamond Kursiv

ABCDEFGHIJKLMNOPQRSTUVWXYZ

abcdefghijklmnopqrstuvwxyz

1234567890?!$%&

Adobe Systems, Inc.

Garamond Halbfett

ABCDEFGHIJKLMNOPQRSTUVWXYZ

abcdefghijklmnopqrstuvwxyz

1234567890?!$%&

Adobe Systems, Inc.

Garamond Kursiv Halbfett

ABCDEFGHIJKLMNOPQRSTUVWXYZ

abcdefghijklmnopqrstuvwxyz

1234567890?!$%&

Adobe Systems, Inc.

ITC Garamond® Bold

ABCDEFGHIJKLMNOPQRSTUVWXYZ

abcdefghijklmnopqrstuvwxyz

1234567890?!$%&

Adobe Systems, Inc.

ITC Garamond Bold Italic

ABCDEFGHIJKLMNOPQRSTUVWXYZ

abcdefghijklmnopqrstuvwxyz

1234567890?!$%&

Adobe Systems, Inc. / Bitstream, Inc.

ITC Garamond Light

ABCDEFGHIJKLMNOPQRSTUVWXYZ
abcdefghijklmnopqrstuvwxyz
1234567890?!$%&
Adobe Systems, Inc.

ITC Garamond Light Italic

ABCDEFGHIJKLMNOPQRSTUVWXYZ
abcdefghijklmnopqrstuvwxyz
1234567890?!$%&
Adobe Systems, Inc.

Stempel Garamond™ Roman

ABCDEFGHIJKLMNOPQRSTUVWXYZ
abcdefghijklmnopqrstuvwxyz
1234567890?!$%&
Adobe Systems, Inc.

Stempel Garamond Italic

ABCDEFGHIJKLMNOPQRSTUVWXYZ
abcdefghijklmnopqrstuvwxyz
1234567890?!$%&
Adobe Systems, Inc.

Stempel Garamond Bold

ABCDEFGHIJKLMNOPQRSTUVWXYZ
abcdefghijklmnopqrstuvwxyz
1234567890?!$%&
Adobe Systems, Inc.

Stempel Garamond Bold Italic

ABCDEFGHIJKLMNOPQRSTUVWXYZ

abcdefghijklmnopqrstuvwxyz

1234567890?!$%&

Adobe Systems, Inc.

Gatsby

ABCDEFGHIJKLMNOPQRSTUVWXYZ

abcdefghijklmnopqrstuvwxyz

1234567890?!$%&

Casady & Greene, Inc.

Gatsby Italic

ABCDEFGHIJKLMNOPQRSTUVWXYZ

abcdefghijklmnopqrstuvwxyz

1234567890?!$%&

Casady & Greene, Inc.

Gatsby Demi Bold

ABCDEFGHIJKLMNOPQRSTUVWXYZ

abcdefghijklmnopqrstuvwxyz

1234567890?!$%&

Casady & Greene, Inc.

Gatsby Demi Bold Italic

ABCDEFGHIJKLMNOPQRSTUVWXYZ

abcdefghijklmnopqrstuvwxyz

1234567890?!$%&

Casady & Greene, Inc.

Gazelle

ABCDEFGHIJKLMNOPQRSTUVWXYZ
abcdefghijklmnopqrstuvwxyz
1234567890?!$%&
Casady & Greene, Inc.

Giotto

ABCDEFGHIJKLMNOPQRSTUVWXYZ
abcdefghijklmnopqrstuvwxyz
1234567890?!$%&
Casady & Greene, Inc.

Giotto Bold

ABCDEFGHIJKLMNOPQRSTUVWXYZ
abcdefghijklmnopqrstuvwxyz
1234567890?!$%&
Casady & Greene, Inc.

Glypha™

ABCDEFGHIJKLMNOPQRSTUVWXYZ
abcdefghijklmnopqrstuvwxyz
1234567890?!$%&
Adobe Systems, Inc.

Glypha Oblique

ABCDEFGHIJKLMNOPQRSTUVWXYZ
abcdefghijklmnopqrstuvwxyz
1234567890?!$%&
Adobe Systems, Inc.

Glypha Bold

ABCDEFGHIJKLMNOPQRSTUVWXYZ
abcdefghijklmnopqrstuvwxyz
1234567890?!$%&

Adobe Systems, Inc.

Glypha Bold Oblique

ABCDEFGHIJKLMNOPQRSTUVWXYZ
abcdefghijklmnopqrstuvwxyz
1234567890?!$%&

Adobe Systems, Inc.

Gothic 13

ABCDEFGHIJKLMNOPQRSTUVWXYZ
abcdefghijklmnopqrstuvwxyz
1234567890?!$%&

Adobe Systems, Inc.

Goudy Extra Bold

ABCDEFGHIJKLMNOPQRSTUVWXYZ
abcdefghijklmnopqrstuvwxyz
1234567890?!$%&

Adobe Systems, Inc.

Goudy Heavyface

ABCDEFGHIJKLMNOPQRSTUVWXYZ
abcdefghijklmnopqrstuvwxyz
1234567890?!$%&

Adobe Systems, Inc.

Goudy Heavyface Italic

ABCDEFGHIJKLMNOPQRSTUVWXYZ

abcdefghijklmnopqrstuvwxyz

1234567890?!$%&

Adobe Systems, Inc.

Goudy Heavyface Condensed

ABCDEFGHIJKLMNOPQRSTUVWXYZ

abcdefghijklmnopqrstuvwxyz

1234567890?!$%&

Adobe Systems, Inc.

Goudy Old Style

ABCDEFGHIJKLMNOPQRSTUVWXYZ

abcdefghijklmnopqrstuvwxyz

1234567890?!$%&

Adobe Systems, Inc.

Goudy Old Style

ABCDEFGHIJKLMNOPQRSTUVWXYZ

abcdefghijklmnopqrstuvwxyz

1234567890?!$%&

Bitstream, Inc.

Goudy Old Style Italic

ABCDEFGHIJKLMNOPQRSTUVWXYZ

abcdefghijklmnopqrstuvwxyz

1234567890?!$%&

Adobe Systems, Inc.

Goudy Old Style Italic

ABCDEFGHIJKLMNOPQRSTUVWXYZ

abcdefghijklmnopqrstuvwxyz

1234567890?!$%&

Bitstream, Inc.

Goudy Old Style Bold

ABCDEFGHIJKLMNOPQRSTUVWXYZ

abcdefghijklmnopqrstuvwxyz

1234567890?!$%&

Adobe Systems, Inc.

Goudy Bold

ABCDEFGHIJKLMNOPQRSTUVWXYZ

abcdefghijklmnopqrstuvwxyz

1234567890?!$%&

Bitstream, Inc.

Goudy Extra Bold

ABCDEFGHIJKLMNOPQRSTUVWXYZ

abcdefghijklmnopqrstuvwxyz

1234567890?!$%&

Bitstream, Inc.

Goudy Old Style Bold Italic

ABCDEFGHIJKLMNOPQRSTUVWXYZ

abcdefghijklmnopqrstuvwxyz

1234567890?!$%&

Adobe Systems, Inc.

Gregorian

ABCDEFGHIJKLMNOPQRSTUVWXYZ

abcdefghijklmnopqrstuvwxyz

1234567890?!$%&

Casady & Greene, Inc.

Hammersmith Roman

ABCDEFGHIJKLMNOPQRSTUVWXYZ

abcdefghijklmnopqrstuvwxyz

1234567890?!$%&

Bitstream, Inc.

Hammersmith Italic

ABCDEFGHIJKLMNOPQRSTUVWXYZ

abcdefghijklmnopqrstuvwxyz

1234567890?!$%&

Bitstream, Inc.

Hammersmith Bold

ABCDEFGHIJKLMNOPQRSTUVWXYZ

abcdefghijklmnopqrstuvwxyz

1234567890?!$%&

Bitstream, Inc.

Hammersmith Bold Italic

ABCDEFGHIJKLMNOPQRSTUVWXYZ

abcdefghijklmnopqrstuvwxyz

1234567890?!$%&

Bitstream, Inc.

Handel Gothic

ABCDEFGHIJKLMNOPQRSTUVWXYZ
abcdefghijklmnopqrstuvwxyz
1234567890?!$%&

Bitstream, Inc.

Helvetica™ Black

ABCDEFGHIJKLMNOPQRSTUVWXYZ
abcdefghijklmnopqrstuvwxyz
1234567890?!$%&

Adobe Systems, Inc.

Helvetica Black Oblique

ABCDEFGHIJKLMNOPQRSTUVWXYZ
abcdefghijklmnopqrstuvwxyz
1234567890?!$%&

Adobe Systems, Inc.

Helvetica Light

ABCDEFGHIJKLMNOPQRSTUVWXYZ
abcdefghijklmnopqrstuvwxyz
1234567890?!$%&

Adobe Systems, Inc.

Helvetica Light Oblique

ABCDEFGHIJKLMNOPQRSTUVWXYZ
abcdefghijklmnopqrstuvwxyz
1234567890?!$%&

Adobe Systems, Inc.

Helvetica Condensed

ABCDEFGHIJKLMNOPQRSTUVWXYZ

abcdefghijklmnopqrstuvwxyz

1234567890?!$%&

Adobe Systems, Inc.

Helvetica Condensed Oblique

ABCDEFGHIJKLMNOPQRSTUVWXYZ

abcdefghijklmnopqrstuvwxyz

1234567890?!$%&

Adobe Systems, Inc.

Helvetica Condensed Bold

ABCDEFGHIJKLMNOPQRSTUVWXYZ

abcdefghijklmnopqrstuvwxyz

1234567890?!$%&

Adobe Systems, Inc.

Helvetica Condensed Black

ABCDEFGHIJKLMNOPQRSTUVWXYZ

abcdefghijklmnopqrstuvwxyz

1234567890?!$%&

Adobe Systems, Inc.

Helvetica Condensed Bold Oblique

ABCDEFGHIJKLMNOPQRSTUVWXYZ

abcdefghijklmnopqrstuvwxyz

1234567890?!$%&

Adobe Systems, Inc.

Helvetica Condensed Light

ABCDEFGHIJKLMNOPQRSTUVWXYZ
abcdefghijklmnopqrstuvwxyz
1234567890?!$%&

Adobe Systems, Inc.

Helvetica Condensed Light Oblique

ABCDEFGHIJKLMNOPQRSTUVWXYZ
abcdefghijklmnopqrstuvwxyz
1234567890?!$%&

Adobe Systems, Inc.

Helvetica Compressed

ABCDEFGHIJKLMNOPQRSTUVWXYZ
abcdefghijklmnopqrstuvwxyz
1234567890?!$%&

Adobe Systems, Inc.

Helvetica Compressed Extra

ABCDEFGHIJKLMNOPQRSTUVWXYZ
abcdefghijklmnopqrstuvwxyz
1234567890?!$%&

Adobe Systems, Inc.

Helvetica Condensed Black Oblique

ABCDEFGHIJKLMNOPQRSTUVWXYZ
abcdefghijklmnopqrstuvwxyz
1234567890?!$%&

Adobe Systems, Inc.

Helvetica Compressed Ultra

ABCDEFGHIJKLMNOPQRSTUVWXYZ
abcdefghijklmnopqrstuvwxyz
1234567890?!$%&
Adobe Systems, Inc.

Helvetica Inserat

ABCDEFGHIJKLMNOPQRSTUVWXYZ
abcdefghijklmnopqrstuvwxyz
1234567890?!$%&
Adobe Systems, Inc.

Helvetica 25 Ultra Light

ABCDEFGHIJKLMNOPQRSTUVWXYZ
abcdefghijklmnopqrstuvwxyz
1234567890?!$%&
Adobe Systems, Inc.

Helvetica 26 Ultra Light Italic

ABCDEFGHIJKLMNOPQRSTUVWXYZ
abcdefghijklmnopqrstuvwxyz
1234567890?!$%&
Adobe Systems, Inc.

Helvetica 35 Thin

ABCDEFGHIJKLMNOPQRSTUVWXYZ
abcdefghijklmnopqrstuvwxyz
1234567890?!$%&
Adobe Systems, Inc.

Helvetica 36 Thin Italic

ABCDEFGHIJKLMNOPQRSTUVWXYZ

abcdefghijklmnopqrstuvwxyz

1234567890?!$%&

Adobe Systems, Inc.

Helvetica 45 Light

ABCDEFGHIJKLMNOPQRSTUVWXYZ

abcdefghijklmnopqrstuvwxyz

1234567890?!$%&

Adobe Systems, Inc.

Helvetica 46 Light Italic

ABCDEFGHIJKLMNOPQRSTUVWXYZ

abcdefghijklmnopqrstuvwxyz

1234567890?!$%&

Adobe Systems, Inc.

Helvetica 55 Roman

ABCDEFGHIJKLMNOPQRSTUVWXYZ

abcdefghijklmnopqrstuvwxyz

1234567890?!$%&

Adobe Systems, Inc.

Helvetica 56 Italic

ABCDEFGHIJKLMNOPQRSTUVWXYZ

abcdefghijklmnopqrstuvwxyz

1234567890?!$%&

Adobe Systems, Inc.

Helvetica 65 Medium

ABCDEFGHIJKLMNOPQRSTUVWXYZ
abcdefghijklmnopqrstuvwxyz
1234567890?!$%&
Adobe Systems, Inc.

Helvetica 66 Medium Italic

ABCDEFGHIJKLMNOPQRSTUVWXYZ
abcdefghijklmnopqrstuvwxyz
1234567890?!$%&
Adobe Systems, Inc.

Helvetica 75 Bold

ABCDEFGHIJKLMNOPQRSTUVWXYZ
abcdefghijklmnopqrstuvwxyz
1234567890?!$%&
Adobe Systems, Inc.

Helvetica 76 Bold Italic

ABCDEFGHIJKLMNOPQRSTUVWXYZ
abcdefghijklmnopqrstuvwxyz
1234567890?!$%&
Adobe Systems, Inc.

Helvetica 85 Heavy

ABCDEFGHIJKLMNOPQRSTUVWXYZ
abcdefghijklmnopqrstuvwxyz
1234567890?!$%&
Adobe Systems, Inc.

Helvetica 86 Heavy Italic

ABCDEFGHIJKLMNOPQRSTUVWXYZ

abcdefghijklmnopqrstuvwxyz

1234567890?!$%&

Adobe Systems, Inc.

Helvetica 95 Black

ABCDEFGHIJKLMNOPQRSTUVWXYZ

abcdefghijklmnopqrstuvwxyz

1234567890?!$%&

Adobe Systems, Inc.

Helvetica 96 Black Italic

ABCDEFGHIJKLMNOPQRSTUVWXYZ

abcdefghijklmnopqrstuvwxyz

1234567890?!$%&

Adobe Systems, Inc.

Hiroshige Medium

ABCDEFGHIJKLMNOPQRSTUVWXYZ

abcdefghijklmnopqrstuvwxyz

1234567890?!$%&

Adobe Systems, Inc.

Hiroshige Book

ABCDEFGHIJKLMNOPQRSTUVWXYZ

abcdefghijklmnopqrstuvwxyz

1234567890?!$%&

Adobe Systems, Inc.

Hiroshige Medium Italic

ABCDEFGHIJKLMNOPQRSTUVWXYZ
abcdefghijklmnopqrstuvwxyz
1234567890?!$%&
Adobe Systems, Inc.

Hiroshige Book Italic

ABCDEFGHIJKLMNOPQRSTUVWXYZ
abcdefghijklmnopqrstuvwxyz
1234567890?!$%&
Adobe Systems, Inc.

Hiroshige Bold

ABCDEFGHIJKLMNOPQRSTUVWXYZ
abcdefghijklmnopqrstuvwxyz
1234567890?!$%&
Adobe Systems, Inc.

Hiroshige™ Black

ABCDEFGHIJKLMNOPQRSTUVWXYZ
abcdefghijklmnopqrstuvwxyz
1234567890?!$%&
Adobe Systems, Inc.

Hiroshige Bold Italic

ABCDEFGHIJKLMNOPQRSTUVWXYZ
abcdefghijklmnopqrstuvwxyz
1234567890?!$%&
Adobe Systems, Inc.

Hiroshige Black Italic

ABCDEFGHIJKLMNOPQRSTUVWXYZ

abcdefghijklmnopqrstuvwxyz

1234567890?!$%&

Adobe Systems, Inc.

Hobo

ABCDEFGHIJKLMNOPQRSTUVWXYZ

abcdefghijklmnopqrstuvwxyz

1234567890?!$%&

Adobe Systems, Inc.

Impressum Roman

ABCDEFGHIJKLMNOPQRSTUVWXYZ

abcdefghijklmnopqrstuvwxyz

1234567890?!$%&

Adobe Systems, Inc.

Impressum Italic

ABCDEFGHIJKLMNOPQRSTUVWXYZ

abcdefghijklmnopqrstuvwxyz

1234567890?!$%&

Adobe Systems, Inc.

Impressum® Bold

ABCDEFGHIJKLMNOPQRSTUVWXYZ

abcdefghijklmnopqrstuvwxyz

1234567890?!$%&

Adobe Systems, Inc.

Italia Medium

ABCDEFGHIJKLMNOPQRSTUVWXYZ
abcdefghijklmnopqrstuvwxyz
1234567890?!$%&
Adobe Systems, Inc.

Italia Book

ABCDEFGHIJKLMNOPQRSTUVWXYZ
abcdefghijklmnopqrstuvwxyz
1234567890?!$%&
Adobe Systems, Inc.

Italia Bold

ABCDEFGHIJKLMNOPQRSTUVWXYZ
abcdefghijklmnopqrstuvwxyz
1234567890?!$%&
Adobe Systems, Inc.

Janson Text™

ABCDEFGHIJKLMNOPQRSTUVWXYZ
abcdefghijklmnopqrstuvwxyz
1234567890?!$%&
Adobe Systems, Inc.

Janson Text Italic

ABCDEFGHIJKLMNOPQRSTUVWXYZ
abcdefghijklmnopqrstuvwxyz
1234567890?!$%&
Adobe Systems, Inc.

Janson Text Bold

ABCDEFGHIJKLMNOPQRSTUVWXYZ

abcdefghijklmnopqrstuvwxyz

1234567890?!$%&

Adobe Systems, Inc.

Janson Text Bold Italic

ABCDEFGHIJKLMNOPQRSTUVWXYZ

abcdefghijklmnopqrstuvwxyz

1234567890?!$%&

Adobe Systems, Inc.

Jott Casual

ABCDEFGHIJKLMNOPQRSTUVWXYZ

abcdefghijklmnopqrstuvwxyz

1234567890?!$%&

Casady & Greene, Inc.

Jott Light

ABCDEFGHIJKLMNOPQRSTUVWXYZ

abcdefghijklmnopqrstuvwxyz

1234567890?!$%&

Casady & Greene, Inc.

Jott Quick

ABCDEFGHIJKLMNOPQRSTUVWXYZ

abcdefghijklmnopqrstuvwxyz

1234567890?!$%&

Casady & Greene, Inc.

Jott Quick Light

ABCDEFGHIJKLMNOPQRSTUVWXYZ

abcdefghijklmnopqrstuvwxyz

1234567890?!$%&

Casady & Greene, Inc.

ITC Kabel Medium

ABCDEFGHIJKLMNOPQRSTUVWXYZ

abcdefghijklmnopqrstuvwxyz

1234567890?!$%&

Adobe Systems, Inc.

ITC Kabel Book

ABCDEFGHIJKLMNOPQRSTUVWXYZ

abcdefghijklmnopqrstuvwxyz

1234567890?!$%&

Adobe Systems, Inc.

ITC Kabel® Bold

ABCDEFGHIJKLMNOPQRSTUVWXYZ

abcdefghijklmnopqrstuvwxyz

1234567890?!$%&

Adobe Systems, Inc

ITC Kabel Demi

ABCDEFGHIJKLMNOPQRSTUVWXYZ

abcdefghijklmnopqrstuvwxyz

1234567890?!$%&

Adobe Systems, Inc.

ITC Kabel Ultra

ABCDEFGHIJKLMNOPQRSTUVWXYZ
abcdefghijklmnopqrstuvwxyz
1234567890?!$%&

Adobe Systems, Inc.

Kaufmann®

ABCDEFGHIJKLMNOPQRSTUVWXYZ
abcdefghijklmnopqrstuvwxyz
1234567890?!$%&

Adobe Systems, Inc.

Kaufmann Bold

ABCDEFGHIJKLMNOPQRSTUVWXYZ
abcdefghijklmnopqrstuvwxyz
1234567890?!$%&

Adobe Systems, Inc.

Kaufmann Bold

ABCDEFGHIJKLMNOPQRSTUVWXYZ
abcdefghijklmnopqrstuvwxyz
1234567890?!$%&

Bitstream, Inc.

Kells

ABCDEFGHIJKLMNOPQRSTUVWXYZ
abcdefghijklmnopqrstuvwxyz
1234567890?!$%&

Casady & Greene, Inc.

ITC Korinna Regular

ABCDEFGHIJKLMNOPQRSTUVWXYZ

abcdefghijklmnopqrstuvwxyz

1234567890?!$%&

Adobe Systems, Inc. / Bitstream, Inc.

ITC Korinna Kursiv Regular

ABCDEFGHIJKLMNOPQRSTUVWXYZ

abcdefghijklmnopqrstuvwxyz

1234567890?!$%&

Adobe Systems, Inc. / Bitstream, Inc.

ITC Korinna® Bold

ABCDEFGHIJKLMNOPQRSTUVWXYZ

abcdefghijklmnopqrstuvwxyz

1234567890?!$%&

Adobe Systems, Inc.

ITC Korinna Kursiv Bold

ABCDEFGHIJKLMNOPQRSTUVWXYZ

abcdefghijklmnopqrstuvwxyz

1234567890?!$%&

Adobe Systems, Inc.

Letter Gothic

ABCDEFGHIJKLMNOPQRSTUVWXYZ

abcdefghijklmnopqrstuvwxyz

1234567890?!$%&

Adobe Systems, Inc.

Letter Gothic Slanted

ABCDEFGHIJKLMNOPQRSTUVWXYZ

abcdefghijklmnopqrstuvwxyz

1234567890?!$%&

Adobe Systems, Inc.

Letter Gothic Bold Slanted

ABCDEFGHIJKLMNOPQRSTUVWXYZ

abcdefghijklmnopqrstuvwxyz

1234567890?!$%&

Adobe Systems, Inc.

Letter Gothic Bold

ABCDEFGHIJKLMNOPQRSTUVWXYZ

abcdefghijklmnopqrstuvwxyz

1234567890?!$%&

Adobe Systems, Inc.

Life Roman

ABCDEFGHIJKLMNOPQRSTUVWXYZ

abcdefghijklmnopqrstuvwxyz

1234567890?!$%&

Adobe Systems, Inc.

Life Italic

ABCDEFGHIJKLMNOPQRSTUVWXYZ

abcdefghijklmnopqrstuvwxyz

1234567890?!$%&

Adobe Systems, Inc.

Life® Bold

ABCDEFGHIJKLMNOPQRSTUVWXYZ
abcdefghijklmnopqrstuvwxyz
1234567890?!$%&
Adobe Systems, Inc.

Linoscript™

ABCDEFGHIJKLMNOPQRSTUVWXYZ
abcdefghijklmnopqrstuvwxyz
1234567890?!$%&
Adobe Systems, Inc.

Linotext™

ABCDEFGHIJKLMNOPQRSTUVWXYZ
abcdefghijklmnopqrstuvwxyz
1234567890?!$%&
Adobe Systems, Inc.

Linotype Centennial™ 45 Light

ABCDEFGHIJKLMNOPQRSTUVWXYZ
abcdefghijklmnopqrstuvwxyz
1234567890?!$%&
Adobe Systems, Inc.

Linotype Centennial 46 Light Italic

ABCDEFGHIJKLMNOPQRSTUVWXYZ
abcdefghijklmnopqrstuvwxyz
1234567890?!$%&
Adobe Systems, Inc.

Linotype Centennial 55
ABCDEFGHIJKLMNOPQRSTUVWXYZ
abcdefghijklmnopqrstuvwxyz
1234567890?!$%&
Adobe Systems, Inc.

Linotype Centennial 56 Italic
ABCDEFGHIJKLMNOPQRSTUVWXYZ
abcdefghijklmnopqrstuvwxyz
1234567890?!$%&
Adobe Systems, Inc.

Linotype Centennial 75 Bold
ABCDEFGHIJKLMNOPQRSTUVWXYZ
abcdefghijklmnopqrstuvwxyz
1234567890?!$%&
Adobe Systems, Inc.

Linotype Centennial 76 Bold Italic
ABCDEFGHIJKLMNOPQRSTUVWXYZ
abcdefghijklmnopqrstuvwxyz
1234567890?!$%&
Adobe Systems, Inc.

Linotype Centennial 95 Black
ABCDEFGHIJKLMNOPQRSTUVWXYZ
abcdefghijklmnopqrstuvwxyz
1234567890?!$%&
Adobe Systems, Inc.

Linotype Centennial 96 Black Italic

ABCDEFGHIJKLMNOPQRSTUVWXYZ

abcdefghijklmnopqrstuvwxyz

1234567890?!$%&

Adobe Systems, Inc.

ITC Lubalin Graph® Book

ABCDEFGHIJKLMNOPQRSTUVWXYZ

abcdefghijklmnopqrstuvwxyz

1234567890?!$%&

Adobe Systems, Inc. / Bitstream, Inc.

ITC Lubalin Graph Book Oblique

ABCDEFGHIJKLMNOPQRSTUVWXYZ

abcdefghijklmnopqrstuvwxyz

1234567890?!$%&

Adobe Systems, Inc.

ITC Lubalin Graph Demi

ABCDEFGHIJKLMNOPQRSTUVWXYZ

abcdefghijklmnopqrstuvwxyz

1234567890?!$%&

Adobe Systems, Inc. / Bitstream, Inc.

ITC Lubalin Graph Demi Oblique

ABCDEFGHIJKLMNOPQRSTUVWXYZ

abcdefghijklmnopqrstuvwxyz

1234567890?!$%&

Adobe Systems, Inc.

Lucida®

ABCDEFGHIJKLMNOPQRSTUVWXYZ
abcdefghijklmnopqrstuvwxyz
1234567890?!$%&

Adobe Systems, Inc.

Lucida Italic

ABCDEFGHIJKLMNOPQRSTUVWXYZ
abcdefghijklmnopqrstuvwxyz
1234567890?!$%&

Adobe Systems, Inc.

Lucida Bold

ABCDEFGHIJKLMNOPQRSTUVWXYZ
abcdefghijklmnopqrstuvwxyz
1234567890?!$%&

Adobe Systems, Inc.

Lucida Bold Italic

ABCDEFGHIJKLMNOPQRSTUVWXYZ
abcdefghijklmnopqrstuvwxyz
1234567890?!$%&

Adobe Systems, Inc.

Lucida Sans Roman

ABCDEFGHIJKLMNOPQRSTUVWXYZ
abcdefghijklmnopqrstuvwxyz
1234567890?!$%&

Adobe Systems, Inc.

Lucida Sans Italic

ABCDEFGHIJKLMNOPQRSTUVWXYZ

abcdefghijklmnopqrstuvwxyz

1234567890?!$%&

Adobe Systems, Inc.

Lucida Sans Bold

ABCDEFGHIJKLMNOPQRSTUVWXYZ

abcdefghijklmnopqrstuvwxyz

1234567890?!$%&

Adobe Systems, Inc.

Lucida Sans Bold Italic

ABCDEFGHIJKLMNOPQRSTUVWXYZ

abcdefghijklmnopqrstuvwxyz

1234567890?!$%&

Adobe Systems, Inc.

ITC MACHINE

ABCDEFGHIJKLMNOPQRSTUVWXYZ

1234567890?!$%&

Adobe Systems, Inc.

Meath

ABCDEFGHIJKLMNOPQRSTUVWXYZ

abcdefghijklmnopqrstuvwxyz

1234567890?!$%&

Casady & Greene, Inc.

Melior™

ABCDEFGHIJKLMNOPQRSTUVWXYZ
abcdefghijklmnopqrstuvwxyz
1234567890?!$%&

Adobe Systems, Inc.

Melior Italic

ABCDEFGHIJKLMNOPQRSTUVWXYZ
abcdefghijklmnopqrstuvwxyz
1234567890?!$%&

Adobe Systems, Inc.

Melior Bold

ABCDEFGHIJKLMNOPQRSTUVWXYZ
abcdefghijklmnopqrstuvwxyz
1234567890?!$%&

Adobe Systems, Inc.

Melior Bold Italic

ABCDEFGHIJKLMNOPQRSTUVWXYZ
abcdefghijklmnopqrstuvwxyz
1234567890?!$%&

Adobe Systems, Inc.

Memphis Medium

ABCDEFGHIJKLMNOPQRSTUVWXYZ
abcdefghijklmnopqrstuvwxyz
1234567890?!$%&

Adobe Systems, Inc.

Memphis Medium Italic

ABCDEFGHIJKLMNOPQRSTUVWXYZ

abcdefghijklmnopqrstuvwxyz

1234567890?!$%&

Adobe Systems, Inc.

Memphis Bold

ABCDEFGHIJKLMNOPQRSTUVWXYZ

abcdefghijklmnopqrstuvwxyz

1234567890?!$%&

Adobe Systems, Inc.

Memphis Bold Italic

ABCDEFGHIJKLMNOPQRSTUVWXYZ

abcdefghijklmnopqrstuvwxyz

1234567890?!$%&

Adobe Systems, Inc.

Memphis Extra Bold

ABCDEFGHIJKLMNOPQRSTUVWXYZ

abcdefghijklmnopqrstuvwxyz

1234567890?!$%&

Adobe Systems, Inc.

Memphis Light

ABCDEFGHIJKLMNOPQRSTUVWXYZ

abcdefghijklmnopqrstuvwxyz

1234567890?!$%&

Adobe Systems, Inc.

Memphis Light Italic

ABCDEFGHIJKLMNOPQRSTUVWXYZ

abcdefghijklmnopqrstuvwxyz

1234567890?!$%&

Adobe Systems, Inc.

Mermaid

ABCDEFGHIJKLMNOPQRSTUVWXYZ

abcdefghijklmnopqrstuvwxyz

1234567890?!$%&

Bitstream, Inc.

Micro

ABCDEFGHIJKLMNOPQRSTUVWXYZ

abcdefghijklmnopqrstuvwxyz

1234567890?!$%&

Casady & Greene, Inc.

Micro Italic

ABCDEFGHIJKLMNOPQRSTUVWXYZ

abcdefghijklmnopqrstuvwxyz

1234567890?!$%&

Casady & Greene, Inc.

Micro Bold

ABCDEFGHIJKLMNOPQRSTUVWXYZ

abcdefghijklmnopqrstuvwxyz

1234567890?!$%&

Casady & Greene, Inc.

Micro Bold Italic

ABCDEFGHIJKLMNOPQRSTUVWXYZ

abcdefghijklmnopqrstuvwxyz

1234567890?!$%&

Casady & Greene, Inc.

Micro Extended

ABCDEFGHIJKLMNOPQRSTUVWXYZ

abcdefghijklmnopqrstuvwxyz

1234567890?!$%&

Casady & Greene, Inc.

Micro Extended Italic

ABCDEFGHIJKLMNOPQRSTUVWXYZ

abcdefghijklmnopqrstuvwxyz

1234567890?!$%&

Casady & Greene, Inc.

Micro Extended Bold

ABCDEFGHIJKLMNOPQRSTUVWXYZ

abcdefghijklmnopqrstuvwxyz

1234567890?!$%&

Casady & Greene, Inc.

Micro Extended Bold Italic

ABCDEFGHIJKLMNOPQRSTUVWXYZ

abcdefghijklmnopqrstuvwxyz

1234567890?!$%&

Casady & Greene, Inc.

MONTEREY MEDIUM

ABCDEFGHIJKLMNOPQRSTUVWXYZ

abcdefghijklmnopqrstuvwxyz

1234567890?!$%&

Casady & Greene, Inc.

MONTEREY ITALIC

ABCDEFGHIJKLMNOPQRSTUVWXYZ

abcdefghijklmnopqrstuvwxyz

1234567890?!$%&

Casady & Greene, Inc.

MONTEREY Bold

ABCDEFGHIJKLMNOPQRSTUVWXYZ

abcdefghijklmnopqrstuvwxyz

1234567890?!$%&

Casady & Greene, Inc.

MONTEREY Bold ITALIC

ABCDEFGHIJKLMNOPQRSTUVWXYZ

abcdefghijklmnopqrstuvwxyz

1234567890?!$%&

Casady & Greene, Inc.

New Aster®

ABCDEFGHIJKLMNOPQRSTUVWXYZ

abcdefghijklmnopqrstuvwxyz

1234567890?!$%&

Adobe Systems, Inc.

New Aster Italic

ABCDEFGHIJKLMNOPQRSTUVWXYZ
abcdefghijklmnopqrstuvwxyz
1234567890?!$%&
Adobe Systems, Inc.

New Aster Bold

ABCDEFGHIJKLMNOPQRSTUVWXYZ
abcdefghijklmnopqrstuvwxyz
1234567890?!$%&
Adobe Systems, Inc.

New Aster Black

ABCDEFGHIJKLMNOPQRSTUVWXYZ
abcdefghijklmnopqrstuvwxyz
1234567890?!$%&
Adobe Systems, Inc.

New Aster Semibold

ABCDEFGHIJKLMNOPQRSTUVWXYZ
abcdefghijklmnopqrstuvwxyz
1234567890?!$%&
Adobe Systems, Inc.

New Aster Bold Italic

ABCDEFGHIJKLMNOPQRSTUVWXYZ
abcdefghijklmnopqrstuvwxyz
1234567890?!$%&
Adobe Systems, Inc.

New Aster Black Italic

ABCDEFGHIJKLMNOPQRSTUVWXYZ

abcdefghijklmnopqrstuvwxyz

1234567890?!$%&

Adobe Systems, Inc.

New Aster Semibold Italic

ABCDEFGHIJKLMNOPQRSTUVWXYZ

abcdefghijklmnopqrstuvwxyz

1234567890?!$%&

Adobe Systems, Inc.

ITC New Baskerville Roman

ABCDEFGHIJKLMNOPQRSTUVWXYZ

abcdefghijklmnopqrstuvwxyz

1234567890?!$%&

Adobe Systems, Inc.

ITC New Baskerville Italic

ABCDEFGHIJKLMNOPQRSTUVWXYZ

abcdefghijklmnopqrstuvwxyz

1234567890?!$%&

Adobe Systems, Inc.

ITC New Baskerville® Bold

ABCDEFGHIJKLMNOPQRSTUVWXYZ

abcdefghijklmnopqrstuvwxyz

1234567890?!$%&

Adobe Systems, Inc.

ITC New Baskerville Bold Italic

ABCDEFGHIJKLMNOPQRSTUVWXYZ

abcdefghijklmnopqrstuvwxyz

1234567890?!$%&

Adobe Systems, Inc.

New Caledonia™

ABCDEFGHIJKLMNOPQRSTUVWXYZ

abcdefghijklmnopqrstuvwxyz

1234567890?!$%&

Adobe Systems, Inc.

New Caledonia Italic

ABCDEFGHIJKLMNOPQRSTUVWXYZ

abcdefghijklmnopqrstuvwxyz

1234567890?!$%&

Adobe Systems, Inc.

New Caledonia Bold

ABCDEFGHIJKLMNOPQRSTUVWXYZ

abcdefghijklmnopqrstuvwxyz

1234567890?!$%&

Adobe Systems, Inc.

New Caledonia Black

ABCDEFGHIJKLMNOPQRSTUVWXYZ

abcdefghijklmnopqrstuvwxyz

1234567890?!$%&

Adobe Systems, Inc.

New Caledonia Semi Bold

ABCDEFGHIJKLMNOPQRSTUVWXYZ

abcdefghijklmnopqrstuvwxyz

1234567890?!$%&

Adobe Systems, Inc.

New Caledonia Bold Italic

ABCDEFGHIJKLMNOPQRSTUVWXYZ

abcdefghijklmnopqrstuvwxyz

1234567890?!$%&

Adobe Systems, Inc.

New Caledonia Black Italic

ABCDEFGHIJKLMNOPQRSTUVWXYZ

abcdefghijklmnopqrstuvwxyz

1234567890?!$%&

Adobe Systems, Inc.

New Caledonia Semi Bold Italic

ABCDEFGHIJKLMNOPQRSTUVWXYZ

abcdefghijklmnopqrstuvwxyz

1234567890?!$%&

Adobe Systems, Inc.

New Century Schoolbook

ABCDEFGHIJKLMNOPQRSTUVWXYZ

abcdefghijklmnopqrstuvwxyz

1234567890?!$%&

Adobe Systems, Inc.

New Century Schoolbook Italic

ABCDEFGHIJKLMNOPQRSTUVWXYZ

abcdefghijklmnopqrstuvwxyz

1234567890?!$%&

Adobe Systems, Inc.

New Century Schoolbook Bold

ABCDEFGHIJKLMNOPQRSTUVWXYZ

abcdefghijklmnopqrstuvwxyz

1234567890?!$%&

Adobe Systems, Inc.

New Century Schoolbook Bold Italic

ABCDEFGHIJKLMNOPQRSTUVWXYZ

abcdefghijklmnopqrstuvwxyz

1234567890?!$%&

Adobe Systems, Inc.

News Gothic

ABCDEFGHIJKLMNOPQRSTUVWXYZ

abcdefghijklmnopqrstuvwxyz

1234567890?!$%&

Adobe Systems, Inc.

News Gothic Oblique

ABCDEFGHIJKLMNOPQRSTUVWXYZ

abcdefghijklmnopqrstuvwxyz

1234567890?!$%&

Adobe Systems, Inc.

News Gothic Bold

ABCDEFGHIJKLMNOPQRSTUVWXYZ
abcdefghijklmnopqrstuvwxyz
1234567890?!$%&

Adobe Systems, Inc.

News Gothic Bold Oblique

ABCDEFGHIJKLMNOPQRSTUVWXYZ
abcdefghijklmnopqrstuvwxyz
1234567890?!$%&

Adobe Systems, Inc.

OCRA

ABCDEFGHIJKLMNOPQRSTUVWXYZ
abcdefghijklmnopqrstuvwxyz
1234567890?!$%&

Adobe Systems, Inc.

OCRB

ABCDEFGHIJKLMNOPQRSTUVWXYZ
abcdefghijklmnopqrstuvwxyz
1234567890?!$%&

Adobe Systems, Inc.

Optima™

ABCDEFGHIJKLMNOPQRSTUVWXYZ
abcdefghijklmnopqrstuvwxyz
1234567890?!$%&

Adobe Systems, Inc.

Optima Oblique

ABCDEFGHIJKLMNOPQRSTUVWXYZ
abcdefghijklmnopqrstuvwxyz
1234567890?!$%&
Adobe Systems, Inc.

Optima Bold

ABCDEFGHIJKLMNOPQRSTUVWXYZ
abcdefghijklmnopqrstuvwxyz
1234567890?!$%&
Adobe Systems, Inc.

Optima Bold Oblique

ABCDEFGHIJKLMNOPQRSTUVWXYZ
abcdefghijklmnopqrstuvwxyz
1234567890?!$%&
Adobe Systems, Inc.

ORATOR

ABCDEFGHIJKLMNOPQRSTUVWXYZ
ABCDEFGHIJKLMNOPQRSTUVWXYZ
1234567890?!$%&
Adobe Systems, Inc.

ORATOR SLANTED

ABCDEFGHIJKLMNOPQRSTUVWXYZ
ABCDEFGHIJKLMNOPQRSTUVWXYZ
1234567890?!$%&
Adobe Systems, Inc.

P.T. Barnum

ABCDEFGHIJKLMNOPQRSTUVWXYZ
abcdefghijklmnopqrstuvwxyz
1234567890?!$%&
Bitstream, Inc.

Paladin

ABCDEFGHIJKLMNOPQRSTUVWXYZ
abcdefghijklmnopqrstuvwxyz
1234567890?!$%&
Casady & Greene, Inc.

Palatino™

ABCDEFGHIJKLMNOPQRSTUVWXYZ
abcdefghijklmnopqrstuvwxyz
1234567890?!$%&
Adobe Systems, Inc.

Palatino Italic

ABCDEFGHIJKLMNOPQRSTUVWXYZ
abcdefghijklmnopqrstuvwxyz
1234567890?!$%&
Adobe Systems, Inc.

Palatino Bold

ABCDEFGHIJKLMNOPQRSTUVWXYZ
abcdefghijklmnopqrstuvwxyz
1234567890?!$%&
Adobe Systems, Inc.

Palatino Bold Italic

ABCDEFGHIJKLMNOPQRSTUVWXYZ

abcdefghijklmnopqrstuvwxyz

1234567890?!$%&

Adobe Systems, Inc.

Park Avenue®

ABCDEFGHIJKLMNOPQRSTUVWXYZ

abcdefghijklmnopqrstuvwxyz

1234567890?!$%&

Adobe Systems, Inc.

Park Avenue

ABCDEFGHIJKLMNOPQRSTUVWXYZ

abcdefghijklmnopqrstuvwxyz

1234567890?!$%&

Bitstream, Inc.

Peignot™ Bold

ABCDEFGHIJKLMNOPQRSTUVWXYZ

abcdefghijklmnopqrstuvwxyz

1234567890?!$%&

Adobe Systems, Inc.

Peignot Demi

ABCDEFGHIJKLMNOPQRSTUVWXYZ

abcdefghijklmnopqrstuvwxyz

1234567890?!$%&

Adobe Systems, Inc.

Peignot Light

ABCDEFGHIJKLMNOPQRSTUVWXYZ

abcdefghijklmnopqrstuvwxyz

1234567890?!$%&

Adobe Systems, Inc.

Post Antiqua™

ABCDEFGHIJKLMNOPQRSTUVWXYZ

abcdefghijklmnopqrstuvwxyz

1234567890?!$%&

Adobe Systems, Inc.

Post Antiqua Bold

ABCDEFGHIJKLMNOPQRSTUVWXYZ

abcdefghijklmnopqrstuvwxyz

1234567890?!$%&

Adobe Systems, Inc.

Prelude Script

ABCDEFGHIJKLMNOPQRSTUVWXYZ

abcdefghijklmnopqrstuvwxyz

1234567890?!$%&

Casady & Greene, Inc.

Prelude Script Bold

ABCDEFGHIJKLMNOPQRSTUVWXYZ

abcdefghijklmnopqrstuvwxyz

1234567890?!$%&

Casady & Greene, Inc.

Prelude Script Bold Slant

ABCDEFGHIJKLMNOPQRSTUVWXYZ

abcdefghijklmnopqrstuvwxyz

1234567890?!$%&

Casady & Greene, Inc.

Prelude Script Light Slant

ABCDEFGHIJKLMNOPQRSTUVWXYZ

abcdefghijklmnopqrstuvwxyz

1234567890?!$%&

Casady & Greene, Inc.

Present™ Script

ABCDEFGHIJKLMNOPQRSTUVWXYZ

abcdefghijklmnopqrstuvwxyz

1234567890?!$%&

Adobe Systems, Inc.

Prestige Elite

ABCDEFGHIJKLMNOPQRSTUVWXYZ

abcdefghijklmnopqrstuvwxyz

1234567890?!$%&

Adobe Systems, Inc.

Prestige Elite Slanted

ABCDEFGHIJKLMNOPQRSTUVWXYZ

abcdefghijklmnopqrstuvwxyz

1234567890?!$%&

Adobe Systems, Inc.

Prestige Elite Bold

ABCDEFGHIJKLMNOPQRSTUVWXYZ

abcdefghijklmnopqrstuvwxyz

1234567890?!$%&

Adobe Systems, Inc.

Prestige Elite Bold Slanted

ABCDEFGHIJKLMNOPQRSTUVWXYZ

abcdefghijklmnopqrstuvwxyz

1234567890?!$%&

Adobe Systems, Inc.

Provence Roman

ABCDEFGHIJKLMNOPQRSTUVWXYZ

abcdefghijklmnopqrstuvwxyz

1234567890?!$%&

Bitstream, Inc.

Provence Italic

ABCDEFGHIJKLMNOPQRSTUVWXYZ

abcdefghijklmnopqrstuvwxyz

1234567890?!$%&

Bitstream, Inc.

Provence Black

ABCDEFGHIJKLMNOPQRSTUVWXYZ

abcdefghijklmnopqrstuvwxyz

1234567890?!$%&

Bitstream, Inc.

Provence Compact

ABCDEFGHIJKLMNOPQRSTUVWXYZ
abcdefghijklmnopqrstuvwxyz
1234567890?!$%&

Bitstream, Inc.

Regency Script

ABCDEFGHIJKLMNOPQRSTUVWXYZ
abcdefghijklmnopqrstuvwxyz
1234567890?!$%&

Casady & Greene, Inc.

Revue

ABCDEFGHIJKLMNOPQRSTUVWXYZ
abcdefghijklmnopqrstuvwxyz
1234567890?!$%&

Adobe Systems, Inc.

Right Bank

ABCDEFGHIJKLMNOPQRSTUVWXYZ
ABCDEFGHIJKLMNOPQRSTUVWXYZ
1234567890?!$%&

Casady & Greene, Inc.

Ritz

ABCDEFGHIJKLMNOPQRSTUVWXYZ
abcdefghijklmnopqrstuvwxyz
1234567890?!$%&

Casady & Greene, Inc.

Ritz Italic

ABCDEFGHIJKLMNOPQRSTUVWXYZ

abcdefghijklmnopqrstuvwxyz

1234567890?!$%&

Casady & Greene, Inc.

Ritz Condensed

ABCDEFGHIJKLMNOPQRSTUVWXYZ

abcdefghijklmnopqrstuvwxyz

1234567890?!$%&

Casady & Greene, Inc.

Sabon™

ABCDEFGHIJKLMNOPQRSTUVWXYZ

abcdefghijklmnopqrstuvwxyz

1234567890?!$%&

Adobe Systems, Inc.

Sabon Italic

ABCDEFGHIJKLMNOPQRSTUVWXYZ

abcdefghijklmnopqrstuvwxyz

1234567890?!$%&

Adobe Systems, Inc.

Sabon Bold

ABCDEFGHIJKLMNOPQRSTUVWXYZ

abcdefghijklmnopqrstuvwxyz

1234567890?!$%&

Adobe Systems, Inc.

Sabon Bold Italic

ABCDEFGHIJKLMNOPQRSTUVWXYZ

abcdefghijklmnopqrstuvwxyz

1234567890?!$%&

Adobe Systems, Inc.

Sans Serif

ABCDEFGHIJKLMNOPQRSTUVWXYZ

abcdefghijklmnopqrstuvwxyz

1234567890?!$%&

Casady & Greene, Inc.

Sans Serif Book

ABCDEFGHIJKLMNOPQRSTUVWXYZ

abcdefghijklmnopqrstuvwxyz

1234567890?!$%&

Casady & Greene, Inc.

Sans Serif Italic

ABCDEFGHIJKLMNOPQRSTUVWXYZ

abcdefghijklmnopqrstuvwxyz

1234567890?!$%&

Casady & Greene, Inc.

Sans Serif Book Italic

ABCDEFGHIJKLMNOPQRSTUVWXYZ

abcdefghijklmnopqrstuvwxyz

1234567890?!$%&

Casady & Greene, Inc.

Sans Serif Bold

ABCDEFGHIJKLMNOPQRSTUVWXYZ

abcdefghijklmnopqrstuvwxyz

1234567890?!$%&

Casady & Greene, Inc.

Sans Serif Extra Bold

ABCDEFGHIJKLMNOPQRSTUVWXYZ

abcdefghijklmnopqrstuvwxyz

1234567890?!$%&

Casady & Greene, Inc.

Sans Serif Demi Bold

ABCDEFGHIJKLMNOPQRSTUVWXYZ

abcdefghijklmnopqrstuvwxyz

1234567890?!$%&

Casady & Greene, Inc.

Sans Serif Bold Italic

ABCDEFGHIJKLMNOPQRSTUVWXYZ

abcdefghijklmnopqrstuvwxyz

1234567890?!$%&

Casady & Greene, Inc.

Sans Serif Extra Bold Italic

ABCDEFGHIJKLMNOPQRSTUVWXYZ

abcdefghijklmnopqrstuvwxyz

1234567890?!$%&

Casady & Greene, Inc.

Sans Serif Demi Italic

ABCDEFGHIJKLMNOPQRSTUVWXYZ

abcdefghijklmnopqrstuvwxyz

1234567890?!$%&

Casady & Greene, Inc.

Sans Serif Bold Condensed

ABCDEFGHIJKLMNOPQRSTUVWXYZ

abcdefghijklmnopqrstuvwxyz

1234567890?!$%&

Casady & Greene, Inc.

Sans Serif Extra Bold Condensed

ABCDEFGHIJKLMNOPQRSTUVWXYZ

abcdefghijklmnopqrstuvwxyz

1234567890?!$%&

Casady & Greene, Inc.

Sans Serif Bold Condensed Italic

ABCDEFGHIJKLMNOPQRSTUVWXYZ

abcdefghijklmnopqrstuvwxyz

1234567890?!$%&

Casady & Greene, Inc.

Sans Serif Extra Bold Condensed Italic

ABCDEFGHIJKLMNOPQRSTUVWXYZ

abcdefghijklmnopqrstuvwxyz

1234567890?!$%&

Casady & Greene, Inc.

ITC Serif Gothic®

ABCDEFGHIJKLMNOPQRSTUVWXYZ
abcdefghijklmnopqrstuvwxyz
1234567890?!$%&

Adobe Systems, Inc.

ITC Serif Gothic Bold

ABCDEFGHIJKLMNOPQRSTUVWXYZ
abcdefghijklmnopqrstuvwxyz
1234567890?!$%&

Adobe Systems, Inc.

ITC Serif Gothic Extra Bold

ABCDEFGHIJKLMNOPQRSTUVWXYZ
abcdefghijklmnopqrstuvwxyz
1234567890?!$%&

Adobe Systems, Inc.

ITC Serif Gothic Black

ABCDEFGHIJKLMNOPQRSTUVWXYZ
abcdefghijklmnopqrstuvwxyz
1234567890?!$%&

Adobe Systems, Inc.

ITC Serif Gothic Heavy

ABCDEFGHIJKLMNOPQRSTUVWXYZ
abcdefghijklmnopqrstuvwxyz
1234567890?!$%&

Adobe Systems, Inc.

ITC Serif Gothic Light

ABCDEFGHIJKLMNOPQRSTUVWXYZ

abcdefghijklmnopqrstuvwxyz

1234567890?!$%&

Adobe Systems, Inc.

Serifa® 45 Light

ABCDEFGHIJKLMNOPQRSTUVWXYZ

abcdefghijklmnopqrstuvwxyz

1234567890?!$%&

Adobe Systems, Inc.

Serifa 46 Light Italic

ABCDEFGHIJKLMNOPQRSTUVWXYZ

abcdefghijklmnopqrstuvwxyz

1234567890?!$%&

Adobe Systems, Inc.

Serifa 55

ABCDEFGHIJKLMNOPQRSTUVWXYZ

abcdefghijklmnopqrstuvwxyz

1234567890?!$%&

Adobe Systems, Inc.

Serifa 56 Italic

ABCDEFGHIJKLMNOPQRSTUVWXYZ

abcdefghijklmnopqrstuvwxyz

1234567890?!$%&

Adobe Systems, Inc.

Serifa 65 Bold

ABCDEFGHIJKLMNOPQRSTUVWXYZ
abcdefghijklmnopqrstuvwxyz
1234567890?!$%&

Adobe Systems, Inc.

Serifa 75 Black

ABCDEFGHIJKLMNOPQRSTUVWXYZ
abcdefghijklmnopqrstuvwxyz
1234567890?!$%&

Adobe Systems, Inc.

ITC Souvenir®

ABCDEFGHIJKLMNOPQRSTUVWXYZ
abcdefghijklmnopqrstuvwxyz
1234567890?!$%&

Adobe Systems, Inc.

ITC Souvenir Demi

ABCDEFGHIJKLMNOPQRSTUVWXYZ
abcdefghijklmnopqrstuvwxyz
1234567890?!$%&

Adobe Systems, Inc. / Bitstream, Inc.

ITC Souvenir Demi Italic

ABCDEFGHIJKLMNOPQRSTUVWXYZ
abcdefghijklmnopqrstuvwxyz
1234567890?!$%&

Adobe Systems, Inc. / Bitstream, Inc.

ITC Souvenir Light

ABCDEFGHIJKLMNOPQRSTUVWXYZ
abcdefghijklmnopqrstuvwxyz
1234567890?!$%&

Bitstream, Inc.

ITC Souvenir Light Italic

ABCDEFGHIJKLMNOPQRSTUVWXYZ
abcdefghijklmnopqrstuvwxyz
1234567890?!$%&

Adobe Systems, Inc. / Bitstream, Inc.

STENCIL

ABCDEFGHIJKLMNOPQRSTUVWXYZ
1234567890?!$%&

Adobe Systems, Inc.

Stone® Informal

ABCDEFGHIJKLMNOPQRSTUVWXYZ
abcdefghijklmnopqrstuvwxyz
1234567890?!$%&

Adobe Systems, Inc.

Stone Informal Italic

ABCDEFGHIJKLMNOPQRSTUVWXYZ
abcdefghijklmnopqrstuvwxyz
1234567890?!$%&

Adobe Systems, Inc.

Stone Informal Bold

ABCDEFGHIJKLMNOPQRSTUVWXYZ
abcdefghijklmnopqrstuvwxyz
1234567890?!$%&

Adobe Systems, Inc.

Stone Informal Semibold

ABCDEFGHIJKLMNOPQRSTUVWXYZ
abcdefghijklmnopqrstuvwxyz
1234567890?!$%&

Adobe Systems, Inc.

Stone Informal Bold Italic

ABCDEFGHIJKLMNOPQRSTUVWXYZ
abcdefghijklmnopqrstuvwxyz
1234567890?!$%&

Adobe Systems, Inc.

Stone Informal Semibold Italic

ABCDEFGHIJKLMNOPQRSTUVWXYZ
abcdefghijklmnopqrstuvwxyz
1234567890?!$%&

Adobe Systems, Inc.

Stone Sans

ABCDEFGHIJKLMNOPQRSTUVWXYZ
abcdefghijklmnopqrstuvwxyz
1234567890?!$%&

Adobe Systems, Inc.

Stone Sans Italic

ABCDEFGHIJKLMNOPQRSTUVWXYZ

abcdefghijklmnopqrstuvwxyz

1234567890?!$%&

Adobe Systems, Inc.

Stone Sans Bold

ABCDEFGHIJKLMNOPQRSTUVWXYZ

abcdefghijklmnopqrstuvwxyz

1234567890?!$%&

Adobe Systems, Inc.

Stone Sans Semibold

ABCDEFGHIJKLMNOPQRSTUVWXYZ

abcdefghijklmnopqrstuvwxyz

1234567890?!$%&

Adobe Systems, Inc.

Stone Sans Bold Italic

ABCDEFGHIJKLMNOPQRSTUVWXYZ

abcdefghijklmnopqrstuvwxyz

1234567890?!$%&

Adobe Systems, Inc.

Stone Sans Semibold Italic

ABCDEFGHIJKLMNOPQRSTUVWXYZ

abcdefghijklmnopqrstuvwxyz

1234567890?!$%&

Adobe Systems, Inc.

Stone Serif

ABCDEFGHIJKLMNOPQRSTUVWXYZ
abcdefghijklmnopqrstuvwxyz
1234567890?!$%&
Adobe Systems, Inc.

Stone Serif Italic

ABCDEFGHIJKLMNOPQRSTUVWXYZ
abcdefghijklmnopqrstuvwxyz
1234567890?!$%&
Adobe Systems, Inc.

Stone Serif Bold

ABCDEFGHIJKLMNOPQRSTUVWXYZ
abcdefghijklmnopqrstuvwxyz
1234567890?!$%&
Adobe Systems, Inc.

Stone Serif Semibold

ABCDEFGHIJKLMNOPQRSTUVWXYZ
abcdefghijklmnopqrstuvwxyz
1234567890?!$%&
Adobe Systems, Inc.

Stone Serif Bold Italic

ABCDEFGHIJKLMNOPQRSTUVWXYZ
abcdefghijklmnopqrstuvwxyz
1234567890?!$%&
Adobe Systems, Inc

Stone Serif Semibold Italic

ABCDEFGHIJKLMNOPQRSTUVWXYZ
abcdefghijklmnopqrstuvwxyz
1234567890?!$%&

Adobe Systems, Inc.

Swiss Roman

ABCDEFGHIJKLMNOPQRSTUVWXYZ
abcdefghijklmnopqrstuvwxyz
1234567890?!$%&

Bitstream, Inc.

Swiss Italic

ABCDEFGHIJKLMNOPQRSTUVWXYZ
abcdefghijklmnopqrstuvwxyz
1234567890?!$%&

Bitstream, Inc.

Swiss Bold

ABCDEFGHIJKLMNOPQRSTUVWXYZ
abcdefghijklmnopqrstuvwxyz
1234567890?!$%&

Bitstream, Inc.

Swiss Bold Italic

ABCDEFGHIJKLMNOPQRSTUVWXYZ
abcdefghijklmnopqrstuvwxyz
1234567890?!$%&

Bitstream, Inc.

Swiss Condensed Roman

ABCDEFGHIJKLMNOPQRSTUVWXYZ

abcdefghijklmnopqrstuvwxyz

1234567890?!$%&

Bitstream, Inc.

Swiss Condensed Italic

ABCDEFGHIJKLMNOPQRSTUVWXYZ

abcdefghijklmnopqrstuvwxyz

1234567890?!$%&

Bitstream, Inc.

Swiss Bold Condensed

ABCDEFGHIJKLMNOPQRSTUVWXYZ

abcdefghijklmnopqrstuvwxyz

1234567890?!$%&

Bitstream, Inc.

Swiss Black Condensed

ABCDEFGHIJKLMNOPQRSTUVWXYZ

abcdefghijklmnopqrstuvwxyz

1234567890?!$%&

Bitstream, Inc.

Swiss Light

ABCDEFGHIJKLMNOPQRSTUVWXYZ

abcdefghijklmnopqrstuvwxyz

1234567890?!$%&

Bitstream, Inc.

Swiss Light Italic

ABCDEFGHIJKLMNOPQRSTUVWXYZ
abcdefghijklmnopqrstuvwxyz
1234567890?!$%&

Bitstream, Inc.

Swiss Black

ABCDEFGHIJKLMNOPQRSTUVWXYZ
abcdefghijklmnopqrstuvwxyz
1234567890?!$%&

Bitstream, Inc.

Swiss Black Italic

ABCDEFGHIJKLMNOPQRSTUVWXYZ
abcdefghijklmnopqrstuvwxyz
1234567890?!$%&

Bitstream, Inc.

Tempo Heavy Condensed

ABCDEFGHIJKLMNOPQRSTUVWXYZ
abcdefghijklmnopqrstuvwxyz
1234567890?!$%&

Adobe Systems, Inc.

Tempo Heavy Condensed Italic

ABCDEFGHIJKLMNOPQRSTUVWXYZ
abcdefghijklmnopqrstuvwxyz
1234567890?!$%&

Adobe Systems, Inc.

ITC Tiffany®

ABCDEFGHIJKLMNOPQRSTUVWXYZ

abcdefghijklmnopqrstuvwxyz

1234567890?!$%&

Adobe Systems, Inc. / Bitstream, Inc.

ITC Tiffany Italic

ABCDEFGHIJKLMNOPQRSTUVWXYZ

abcdefghijklmnopqrstuvwxyz

1234567890?!$%&

Adobe Systems, Inc. / Bitstream, Inc.

ITC Tiffany Demi

ABCDEFGHIJKLMNOPQRSTUVWXYZ

abcdefghijklmnopqrstuvwxyz

1234567890?!$%&

Adobe Systems, Inc.

ITC Tiffany Heavy

ABCDEFGHIJKLMNOPQRSTUVWXYZ

abcdefghijklmnopqrstuvwxyz

1234567890?!$%&

Adobe Systems, Inc. / Bitstream, Inc.

ITC Tiffany Demi Italic

ABCDEFGHIJKLMNOPQRSTUVWXYZ

abcdefghijklmnopqrstuvwxyz

1234567890?!$%&

Adobe Systems, Inc.

ITC Tiffany Heavy Italic

ABCDEFGHIJKLMNOPQRSTUVWXY

Zabcdefghijklmnopqrstuvwxyz

1234567890?!$%&

Adobe Systems, Inc. / Bitstream, Inc.

Times Ten Roman

ABCDEFGHIJKLMNOPQRSTUVWXYZ

abcdefghijklmnopqrstuvwxyz

1234567890?!$%&

Adobe Systems, Inc.

Times Ten Italic

ABCDEFGHIJKLMNOPQRSTUVWXYZ

abcdefghijklmnopqrstuvwxyz

1234567890?!$%&

Adobe Systems, Inc.

Times™ Ten Bold

ABCDEFGHIJKLMNOPQRSTUVWXYZ

abcdefghijklmnopqrstuvwxyz

1234567890?!$%&

Adobe Systems, Inc.

Times Ten Bold Italic

ABCDEFGHIJKLMNOPQRSTUVWXYZ

abcdefghijklmnopqrstuvwxyz

1234567890?!$%&

Adobe Systems, Inc.

Trump Mediaeval™

ABCDEFGHIJKLMNOPQRSTUVWXYZ
abcdefghijklmnopqrstuvwxyz
1234567890?!$%&

Adobe Systems, Inc.

Trump Mediaeval Italic

ABCDEFGHIJKLMNOPQRSTUVWXYZ
abcdefghijklmnopqrstuvwxyz
1234567890?!$%&

Adobe Systems, Inc.

Trump Mediaeval Bold

ABCDEFGHIJKLMNOPQRSTUVWXYZ
abcdefghijklmnopqrstuvwxyz
1234567890?!$%&

Adobe Systems, Inc.

Trump Mediaeval Bold Italic

ABCDEFGHIJKLMNOPQRSTUVWXYZ
abcdefghijklmnopqrstuvwxyz
1234567890?!$%&

Adobe Systems, Inc.

Univers™ 45 Light

ABCDEFGHIJKLMNOPQRSTUVWXYZ
abcdefghijklmnopqrstuvwxyz
1234567890?!$%&

Adobe Systems, Inc.

Univers 45 Light Oblique

ABCDEFGHIJKLMNOPQRSTUVWXYZ

abcdefghijklmnopqrstuvwxyz

1234567890?!$%&

Adobe Systems, Inc.

Univers 47 Condensed Light

ABCDEFGHIJKLMNOPQRSTUVWXYZ

abcdefghijklmnopqrstuvwxyz

1234567890?!$%&

Adobe Systems, Inc.

Univers 47 Condensed Light Oblique

ABCDEFGHIJKLMNOPQRSTUVWXYZ

abcdefghijklmnopqrstuvwxyz

1234567890?!$%&

Adobe Systems, Inc.

Univers 55

ABCDEFGHIJKLMNOPQRSTUVWXYZ

abcdefghijklmnopqrstuvwxyz

1234567890?!$%&

Adobe Systems, Inc.

Univers 55 Oblique

ABCDEFGHIJKLMNOPQRSTUVWXYZ

abcdefghijklmnopqrstuvwxyz

1234567890?!$%&

Adobe Systems, Inc.

Univers 57 Condensed

ABCDEFGHIJKLMNOPQRSTUVWXYZ
abcdefghijklmnopqrstuvwxyz
1234567890?!$%&

Adobe Systems, Inc.

Univers 57 Condensed Oblique

ABCDEFGHIJKLMNOPQRSTUVWXYZ
abcdefghijklmnopqrstuvwxyz
1234567890?!$%&

Adobe Systems, Inc.

Univers 65 Bold

ABCDEFGHIJKLMNOPQRSTUVWXYZ
abcdefghijklmnopqrstuvwxyz
1234567890?!$%&

Adobe Systems, Inc.

Univers 65 Bold Oblique

ABCDEFGHIJKLMNOPQRSTUVWXYZ
abcdefghijklmnopqrstuvwxyz
1234567890?!$%&

Adobe Systems, Inc.

Univers 67 Condensed Bold

ABCDEFGHIJKLMNOPQRSTUVWXYZ
abcdefghijklmnopqrstuvwxyz
1234567890?!$%&

Adobe Systems, Inc.

Univers 67 Condensed Bold Oblique

ABCDEFGHIJKLMNOPQRSTUVWXYZ

abcdefghijklmnopqrstuvwxyz

1234567890?!$%&

Adobe Systems, Inc.

Univers 75 Black

ABCDEFGHIJKLMNOPQRSTUVWXYZ

abcdefghijklmnopqrstuvwxyz

1234567890?!$%&

Adobe Systems, Inc.

Univers 75 Black Oblique

ABCDEFGHIJKLMNOPQRSTUVWXYZ

abcdefghijklmnopqrstuvwxyz

1234567890?!$%&

Adobe Systems, Inc.

University Roman

ABCDEFGHIJKLMNOPQRSTUVWXYZ

abcdefghijklmnopqrstuvwxyz

1234567890?!$%&

Adobe Systems, Inc. / Bitstream, Inc.

Utopia™

ABCDEFGHIJKLMNOPQRSTUVWXYZ

abcdefghijklmnopqrstuvwxyz

1234567890?!$%&

Adobe Systems, Inc.

Utopia Italic

ABCDEFGHIJKLMNOPQRSTUVWXYZ

abcdefghijklmnopqrstuvwxyz

1234567890?!$%&

Adobe Systems, Inc.

Utopia Bold

ABCDEFGHIJKLMNOPQRSTUVWXYZ

abcdefghijklmnopqrstuvwxyz

1234567890?!$%&

Adobe Systems, Inc.

Utopia Black

ABCDEFGHIJKLMNOPQRSTUVWXYZ

abcdefghijklmnopqrstuvwxyz

1234567890?!$%&

Adobe Systems, Inc.

Utopia Semibold

ABCDEFGHIJKLMNOPQRSTUVWXYZ

abcdefghijklmnopqrstuvwxyz

1234567890?!$%&

Adobe Systems, Inc.

Utopia Bold Italic

ABCDEFGHIJKLMNOPQRSTUVWXYZ

abcdefghijklmnopqrstuvwxyz

1234567890?!$%&

Adobe Systems, Inc.

Utopia Semibold Italic

ABCDEFGHIJKLMNOPQRSTUVWXYZ

abcdefghijklmnopqrstuvwxyz

1234567890?!$%&

Adobe Systems, Inc.

VAG Rounded Bold

ABCDEFGHIJKLMNOPQRSTUVWXYZ

abcdefghijklmnopqrstuvwxyz

1234567890?!$%&

Adobe Systems, Inc.

VAG Rounded Black

ABCDEFGHIJKLMNOPQRSTUVWXYZ

abcdefghijklmnopqrstuvwxyz

1234567890?!$%&

Adobe Systems, Inc.

VAG Rounded Light

ABCDEFGHIJKLMNOPQRSTUVWXYZ

abcdefghijklmnopqrstuvwxyz

1234567890?!$%&

Adobe Systems, Inc.

VAG Rounded Thin

ABCDEFGHIJKLMNOPQRSTUVWXYZ

abcdefghijklmnopqrstuvwxyz

1234567890?!$%&

Adobe Systems, Inc.

Walbaum®

ABCDEFGHIJKLMNOPQRSTUVWXYZ

abcdefghijklmnopqrstuvwxyz

1234567890?!$%&

Adobe Systems, Inc.

Walbaum Italic

ABCDEFGHIJKLMNOPQRSTUVWXYZ

abcdefghijklmnopqrstuvwxyz

1234567890?!$%&

Adobe Systems, Inc.

Walbaum Bold

ABCDEFGHIJKLMNOPQRSTUVWXYZ

abcdefghijklmnopqrstuvwxyz

1234567890?!$%&

Adobe Systems, Inc.

Walbaum Bold Italic

ABCDEFGHIJKLMNOPQRSTUVWXYZ

abcdefghijklmnopqrstuvwxyz

1234567890?!$%&

Adobe Systems, Inc.

Weiss®

ABCDEFGHIJKLMNOPQRSTUVWXYZ

abcdefghijklmnopqrstuvwxyz

1234567890?!$%&

Adobe Systems, Inc.

Weiss Italic

ABCDEFGHIJKLMNOPQRSTUVWXYZ

abcdefghijklmnopqrstuvwxyz

1234567890?!$%&

Adobe Systems, Inc.

Weiss Bold

ABCDEFGHIJKLMNOPQRSTUVWXYZ

abcdefghijklmnopqrstuvwxyz

1234567890?!$%&

Adobe Systems, Inc.

Weiss Extra Bold

ABCDEFGHIJKLMNOPQRSTUVWXYZ

abcdefghijklmnopqrstuvwxyz

1234567890?!$%&

Adobe Systems, Inc.

ITC Zapf Chancery®

ABCDEFGHIJKLMNOPQRSTUVWXYZ

abcdefghijklmnopqrstuvwxyz

1234567890?!$%&

Adobe Systems, Inc.

Zephyr Script

ABCDEFGHIJKLMNOPQRSTUVWXYZ

abcdefghijklmnopqrstuvwxyz

1234567890?!$%&

Casady & Greene, Inc.

Zurich Roman

ABCDEFGHIJKLMNOPQRSTUVWXYZ
abcdefghijklmnopqrstuvwxyz
1234567890?!$%&

Bitstream, Inc.

Zurich Italic

ABCDEFGHIJKLMNOPQRSTUVWXYZ
abcdefghijklmnopqrstuvwxyz
1234567890?!$%&

Bitstream, Inc.

Zurich Bold

ABCDEFGHIJKLMNOPQRSTUVWXYZ
abcdefghijklmnopqrstuvwxyz
1234567890?!$%&

Bitstream, Inc.

Zurich Black

ABCDEFGHIJKLMNOPQRSTUVWXYZ
abcdefghijklmnopqrstuvwxyz
1234567890?!$%&

Bitstream, Inc.

Zurich Bold Italic

ABCDEFGHIJKLMNOPQRSTUVWXYZ
abcdefghijklmnopqrstuvwxyz
1234567890?!$%&

Bitstream, Inc.

Zurich Black Italic

ABCDEFGHIJKLMNOPQRSTUVWXYZ

abcdefghijklmnopqrstuvwxyz

1234567890?!$%&

Bitstream, Inc.

Zurich Light

ABCDEFGHIJKLMNOPQRSTUVWXYZ

abcdefghijklmnopqrstuvwxyz

1234567890?!$%&

Bitstream, Inc.

Zurich Light Italic

ABCDEFGHIJKLMNOPQRSTUVWXYZ

abcdefghijklmnopqrstuvwxyz

1234567890?!$%&

Bitstream, Inc.

Zurich Condensed Roman

ABCDEFGHIJKLMNOPQRSTUVWXYZ

abcdefghijklmnopqrstuvwxyz

1234567890?!$%&

Bitstream, Inc.

Zurich Condensed Italic

ABCDEFGHIJKLMNOPQRSTUVWXYZ

abcdefghijklmnopqrstuvwxyz

1234567890?!$%&

Bitstream, Inc.

Zurich Bold Extended

ABCDEFGHIJKLMNOPQRSTUVWXYZ
abcdefghijklmnopqrstuvwxyz
1234567890?!$%&

Bitstream, Inc.

Zurich Black Extended

ABCDEFGHIJKLMNOPQRSTUVWXY
Zabcdefghijklmnopqrstuvwxyz
1234567890?!$%&

Bitstream, Inc.

4 LaserJet Fonts

The *LaserJet* printers from Hewlett Packard have long been the standard when printing a document from an IBM or IBM-compatible computer. This standard has prompted several companies to produce font styles exclusively for LaserJet printers (LaserJet Series II, IID, IIP, and III) or printers that emulate the LaserJet printers.

This chapter includes hundreds of English-language font styles that are only available for LaserJet printers, including

Bitstream®, Inc.
Good Software Corporation
Hewlett-Packard Company
SoftCraft, Inc.
SWFTE International, Ltd.
VS Software

Some LaserJet fonts come with (or have available) a program that lets you generate the fonts in any size you wish, although unlike PostScript, the fonts need to be generated before you use them in your document. Other font companies offer fonts in specific sizes ranging from 6pt to 48pt.

Most fonts are available in several sizes in a variety of weights. Others are only available in one or two sizes of one or two weights.

When the font is available in 14pt, the font is displayed in that size. The display includes the name of the font, the upper and lower case alphabets, the numbers 0-9, and some popular symbols. Several fonts do not include the lower case alphabet, the numbers and/or the symbols. If the lower case alphabet, numbers, or symbol characters are not displayed then they are not included with the font.

Each font is listed in alphabetical order by font name, except when the name has a prefix such as *CG, ITC, HP, SWFTE*, or *VS*.

Below each font you'll find the name of the company or companies that offer the font for sale. For more information about each font company and its product line, see Chapter 5, *Font Companies*.

ITC American Typewriter®

ABCDEFGHIJKLMNOPQRSTUVWXYZ
abcdefghijklmnopqrstuvwxyz
1234567890?!$%&

Bitstream, Inc.

American Typewriter Bold

ABCDEFGHIJKLMNOPQRSTUVWXYZ
abcdefghijklmnopqrstuvwxyz
1234567890?!$%&

Bitstream, Inc.

Antique Olive

ABCDEFGHIJKLMNOPQRSTUVWXYZ
abcdefghijklmnopqrstuvwxyz
1234567890?!$%&

Hewlett-Packard Company

Antique Olive Medium

ABCDEFGHIJKLMNOPQRSTUVWXYZ
abcdefghijklmnopqrstuvwxyz
1234567890?!$%&

VS Software

Antique Olive Italic

ABCDEFGHIJKLMNOPQRSTUVWXYZ
abcdefghijklmnopqrstuvwxyz
1234567890?!$%&

Hewlett-Packard Company

Antique Olive Bold

ABCDEFGHIJKLMNOPQRSTUVWXYZ
abcdefghijklmnopqrstuvwxyz
1234567890?!$%&

Hewlett-Packard Company

Antique Olive Bold

ABCDEFGHIJKLMNOPQRSTUVWXYZ
abcdefghijklmnopqrstuvwxyz
1234567890?!$%&

VS Software

Antique Olive Thin

ABCDEFGHIJKLMNOPQRSTUVWXYZ
abcdefghijklmnopqrstuvwxyz
1234567890?!$%&

VS Software

ITC Avant Garde Gothic

ABCDEFGHIJKLMNOPQRSTUVWXYZ
abcdefghijklmnopqrstuvwxyz
1234567890?!$%&

Bitstream, Inc. / Good Software Corporation / Hewlett-Packard Company / VS Software

ITC Avant Garde Gothic Oblique

ABCDEFGHIJKLMNOPQRSTUVWXYZ
abcdefghijklmnopqrstuvwxyz
1234567890?!$%&

Bitstream, Inc. / Good Software Corporation / Hewlett-Packard Company / VS Software

ITC Avant Garde Gothic Bold

ABCDEFGHIJKLMNOPQRSTUVWXYZ
abcdefghijklmnopqrstuvwxyz
1234567890?!$%&

Bitstream, Inc. / Good Software Corporation / Hewlett-Packard Company / VS Software

ITC Avant Garde Gothic Bold Oblique

ABCDEFGHIJKLMNOPQRSTUVWXYZ
abcdefghijklmnopqrstuvwxyz
1234567890?!$%&

Bitstream, Inc. / Good Software Corporation / Hewlett-Packard Company / VS Software

Avant Guard

ABCDEFGHIJKLMNOPQRSTUVWXYZ
abcdefghijklmnopqrstuvwxyz
1234567890?!$%&

SWFTE International

Baskerton

ABCDEFGHIJKLMNOPQRSTUVWXYZ
abcdefghijklmnopqrstuvwxyz
1234567890?!$%&

SWFTE International

Baskerville II Medium

ABCDEFGHIJKLMNOPQRSTUVWXYZ
abcdefghijklmnopqrstuvwxyz
1234567890?!$%&

VS Software

Baskerville II Italic

ABCDEFGHIJKLMNOPQRSTUVWXYZ

abcdefghijklmnopqrstuvwxyz

1234567890?!$%&

VS Software

Baskerville II Bold

ABCDEFGHIJKLMNOPQRSTUVWXYZ

abcdefghijklmnopqrstuvwxyz

1234567890?!$%&

VS Software

Baskerville II Bold Italic

ABCDEFGHIJKLMNOPQRSTUVWXYZ

abcdefghijklmnopqrstuvwxyz

1234567890?!$%&

VS Software

ITC Benguiat Book

ABCDEFGHIJKLMNOPQRSTUVWXYZ

abcdefghijklmnopqrstuvwxyz

1234567890?!$%&

Bitstream, Inc. / Good Software Corporation / Hewlett-Packard Company

ITC Benguiat Book Italic

ABCDEFGHIJKLMNOPQRSTUVWXYZ

abcdefghijklmnopqrstuvwxyz

1234567890?!$%&

Bitstream, Inc. / Good Software Corporation / Hewlett-Packard Company / VS Software

ITC Benguiat Bold

ABCDEFGHIJKLMNOPQRSTUVWXYZ
abcdefghijklmnopqrstuvwxyz
1234567890?!$%&

Bitstream, Inc. / Good Software Corporation / Hewlett-Packard Company / VS Software

ITC Benguiat Bold Italic

ABCDEFGHIJKLMNOPQRSTUVWXYZ
abcdefghijklmnopqrstuvwxyz
1234567890?!$%&

Bitstream, Inc. / Good Software Corporation / Hewlett-Packard Company / VS Software

VS BHS Medium

ABCDEFGHIJKLMNOPQRSTUVWXYZ
abcdefghijklmnopqrstuvwxyz
1234567890?!$%&

VS Software

VS BHS Bold

ABCDEFGHIJKLMNOPQRSTUVWXYZ
abcdefghijklmnopqrstuvwxyz
1234567890?!$%&

VS Software

VS BHS Extra Bold

ABCDEFGHIJKLMNOPQRSTUVWXYZ
abcdefghijklmnopqrstuvwxyz
1234567890?!$%&

VS Software

Block Outline

ABCDEFGHIJKLMNOPQRSTUV
WXYZabcdefghijklmno
pqrstuvwxyz123456789
0?!$%&

SoftCraft, Inc.

Bodoni Book

ABCDEFGHIJKLMNOPQRSTUVWXYZ
abcdefghijklmnopqrstuvwxyz
1234567890?!$%&

Bitstream, Inc.

Bodoni Book Italic

ABCDEFGHIJKLMNOPQRSTUVWXYZ
abcdefghijklmnopqrstuvwxyz
1234567890?!$%&

Bitstream, Inc.

Bodoni Bold

ABCDEFGHIJKLMNOPQRSTUVWXYZ
abcdefghijklmnopqrstuvwxyz
1234567890?!$%&

Bitstream, Inc.

Bodoni Bold Italic

ABCDEFGHIJKLMNOPQRSTUVWXYZ
abcdefghijklmnopqrstuvwxyz
1234567890?!$%&

Bitstream, Inc.

ITC Bolt Bold

ABCDEFGHIJKLMNOPQRSTUVWXYZ
abcdefghijklmnopqrstuvwxyz
1234567890?!$%&

Bitstream, Inc.

Bongo Black

ABCDEFGHIJKLMNOPQRSTUVWXYZ
abcdefghijklmnopqrstuvwxyz
1234567890?!$%&

SWFTE International

ITC Bookman Demi

ABCDEFGHIJKLMNOPQRSTUVWXYZ
abcdefghijklmnopqrstuvwxyz
1234567890?!$%&

Bitstream, Inc. / Hewlett-Packard Company

ITC Bookman Demi Italic

ABCDEFGHIJKLMNOPQRSTUVWXYZ
abcdefghijklmnopqrstuvwxyz
1234567890?!$%&

Bitstream, Inc. / Hewlett-Packard Company

ITC Bookman Light

ABCDEFGHIJKLMNOPQRSTUVWXYZ
abcdefghijklmnopqrstuvwxyz
1234567890?!$%&

Bitstream, Inc. / Hewlett-Packard Company

ITC Bookman Light Italic

ABCDEFGHIJKLMNOPQRSTUVWXYZ

abcdefghijklmnopqrstuvwxyz

1234567890?!$%&

Bitstream, Inc. / Hewlett-Packard Company

VS Bookman Medium

ABCDEFGHIJKLMNOPQRSTUVWXYZ

abcdefghijklmnopqrstuvwxyz

1234567890?!$%&

VS Software

VS Bookman Italic

ABCDEFGHIJKLMNOPQRSTUVWXYZ

abcdefghijklmnopqrstuvwxyz

1234567890?!$%&

VS Software

VS Bookman Bold

ABCDEFGHIJKLMNOPQRSTUVWXYZ

abcdefghijklmnopqrstuvwxyz

1234567890?!$%&

VS Software

VS Bookman Bold Italic

ABCDEFGHIJKLMNOPQRSTUVWXYZ

abcdefghijklmnopqrstuvwxyz

1234567890?!$%&

VS Software

Broadway

ABCDEFGHIJKLMNOPQRSTUVWXYZ
abcdefghijklmnopqrstuvwxyz
1234567890?!$%&

Bitstream, Inc.

Broadway

ABCDEFGHIJKLMNOPQRSTUVWXYZ
abcdefghijklmnopqrstuvwxyz
1234567890?!$%&

VS Software

Broadway Engraved

ABCDEFGHIJKLMNOPQRSTUVWXYZ
abcdefghijklmnopqrstuvwxyz
1234567890?!$%&

VS Software

Brush

ABCDEFGHIJKLMNOPQRSTUVWXYZ
abcdefghijklmnopqrstuvwxyz
1234567890?!$%&

Good Software Corporation

Brush

ABCDEFGHIJKLMNOPQRSTUVWXYZ
abcdefghijklmnopqrstuvwxyz
1234567890?!$%&

Hewlett-Packard Company

Brush

ABCDEFGHIJKLMNOPQRSTUVWXYZ
abcdefghijklmnopqrstuvwxyz
1234567890?!$% &
VS Software

Buckingham

ABCDEFGHIJKLMNOPQRSTUVWXYZ
abcdefghijklmnopqrstuvwxyz
1234567890?!$%&
SWFTE International

Calligrapher

ABCDEFGHIJKLMNOPQRSTUVWXYZ
abcdefghijklmnopqrstuvwxyz
1234567890?!$¢&
SoftCraft, Inc.

CARIBBEAN

ABCDEFGHIJKLMNOPQRSTUVWXYZ
SoftCraft, Inc.

VS Century Medium

ABCDEFGHIJKLMNOPQRSTUVWXYZ
abcdefghijklmnopqrstuvwxyz
1234567890?!$%&
VS Software

VS Century Italic

ABCDEFGHIJKLMNOPQRSTUVWXYZ

abcdefghijklmnopqrstuvwxyz

1234567890?!$%&

VS Software

VS Century Bold

ABCDEFGHIJKLMNOPQRSTUVWXYZ

abcdefghijklmnopqrstuvwxyz

1234567890?!$%&

VS Software

VS Century Bold Italic

ABCDEFGHIJKLMNOPQRSTUVWXYZ

abcdefghijklmnopqrstuvwxyz

1234567890?!$%&

VS Software

VS CENTURY CAPS

ABCDEFGHIJKLMNOPQRSTUVWXYZ

ABCDEFGHIJKLMNOPQRSTUVWXYZ

1234567890?!$%&

VS Software

VS Century Slant

ABCDEFGHIJKLMNOPQRSTUVWXYZ

abcdefghijklmnopqrstuvwxyz

1234567890?!$%&

VS Software

VS Century Bold Slant

ABCDEFGHIJKLMNOPQRSTUVWXYZ

abcdefghijklmnopqrstuvwxyz

1234567890?!$%&

VS Software

Century II Bold

ABCDEFGHIJKLMNOPQRSTUVWXYZ

abcdefghijklmnopqrstuvwxyz

1234567890?!$%&

VS Software

Century II Bold Italic

ABCDEFGHIJKLMNOPQRSTUVWXYZ

abcdefghijklmnopqrstuvwxyz

1234567890?!$%&

VS Software

Century II Light

ABCDEFGHIJKLMNOPQRSTUVWXYZ

abcdefghijklmnopqrstuvwxyz

1234567890?!$%&

VS Software

Century II Light Italic

ABCDEFGHIJKLMNOPQRSTUVWXYZ

abcdefghijklmnopqrstuvwxyz

1234567890?!$%&

VS Software

Century Schoolbook Medium

ABCDEFGHIJKLMNOPQRSTUVWXYZ

abcdefghijklmnopqrstuvwxyz

1234567890?!$%&

Good Software Corporation

Century Schoolbook Italic

ABCDEFGHIJKLMNOPQRSTUVWXYZ

abcdefghijklmnopqrstuvwxyz

1234567890?!$%&

Good Software Corporation

Century Schoolbook Bold

ABCDEFGHIJKLMNOPQRSTUVWXYZ

abcdefghijklmnopqrstuvwxyz

1234567890?!$%&

Good Software Corporation

Century Schoolbook Bold Italic

ABCDEFGHIJKLMNOPQRSTUVWXYZ

abcdefghijklmnopqrstuvwxyz

1234567890?!$%&

Good Software Corporation

CG Century Schoolbook

ABCDEFGHIJKLMNOPQRSTUVWXYZ

abcdefghijklmnopqrstuvwxyz

1234567890?!$%&

Hewlett-Packard Company

CG Century Schoolbook Italic
ABCDEFGHIJKLMNOPQRSTUVWXYZ
abcdefghijklmnopqrstuvwxyz
1234567890?!$%&
Hewlett-Packard Company

CG Century Schoolbook Bold
ABCDEFGHIJKLMNOPQRSTUVWXYZ
abcdefghijklmnopqrstuvwxyz
1234567890?!$%&
Hewlett-Packard Company

CG Century Schoolbook Bold Italic
ABCDEFGHIJKLMNOPQRSTUVWXYZ
abcdefghijklmnopqrstuvwxyz
1234567890?!$%&
Hewlett-Packard Company

Century Textbook Medium
ABCDEFGHIJKLMNOPQRSTUVWXYZ
abcdefghijklmnopqrstuvwxyz
1234567890?!$%&
VS Software

Century Textbook Italic
ABCDEFGHIJKLMNOPQRSTUVWXYZ
abcdefghijklmnopqrstuvwxyz
1234567890?!$%&
VS Software

Century Textbook Bold

ABCDEFGHIJKLMNOPQRSTUVWXYZ

abcdefghijklmnopqrstuvwxyz

1234567890?!$%&

VS Software

Classic Shadow

ABCDEFGHIJKLMNOPQRSTUVWXYZ

abcdefghijklmnopqrstuvwxyz

1234567890?!$%&

SoftCraft, Inc.

Classic Typewriter

ABCDEFGHIJKLMNOPQRSTUVWXYZ

abcdefghijklmnopqrstuvwxyz

1234567890?!$%&

SWFTE International

ITC Clearface Regular

ABCDEFGHIJKLMNOPQRSTUVWXYZ

abcdefghijklmnopqrstuvwxyz

1234567890?!$%&

Bitstream, Inc.

ITC Clearface Regular Italic

ABCDEFGHIJKLMNOPQRSTUVWXYZ

abcdefghijklmnopqrstuvwxyz

1234567890?!$%&

Bitstream, Inc.

ITC Clearface Heavy

ABCDEFGHIJKLMNOPQRSTUVWXYZ
abcdefghijklmnopqrstuvwxyz
1234567890?!$%&
Bitstream, Inc.

ITC Clearface Heavy Italic

ABCDEFGHIJKLMNOPQRSTUVWXYZ
abcdefghijklmnopqrstuvwxyz
1234567890?!$%&
Bitstream, Inc.

Cloister Black

ABCDEFGHIJKLMNOPQRSTUVWXYZ
abcdefghijklmnopqrstuvwxyz
1234567890?!$%&
Bitstream, Inc.

COMPUTER

ABCDEFGHIJKLMNOPQRSTUVWXYZ
SoftCraft, Inc.

Bitstream Cooper Black

ABCDEFGHIJKLMNOPQRSTUVWXYZ
abcdefghijklmnopqrstuvwxyz
1234567890?!$%&
Bitstream, Inc.

Copperfield

ABCDEFGHIJKLMNOPQRSTUVWXYZ
abcdefghijklmnopqrstuvwxyz
1234567890?!$%&
SWFTE International

Courier

ABCDEFGHIJKLMNOPQRSTUVWXYZ
abcdefghijklmnopqrstuvwxyz
1234567890?!$%&
SWFTE International

Courier Medium

ABCDEFGHIJKLMNOPQRSTUVWXYZ
abcdefghijklmnopqrstuvwxyz
1234567890?!$%&
VS Software

Courier Italic

ABCDEFGHIJKLMNOPQRSTUVWXYZ
abcdefghijklmnopqrstuvwxyz
1234567890?!$%&
Good Software Corporation / VS Software

Courier Bold

ABCDEFGHIJKLMNOPQRSTUVWXYZ
abcdefghijklmnopqrstuvwxyz
1234567890?!$%&
Good Software Corporation / VS Software

Courier Bold Italic

ABCDEFGHIJKLMNOPQRSTUVWXYZ
abcdefghijklmnopqrstuvwxyz
1234567890?!$%&

VS Software

Divine Faces

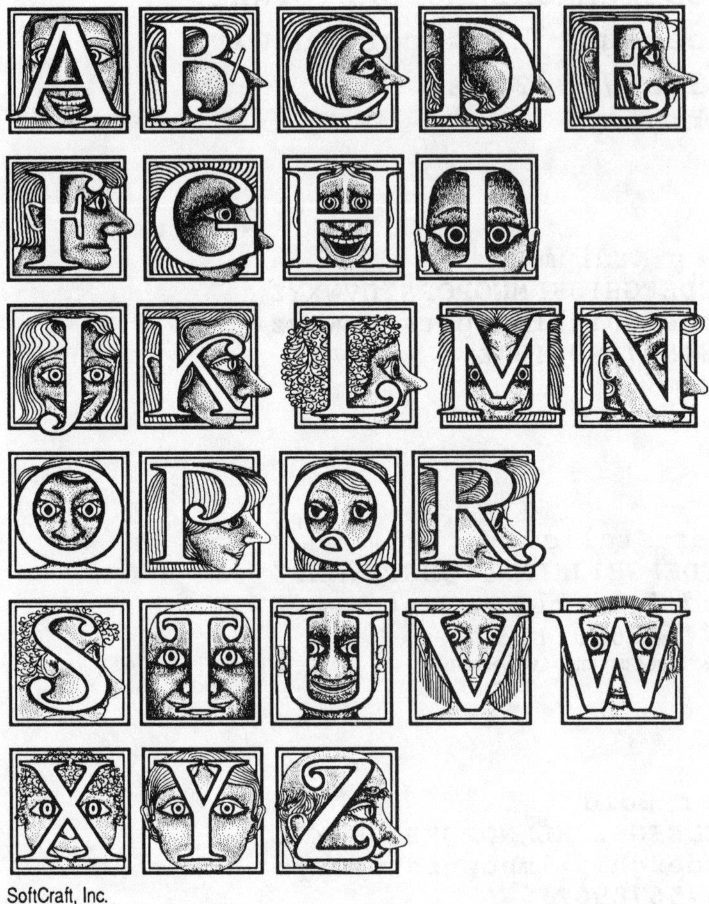

SoftCraft, Inc.

Dom Casual

ABCDEFGHIJKLMNOPQRSTUVWXYZ
abcdefghijklmnopqrstuvwxyz
1234567890?!$%&
Bitstream, Inc.

Dom Casual

ABCDEFGHIJKLMNOPQRSTUVWXYZ
abcdefghijklmnopqrstuvwxyz
1234567890?!$%&
Good Software Corporation

Dom Casual

ABCDEFGHIJKLMNOPQRSTUVWXYZ
abcdefghijklmnopqrstuvwxyz
1234567890?!$%&
Hewlett-Packard Company

Dutch Roman

ABCDEFGHIJKLMNOPQRSTUVWXYZ
abcdefghijklmnopqrstuvwxyz
1234567890?!$%&
Bitstream, Inc.

Dutch Italic

ABCDEFGHIJKLMNOPQRSTUVWXYZ
abcdefghijklmnopqrstuvwxyz
1234567890?!$%&
Bitstream, Inc.

Dutch Bold

ABCDEFGHIJKLMNOPQRSTUVWXYZ
abcdefghijklmnopqrstuvwxyz
1234567890?!$%&

Bitstream, Inc.

Dutch Bold Italic

ABCDEFGHIJKLMNOPQRSTUVWXYZ
abcdefghijklmnopqrstuvwxyz
1234567890?!$%&

Bitstream, Inc.

Elegant Script

ABCDEFGHIJKLMNOPQRSTUVWXYZ
abcdefghijklmnopqrstuvwxyz
1234567890?!$%&

SoftCraft, Inc.

Elite Medium

ABCDEFGHIJKLMNOPQRSTUVWXYZ
abcdefghijklmnopqrstuvwxyz
1234567890?!$%&

VS Software

Elite Italic

ABCDEFGHIJKLMNOPQRSTUVWXYZ
abcdefghijklmnopqrstuvwxyz
1234567890?!$%&

VS Software

Elite Bold

ABCDEFGHIJKLMNOPQRSTUVWXYZ
abcdefghijklmnopqrstuvwxyz
1234567890?!$%&
VS Software

Elite Bold Italic

ABCDEFGHIJKLMNOPQRSTUVWXYZ
abcdefghijklmnopqrstuvwxyz
1234567890?!$%&
VS Software

Eterna

ABCDEFGHIJKLMNOPQRSTUVWXYZ
abcdefghijklmnopqrstuvwxyz
1234567890?!$%&
SWFTE International

Exchequer Script

ABCDEFGHIJKLMNOPQRSTUVWXYZ
abcdefghijklmnopqrstuvwxyz
1234567890?!$%&
SWFTE International

Formal

ABCDEFGHIJKLMNOPQRSTUVWXYZ
abcdefghijklmnopqrstuvwxyz
1234567890?!$%&
SoftCraft, Inc.

Franklin Gothic Roman

ABCDEFGHIJKLMNOPQRSTUVWXYZ
abcdefghijklmnopqrstuvwxyz
1234567890?!$%&

Bitstream, Inc.

Franklin Gothic Italic

ABCDEFGHIJKLMNOPQRSTUVWXYZ
abcdefghijklmnopqrstuvwxyz
1234567890?!$%&

Bitstream, Inc.

Frankin Gothic Extra Condensed

ABCDEFGHIJKLMNOPQRSTUVWXYZ
abcdefghijklmnopqrstuvwxyz
1234567890?!$%&

Bitstream, Inc.

Futura II Medium

ABCDEFGHIJKLMNOPQRSTUVWXYZ
abcdefghijklmnopqrstuvwxyz
1234567890?!$%&

Good Software Corporation

Futura II Book

ABCDEFGHIJKLMNOPQRSTUVWXYZ
abcdefghijklmnopqrstuvwxyz
1234567890?!$%&

VS Software

Futura Book II

ABCDEFGHIJKLMNOPQRSTUVWXYZ
abcdefghijklmnopqrstuvwxyz
1234567890?!$%&

Hewlett-Packard Company

Futura II Italic

ABCDEFGHIJKLMNOPQRSTUVWXYZ
abcdefghijklmnopqrstuvwxyz
1234567890?!$%&

Good Software Corporation

Futura II Book Italic

ABCDEFGHIJKLMNOPQRSTUVWXYZ
abcdefghijklmnopqrstuvwxyz
1234567890?!$%&

VS Software

Futura Book Italic II

ABCDEFGHIJKLMNOPQRSTUVWXYZ
abcdefghijklmnopqrstuvwxyz
1234567890?!$%&

Hewlett-Packard Company

Futura II Bold

ABCDEFGHIJKLMNOPQRSTUVWXYZ
abcdefghijklmnopqrstuvwxyz
1234567890?!$%&

Good Software Corporation

Futura II Bold

ABCDEFGHIJKLMNOPQRSTUVWXYZ
abcdefghijklmnopqrstuvwxyz
1234567890?!$%&

VS Software

Futura Bold II

ABCDEFGHIJKLMNOPQRSTUVWXYZ
abcdefghijklmnopqrstuvwxyz
1234567890?!$%&

Hewlett-Packard Company

Futura II Bold Italic

ABCDEFGHIJKLMNOPQRSTUVWXYZ
abcdefghijklmnopqrstuvwxyz
1234567890?!$%&

Good Software Corporation

Futura II Bold Italic

ABCDEFGHIJKLMNOPQRSTUVWXYZ
abcdefghijklmnopqrstuvwxyz
1234567890?!$%&

VS Software

Futura Bold Italic II

ABCDEFGHIJKLMNOPQRSTUVWXYZ
abcdefghijklmnopqrstuvwxyz
1234567890?!$%&

Hewlett-Packard Company

Garamand

ABCDEFGHIJKLMNOPQRSTUVWXYZ
abcdefghijklmnopqrstuvwxyz
1234567890?!$%&

SWFTE International

Garamond Antiqua

ABCDEFGHIJKLMNOPQRSTUVWXYZ
abcdefghijklmnopqrstuvwxyz
1234567890?!$%&

Good Software Corporation

Garamond Antiqua

ABCDEFGHIJKLMNOPQRSTUVWXYZ
abcdefghijklmnopqrstuvwxyz
1234567890?!$%&

VS Software

Garamond Kursiv

ABCDEFGHIJKLMNOPQRSTUVWXYZ
abcdefghijklmnopqrstuvwxyz
1234567890?!$%&

Good Software Corporation

Garamond Kursiv

ABCDEFGHIJKLMNOPQRSTUVWXYZ
abcdefghijklmnopqrstuvwxyz
1234567890?!$%&

VS Software

Garamond Halbfett

ABCDEFGHIJKLMNOPQRSTUVWXYZ

abcdefghijklmnopqrstuvwxyz

1234567890?!$%&

Good Software Corporation

Garamond Halbfett

ABCDEFGHIJKLMNOPQRSTUVWXYZ

abcdefghijklmnopqrstuvwxyz

1234567890?!$%&

VS Software

Garamond Kursiv Halbfett

ABCDEFGHIJKLMNOPQRSTUVWXYZ

abcdefghijklmnopqrstuvwxyz

1234567890?!$%&

Good Software Corporation

Garamond Kursiv Halbfett

ABCDEFGHIJKLMNOPQRSTUVWXYZ

abcdefghijklmnopqrstuvwxyz

1234567890?!$%&

VS Software

Gibraltar

ABCDEFGHIJKLMNOPQRSTUVWXYZ

abcdefghijklmnopqrstuvwxyz

1234567890?!$%&

SWFTE International

Gill Sans Medium

ABCDEFGHIJKLMNOPQRSTUVWXYZ
abcdefghijklmnopqrstuvwxyz
1234567890?!$%&
VS Software

Gill Sans Medium Italic

ABCDEFGHIJKLMNOPQRSTUVWXYZ
abcdefghijklmnopqrstuvwxyz
1234567890?!$%&
VS Software

Gill Sans Bold

ABCDEFGHIJKLMNOPQRSTUVWXYZ
abcdefghijklmnopqrstuvwxyz
1234567890?!$%&
VS Software

Gill Sans Ultra Bold

ABCDEFGHIJKLMNOPQRSTUVWXYZ
abcdefghijklmnopqrstuvwxyz
1234567890?!$%&
VS Software

Goudy Old Style

ABCDEFGHIJKLMNOPQRSTUVWXYZ
abcdefghijklmnopqrstuvwxyz
1234567890?!$%&
Bitstream, Inc.

Goudy Old Style Italic

ABCDEFGHIJKLMNOPQRSTUVWXYZ

abcdefghijklmnopqrstuvwxyz

1234567890?!$%&

Bitstream, Inc.

Goudy Bold

ABCDEFGHIJKLMNOPQRSTUVWXYZ

abcdefghijklmnopqrstuvwxyz

1234567890?!$%&

Bitstream, Inc.

Goudy Extra Bold

ABCDEFGHIJKLMNOPQRSTUVWXYZ

abcdefghijklmnopqrstuvwxyz

1234567890?!$%&

Bitstream, Inc.

Hammersmith Roman

ABCDEFGHIJKLMNOPQRSTUVWXYZ

abcdefghijklmnopqrstuvwxyz

1234567890?!$%&

Bitstream, Inc.

Hammersmith Italic

ABCDEFGHIJKLMNOPQRSTUVWXYZ

abcdefghijklmnopqrstuvwxyz

1234567890?!$%&

Bitstream, Inc.

Hammersmith Bold

ABCDEFGHIJKLMNOPQRSTUVWXYZ
abcdefghijklmnopqrstuvwxyz
1234567890?!$%&

Bitstream, Inc.

Hammersmith Bold Italic

ABCDEFGHIJKLMNOPQRSTUVWXYZ
abcdefghijklmnopqrstuvwxyz
1234567890?!$%&

Bitstream, Inc.

Handel Gothic

ABCDEFGHIJKLMNOPQRSTUVWXYZ
abcdefghijklmnopqrstuvwxyz
1234567890?!$%&

Bitstream, Inc.

VS Helv Medium

ABCDEFGHIJKLMNOPQRSTUVWXYZ
abcdefghijklmnopqrstuvwxyz
1234567890?!$%&

VS Software

VS Helv Italic

ABCDEFGHIJKLMNOPQRSTUVWXYZ
abcdefghijklmnopqrstuvwxyz
1234567890?!$%&

VS Software

VS Helv Bold

ABCDEFGHIJKLMNOPQRSTUVWXYZ
abcdefghijklmnopqrstuvwxyz
1234567890?!$%&

VS Software

VS Helv Demi Bold

ABCDEFGHIJKLMNOPQRSTUVWXYZ
abcdefghijklmnopqrstuvwxyz
1234567890?!$%&

VS Software

Helvenica

ABCDEFGHIJKLMNOPQRSTUVWXYZ
abcdefghijklmnopqrstuvwxyz
1234567890?!$%&

SWFTE International

Kaufmann Bold

ABCDEFGHIJKLMNOPQRSTUVWXYZ
abcdefghijklmnopqrstuvwxyz
1234567890?!$%&

Bitstream, Inc.

SoftCraft, Inc.

LCD ITALIC

ABCDEFGHIJKLMNOPQRSTUV

WXYZ1234567890?!$¢

SoftCraft, Inc.

SWFTE Letter Gothic

ABCDEFGHIJKLMNOPQRSTUVWXYZ

abcdefghijklmnopqrstuvwxyz

1234567890?!$%&

SWFTE International

ITC Lubalin Graph Book

ABCDEFGHIJKLMNOPQRSTUVWXYZ

abcdefghijklmnopqrstuvwxyz

1234567890?!$%&

Bitstream, Inc. / Good Software Corporation / Hewlett-Packard Company

ITC Lubalin Graph Book Oblique

ABCDEFGHIJKLMNOPQRSTUVWXYZ

abcdefghijklmnopqrstuvwxyz

1234567890?!$%&

Good Software Corporation / Hewlett-Packard Company

ITC Lubalin Graph Demi

ABCDEFGHIJKLMNOPQRSTUVWXYZ

abcdefghijklmnopqrstuvwxyz

1234567890?!$%&

Bitstream, Inc. / Good Software Corporation / Hewlett-Packard Company

ITC Lubalin Graph Demi Oblique

ABCDEFGHIJKLMNOPQRSTUVWXYZ

abcdefghijklmnopqrstuvwxyz

1234567890?!$%&

Good Software Corporation / Hewlett-Packard Company

Manuscript

ABCDEFGHIJKLMNOPQRSTUVWXYZ

abcdefghijklmnopqrstuvwxyz

1234567890?!$%&

SWFTE International

Mermaid

ABCDEFGHIJKLMNOPQRSTUVWXYZ

abcdefghijklmnopqrstuvwxyz

1234567890?!$%&

Bitstream, Inc.

Microstyle Medium

ABCDEFGHIJKLMNOPQRSTUVWXYZ

abcdefghijklmnopqrstuvwxyz

1234567890?!$%&

Good Software Corporation

Microstyle Bold

ABCDEFGHIJKLMNOPQRSTUVWXYZ

abcdefghijklmnopqrstuvwxyz

1234567890?!$%&

Good Software Corporation

Microstyle Extended

ABCDEFGHIJKLMNOPQRSTUVWXYZ
abcdefghijklmnopqrstuvwxyz
1234567890?!$%&

Good Software Corporation

Microstyle Extended Bold

ABCDEFGHIJKLMNOPQRSTUVWXYZ
abcdefghijklmnopqrstuvwxyz
1234567890?!$%&

Good Software Corporation

SoftCraft, Inc.

Modern Medium

ABCDEFGHIJKLMNOPQRSTUVWXYZ
abcdefghijklmnopqrstuvwxyz
1234567890?!$%&

VS Software

Modern Gothic Medium

ABCDEFGHIJKLMNOPQRSTUVWXYZ
abcdefghijklmnopqrstuvwxyz
1234567890?!$%&

VS Software

Modern Gothic Bold

ABCDEFGHIJKLMNOPQRSTUVWXYZ
abcdefghijklmnopqrstuvwxyz
1234567890?!$%&

VS Software

New York Deco

ABCDEFGHIJKLMNOPQRSTUVWXYZ
abcdefghijklmnopqrstuvwxyz
1234567890?!$%&

SWFTE International

Nouveau

ABCDEFGHIJKLMNOPQRSTUV
WXYZabcdefghijklmnopqrstu
vwxyz1234567890?!$%&

SoftCraft, Inc.

Nouveau Bold

ABCDEFGHIJKLMNOPQRSTU
VWXYZabcdefghijklmnopqrs
tuvwxyz1234567890?!$%&

SoftCraft, Inc.

Obelisk

ABCDEFGHIJKLMNOPQRSTUVWXYZ
abcdefghijklmnopqrstuvwxyz
1234567890?!$%&

SWFTE International

Old English Cloistered

ABCDEFGHIJKLMNOPQRSTUVWXYZ

abcdefghijklmnopqrstuvwxyz

1234567890?!$%&

VS Software

Olde English

ABCDEFGHIJKLMNOPQRSTUVWXYZ

abcdefghijklmnopqrstuvwxyz

1234567890?!$%&

SoftCraft, Inc.

Olde English Hollow

ABCDEFGHIJKLMNOPQRSTUVWXYZ

abcdefghijklmnopqrstuvwxyz

1234567890?!$%&

SoftCraft, Inc.

CG Omega

ABCDEFGHIJKLMNOPQRSTUVWXYZ

abcdefghijklmnopqrstuvwxyz

1234567890?!$%&

Hewlett-Packard Company / VS Software

CG Omega Italic

ABCDEFGHIJKLMNOPQRSTUVWXYZ

abcdefghijklmnopqrstuvwxyz

1234567890?!$%&

Hewlett-Packard Company / VS Software

CG Omega Bold

ABCDEFGHIJKLMNOPQRSTUVWXYZ
abcdefghijklmnopqrstuvwxyz
1234567890?!$%&

Hewlett-Packard Company / VS Software

CG Omega Bold Italic

ABCDEFGHIJKLMNOPQRSTUVWXYZ
abcdefghijklmnopqrstuvwxyz
1234567890?!$%&

Hewlett-Packard Company / VS Software

Optical

ABCDEFGHIJKLMNOPQRSTUVWX
YZabcdefghijklmnopqrstuvwxyz
1234567890?!$%&

SoftCraft, Inc.

Orbit

ABCDEFGHIJKLMNOPQRSTUVWXYZ
abcdefghi jklmnopqrstuvwxyz
1234567890?!$%&

SoftCraft, Inc.

Overhead Projector Font

ABCDEFGHIJKLMNOPQRSTUVW
XYZabcdefghijklmnopqrstuvwxyz
1234567890?!$%&

SoftCraft, Inc.

Oxford

ABCDEFGHIJKLMNOPQRSTUVWXYZ
abcdefghijklmnopqrstuvwxyz
1234567890?!$%&
SWFTE International

P.T. Barnum

ABCDEFGHIJKLMNOPQRSTUVWXYZ
abcdefghijklmnopqrstuvwxyz
1234567890?!$%&
Bitstream, Inc.

Park Avenue

ABCDEFGHIJKLMNOPQRSTUVWXYZ
abcdefghijklmnopqrstuvwxyz
1234567890?!$%&
Bitstream, Inc.

Park Avenue

ABCDEFGHIJKLMNOPQRSTUVWXYZ
abcdefghijklmnopqrstuvwxyz
1234567890?!$%&
Good Software Corporation

Park Avenue

ABCDEFGHIJKLMNOPQRSTUVWXYZ
abcdefghijklmnopqrstuvwxyz
1234567890?!$%&
Hewlett-Packard Company

Park Avenue

ABCDEFGHIJKLMNOPQRSTUVWXYZ

abcdefghijklmnopqrstuvwxyz

1234567890?!$%&

VS Software

CG Palacio

ABCDEFGHIJKLMNOPQRSTUVWXYZ

abcdefghijklmnopqrstuvwxyz

1234567890?!$%&

Hewlett-Packard Company

CG Palacio Italic

ABCDEFGHIJKLMNOPQRSTUVWXYZ

abcdefghijklmnopqrstuvwxyz

1234567890?!$%&

Hewlett-Packard Company

CG Palacio Bold

ABCDEFGHIJKLMNOPQRSTUVWXYZ

abcdefghijklmnopqrstuvwxyz

1234567890?!$%&

Hewlett-Packard Company

CG Palacio Bold Italic

ABCDEFGHIJKLMNOPQRSTUVWXYZ

abcdefghijklmnopqrstuvwxyz

1234567890?!$%&

Hewlett-Packard Company

Palatine

ABCDEFGHIJKLMNOPQRSTUVWXYZ
abcdefghijklmnopqrstuvwxyz
1234567890?!$%&
SWFTE International

PC Baby

ABCDEFGHIJKLMNOPQRSTUVWXYZ
abcdefghijklmnopqrstuvwxyz
1234567890?!$%&
VS Software

PC Full Medium

ABCDEFGHIJKLMNOPQRSTUVWXYZ
abcdefghijklmnopqrstuvwxyz
1234567890?!$%&
VS Software

PC Full Bold

ABCDEFGHIJKLMNOPQRSTUVWXYZ
abcdefghijklmnopqrstuvwxyz
1234567890?!$%&
VS Software

Prestige

ABCDEFGHIJKLMNOPQRSTUVWXYZ
abcdefghijklmnopqrstuvwxyz
1234567890?!$%&
SWFTE International

VS Prestige Medium
ABCDEFGHIJKLMNOPQRSTUVWXYZ
abcdefghijklmnopqrstuvwxyz
1234567890?!$%&
VS Software

VS Prestige Italic
ABCDEFGHIJKLMNOPQRSTUVWXYZ
abcdefghijklmnopqrstuvwxyz
1234567890?!$%&
VS Software

VS Prestige Bold
ABCDEFGHIJKLMNOPQRSTUVWXYZ
abcdefghijklmnopqrstuvwxyz
1234567890?!$%&
VS Software

VS Prestige Bold Italic
ABCDEFGHIJKLMNOPQRSTUVWXYZ
abcdefghijklmnopqrstuvwxyz
1234567890?!$%&
VS Software

Provence Roman
ABCDEFGHIJKLMNOPQRSTUVWXYZ
abcdefghijklmnopqrstuvwxyz
1234567890?!$%&
Bitstream, Inc.

Provence Italic

ABCDEFGHIJKLMNOPQRSTUVWXYZ
abcdefghijklmnopqrstuvwxyz
1234567890?!$%&

Bitstream, Inc.

Provence Black

ABCDEFGHIJKLMNOPQRSTUVWXYZ
abcdefghijklmnopqrstuvwxyz
1234567890?!$%&

Bitstream, Inc.

Provence Compact

ABCDEFGHIJKLMNOPQRSTUVWXYZ
abcdefghijklmnopqrstuvwxyz
1234567890?!$%&

Bitstream, Inc.

Rockland

ABCDEFGHIJKLMNOPQRSTUVWXYZ
abcdefghijklmnopqrstuvwxyz
1234567890?!$%&

SWFTE International

Rockwell Medium

ABCDEFGHIJKLMNOPQRSTUVWXYZ
abcdefghijklmnopqrstuvwxyz
1234567890?!$%&

VS Software

Rockwell Italic

ABCDEFGHIJKLMNOPQRSTUVWXYZ

abcdefghijklmnopqrstuvwxyz

1234567890?!$%&

VS Software

Rockwell Bold

ABCDEFGHIJKLMNOPQRSTUVWXYZ

abcdefghijklmnopqrstuvwxyz

1234567890?!$%&

VS Software

Rockwell Extra Bold

ABCDEFGHIJKLMNOPQRSTUVWXYZ

abcdefghijklmnopqrstuvwxyz

1234567890?!$%&

VS Software

Rockwell Bold Italic

ABCDEFGHIJKLMNOPQRSTUVWXYZ

abcdefghijklmnopqrstuvwxyz

1234567890?!$%&

VS Software

Sans Serif Shadow

ABCDEFGHIJKLMNOPQRSTUVWXYZ

abcdefghijklmnopqrstuvwxyz

1234567890?!$%&

SoftCraft, Inc.

Script

ABCDEFGHIJKLMNOPQRSTUVWXYZ

abcdefghijklmnopqrstuvwxyz

1234567890?!$%&

SoftCraft, Inc.

Script Hollow

ABCDEFGHIJKLMNOPQRSTUVWXYZ

abcdefghijklmnopqrstuvwxyz

1234567890?!$%&

SoftCraft, Inc.

ITC Souvenir Demi

ABCDEFGHIJKLMNOPQRSTUVWXYZ

abcdefghijklmnopqrstuvwxyz

1234567890?!$%&

Bitstream, Inc. / Good Software Corporation / Hewlett-Packard Company / VS Software

ITC Souvenir Demi Italic

ABCDEFGHIJKLMNOPQRSTUVWXYZ

abcdefghijklmnopqrstuvwxyz

1234567890?!$%&

Bitstream, Inc. / Good Software Corporation / Hewlett-Packard Company / VS Software

ITC Souvenir Light

ABCDEFGHIJKLMNOPQRSTUVWXYZ

abcdefghijklmnopqrstuvwxyz

1234567890?!$%&

Bitstream, Inc. / Good Software Corporation / Hewlett-Packard Company / VS Software

ITC Souvenir Light Italic

ABCDEFGHIJKLMNOPQRSTUVWXYZ

abcdefghijklmnopqrstuvwxyz

1234567890?!$%&

Bitstream, Inc. / Good Software Corporation / Hewlett-Packard Company / VS Software

Stymie Medium

ABCDEFGHIJKLMNOPQRSTUVWXYZ

abcdefghijklmnopqrstuvwxyz

1234567890?!$%&

Hewlett-Packard Company

Stymie Medium Italic

ABCDEFGHIJKLMNOPQRSTUVWXYZ

abcdefghijklmnopqrstuvwxyz

1234567890?!$%&

Hewlett-Packard Company

Stymie Bold

ABCDEFGHIJKLMNOPQRSTUVWXYZ

abcdefghijklmnopqrstuvwxyz

1234567890?!$%&

Hewlett-Packard Company

Stymie Bold Italic

ABCDEFGHIJKLMNOPQRSTUVWXYZ

abcdefghijklmnopqrstuvwxyz

1234567890?!$%&

Hewlett-Packard Company

Swiss Roman

ABCDEFGHIJKLMNOPQRSTUVWXYZ
abcdefghijklmnopqrstuvwxyz
1234567890?!$%&

Bitstream, Inc.

Swiss Italic

ABCDEFGHIJKLMNOPQRSTUVWXYZ
abcdefghijklmnopqrstuvwxyz
1234567890?!$%&

Bitstream, Inc.

Swiss Bold

ABCDEFGHIJKLMNOPQRSTUVWXYZ
abcdefghijklmnopqrstuvwxyz
1234567890?!$%&

Bitstream, Inc.

Swiss Bold Italic

ABCDEFGHIJKLMNOPQRSTUVWXYZ
abcdefghijklmnopqrstuvwxyz
1234567890?!$%&

Bitstream, Inc.

Swiss Condensed Roman

ABCDEFGHIJKLMNOPQRSTUVWXYZ
abcdefghijklmnopqrstuvwxyz
1234567890?!$%&

Bitstream, Inc.

Swiss Condensed Italic

ABCDEFGHIJKLMNOPQRSTUVWXYZ

abcdefghijklmnopqrstuvwxyz

1234567890?!$%&

Bitstream, Inc.

Swiss Bold Condensed

ABCDEFGHIJKLMNOPQRSTUVWXYZ

abcdefghijklmnopqrstuvwxyz

1234567890?!$%&

Bitstream, Inc.

Swiss Black Condensed

ABCDEFGHIJKLMNOPQRSTUVWXYZ

abcdefghijklmnopqrstuvwxyz

1234567890?!$%&

Bitstream, Inc.

Swiss Light

ABCDEFGHIJKLMNOPQRSTUVWXYZ

abcdefghijklmnopqrstuvwxyz

1234567890?!$%&

Bitstream, Inc.

Swiss Light Italic

ABCDEFGHIJKLMNOPQRSTUVWXYZ

abcdefghijklmnopqrstuvwxyz

1234567890?!$%&

Bitstream, Inc.

Swiss Black

ABCDEFGHIJKLMNOPQRSTUVWXYZ
abcdefghijklmnopqrstuvwxyz
1234567890?!$%&

Bitstream, Inc.

Swiss Black Italic

ABCDEFGHIJKLMNOPQRSTUVWXYZ
abcdefghijklmnopqrstuvwxyz
1234567890?!$%&

Bitstream, Inc.

Tall

ABCDEFGHIJKLMNOPQRSTUVWXYZ
abcdefghijklmnopqrstuvwxyz
1234567890?!$%&

SoftCraft, Inc.

Tall Man

ABCDEFGHIJKLMNOPQRSTUVWXYZ
abcdefghijklmnopqrstuvwxyz
1234567890?!$%&

VS Software

CG Times Medium

ABCDEFGHIJKLMNOPQRSTUVWXYZ
abcdefghijklmnopqrstuvwxyz
1234567890?!$%&

Good Software Corporation / Hewlett-Packard Company / VS Software

CG Times Italic

ABCDEFGHIJKLMNOPQRSTUVWXYZ

abcdefghijklmnopqrstuvwxyz

1234567890?!$%&

Good Software Corporation / Hewlett-Packard Company / VS Software

CG Times Bold

ABCDEFGHIJKLMNOPQRSTUVWXYZ

abcdefghijklmnopqrstuvwxyz

1234567890?!$%&

Good Software Corporation / Hewlett-Packard Company / VS Software

CG Times Bold Italic

ABCDEFGHIJKLMNOPQRSTUVWXYZ

abcdefghijklmnopqrstuvwxyz

1234567890?!$%&

Good Software Corporation / Hewlett-Packard Company / VS Software

VS Times Medium

ABCDEFGHIJKLMNOPQRSTUVWXYZ

abcdefghijklmnopqrstuvwxyz

1234567890?!$%&

VS Software

VS Times Italic

ABCDEFGHIJKLMNOPQRSTUVWXYZ

abcdefghijklmnopqrstuvwxyz

1234567890?!$%&

VS Software

VS Times Bold

ABCDEFGHIJKLMNOPQRSTUVWXYZ

abcdefghijklmnopqrstuvwxyz

1234567890?!$%&

VS Software

VS Times Bold Italic

ABCDEFGHIJKLMNOPQRSTUVWXYZ

abcdefghijklmnopqrstuvwxyz

1234567890?!$%&

VS Software

CG Triumvirate

ABCDEFGHIJKLMNOPQRSTUVWXYZ

abcdefghijklmnopqrstuvwxyz

1234567890?!$%&

Good Software Corporation / Hewlett-Packard Company / VS Software

CG Triumvirate Italic

ABCDEFGHIJKLMNOPQRSTUVWXYZ

abcdefghijklmnopqrstuvwxyz

1234567890?!$%&

Good Software Corporation / Hewlett-Packard Company / VS Software

CG Triumvirate Bold

ABCDEFGHIJKLMNOPQRSTUVWXYZ

abcdefghijklmnopqrstuvwxyz

1234567890?!$%&

Good Software Corporation / Hewlett-Packard Company / VS Software

CG Triumvirate Black

ABCDEFGHIJKLMNOPQRSTUVWXYZ

abcdefghijklmnopqrstuvwxyz

1234567890?!$%&

VS Software

CG Triumvirate Bold Italic

ABCDEFGHIJKLMNOPQRSTUVWXYZ

abcdefghijklmnopqrstuvwxyz

1234567890?!$%&

Good Software Corporation / Hewlett-Packard Company / VS Software

CG Triumvirate Black Italic

ABCDEFGHIJKLMNOPQRSTUVWXYZ

abcdefghijklmnopqrstuvwxyz

1234567890?!$%&

VS Software

CG Triumvirate Light

ABCDEFGHIJKLMNOPQRSTUVWXYZ

abcdefghijklmnopqrstuvwxyz

1234567890?!$%&

VS Software

CG Triumvirate Light Italic

ABCDEFGHIJKLMNOPQRSTUVWXYZ

abcdefghijklmnopqrstuvwxyz

1234567890?!$%&

VS Software

CG Triumvirate Condensed

ABCDEFGHIJKLMNOPQRSTUVWXYZ
abcdefghijklmnopqrstuvwxyz
1234567890?!$%&

Hewlett-Packard Company / VS Software

CG Triumvirate Condensed Italic

ABCDEFGHIJKLMNOPQRSTUVWXYZ
abcdefghijklmnopqrstuvwxyz
1234567890?!$%&

VS Software

CG Triumvirate Bold Condensed

ABCDEFGHIJKLMNOPQRSTUVWXYZ
abcdefghijklmnopqrstuvwxyz
1234567890?!$%&

VS Software

CG Triumvirate Bold Condensed Italic

ABCDEFGHIJKLMNOPQRSTUVWXYZ
abcdefghijklmnopqrstuvwxyz
1234567890?!$%&

VS Software

Twist

ABCDEFGHIJKLMNOPQRSTUVWXYZ
abcdefghijklmnopqrstuvwxyz
1234567890

SoftCraft, Inc.

Tymes Roman

ABCDEFGHIJKLMNOPQRSTUVWXYZ
abcdefghijklmnopqrstuvwxyz
1234567890?!$%&
SWFTE International

Uncial

ABCDEFGHIJKLMNOPQRSTUVWXYZ
abcdefghijklmnopqrstuvwxyz
1234567890?!$%&
Good Software Corporation

Uncial

ABCDEFGHIJKLMNOPQRSTUVWXYZ
abcdefghijklmnopqrstuvwxyz
1234567890?!$%&
Hewlett-Packard Company

Univers Medium

ABCDEFGHIJKLMNOPQRSTUVWXYZ
abcdefghijklmnopqrstuvwxyz
1234567890?!$%&
Good Software Corporation

Univers

ABCDEFGHIJKLMNOPQRSTUVWXYZ
abcdefghijklmnopqrstuvwxyz
1234567890?!$%&
Hewlett-Packard Company

Univers Medium

ABCDEFGHIJKLMNOPQRSTUVWXYZ
abcdefghijklmnopqrstuvwxyz
1234567890?!$%&

VS Software

Univers Italic

ABCDEFGHIJKLMNOPQRSTUVWXYZ
abcdefghijklmnopqrstuvwxyz
1234567890?!$%&

Good Software Corporation

Univers Italic

ABCDEFGHIJKLMNOPQRSTUVWXYZ
abcdefghijklmnopqrstuvwxyz
1234567890?!$%&

Hewlett-Packard Company

Univers Italic

ABCDEFGHIJKLMNOPQRSTUVWXYZ
abcdefghijklmnopqrstuvwxyz
1234567890?!$%&

VS Software

Univers Bold

ABCDEFGHIJKLMNOPQRSTUVWXYZ
abcdefghijklmnopqrstuvwxyz
1234567890?!$%&

Good Software Corporation

Univers Bold

ABCDEFGHIJKLMNOPQRSTUVWXYZ
abcdefghijklmnopqrstuvwxyz
1234567890?!$%&

Hewlett-Packard Company

Univers Bold

ABCDEFGHIJKLMNOPQRSTUVWXYZ
abcdefghijklmnopqrstuvwxyz
1234567890?!$%&

VS Software

Univers Extra Bold

ABCDEFGHIJKLMNOPQRSTUVWXYZ
abcdefghijklmnopqrstuvwxyz
1234567890?!$%&

VS Software

Univers Bold Italic

ABCDEFGHIJKLMNOPQRSTUVWXYZ
abcdefghijklmnopqrstuvwxyz
1234567890?!$%&

Good Software Corporation

Univers Bold Italic

ABCDEFGHIJKLMNOPQRSTUVWXYZ
abcdefghijklmnopqrstuvwxyz
1234567890?!$%&

Hewlett-Packard Company

Univers Condensed Medium

ABCDEFGHIJKLMNOPQRSTUVWXYZ
abcdefghijklmnopqrstuvwxyz
1234567890?!$%&

Good Software Corporation

Univers Condensed Italic

ABCDEFGHIJKLMNOPQRSTUVWXYZ
abcdefghijklmnopqrstuvwxyz
1234567890?!$%&

Good Software Corporation

Univers Condensed Bold

ABCDEFGHIJKLMNOPQRSTUVWXYZ
abcdefghijklmnopqrstuvwxyz
1234567890?!$%&

Good Software Corporation

Univers Condensed Bold Italic

ABCDEFGHIJKLMNOPQRSTUVWXYZ
abcdefghijklmnopqrstuvwxyz
1234567890?!$%&

Good Software Corporation

University Roman

ABCDEFGHIJKLMNOPQRSTUVWXYZ
abcdefghijklmnopqrstuvwxyz
1234567890?!$%&

Bitstream, Inc.

University Ornate

ABCDEFGHIJKLMNOPQRSTUVWXYZ
abcdefghijklmnopqrstuvwxyz
1234567890?!$%&

SWFTE International

Zurich Roman

ABCDEFGHIJKLMNOPQRSTUVWXYZ
abcdefghijklmnopqrstuvwxyz
1234567890?!$%&

Bitstream, Inc.

Zurich Italic

ABCDEFGHIJKLMNOPQRSTUVWXYZ
abcdefghijklmnopqrstuvwxyz
1234567890?!$%&

Bitstream, Inc.

Zurich Black

ABCDEFGHIJKLMNOPQRSTUVWXYZ
abcdefghijklmnopqrstuvwxyz
1234567890?!$%&

Bitstream, Inc.

Zurich Black Italic

ABCDEFGHIJKLMNOPQRSTUVWXYZ
abcdefghijklmnopqrstuvwxyz
1234567890?!$%&

Bitstream, Inc.

Zurich Light

ABCDEFGHIJKLMNOPQRSTUVWXYZ
abcdefghijklmnopqrstuvwxyz
1234567890?!$%&
Bitstream, Inc.

Zurich Light Italic

ABCDEFGHIJKLMNOPQRSTUVWXYZ
abcdefghijklmnopqrstuvwxyz
1234567890?!$%&
Bitstream, Inc.

Zurich Bold

ABCDEFGHIJKLMNOPQRSTUVWXYZ
abcdefghijklmnopqrstuvwxyz
1234567890?!$%&
Bitstream, Inc.

Zurich Bold Italic

ABCDEFGHIJKLMNOPQRSTUVWXYZ
abcdefghijklmnopqrstuvwxyz
1234567890?!$%&
Bitstream, Inc.

Zurich Condensed Roman

ABCDEFGHIJKLMNOPQRSTUVWXYZ
abcdefghijklmnopqrstuvwxyz
1234567890?!$%&
Bitstream, Inc.

Zurich Condensed Italic

ABCDEFGHIJKLMNOPQRSTUVWXYZ

abcdefghijklmnopqrstuvwxyz

1234567890?!$%&

Bitstream, Inc.

Zurich Bold Extended

ABCDEFGHIJKLMNOPQRSTUVWXYZ

abcdefghijklmnopqrstuvwxyz

1234567890?!$%&

Bitstream, Inc.

Zurich Black Extended

ABCDEFGHIJKLMNOPQRSTUVWXY

Zabcdefghijklmnopqrstuvwxyz

1234567890?!$%&

Bitstream, Inc.

5 Font Companies

This chapter shows you a variety of English-language font packages from[1]

Adobe® Systems, Inc.
Bitstream®, Inc.
Casady & Greene, Inc.
Good Software Corporation
Hewlett-Packard Company
SoftCraft, Inc.
SWFTE International
VS Software

In addition to font samples, you'll find each company's address and phone numbers as well as

- A brief company profile.
- A description of the product line.
- A legend that lets you know whether the fonts are available only for IBM and compatible computers, or are also available for the Macintosh.

A list of foreign language and symbol fonts is found in the *Appendix*. For an alphabetical listing of fonts by font name, see Chapter 3, *Postscript Fonts* and Chapter 4, *LaserJet Fonts*.y

[1] Font companies are continually adding to their collections. Contact the companies directly for a list of their newest fonts.

Adobe

Adobe® Systems, Inc.
1585 Charleston Road
P.O. Box 7900
Mountain View, CA 94039
(800) 83-FONTS
(415) 962-2100

IBM
Macintosh

PostScript

Adobe® Systems, Inc. is the owner and licensor of *PostScript,* the most popular and widely-used page-description language for desktop publishing.

Adobe markets the *Adobe Type Library,* an extensive collection of PostScript fonts that are available in both IBM and Mac formats. Many fonts in the Adobe Type Library are created exclusively for Adobe by Adobe's own designers. Other products from Adobe include the

- *Adobe FontFolio,* the entire Adobe Type Library on a hard disk. The *Adobe FontFolio* attaches to any PostScript printer that has a SCSI port.

- *Adobe Type Manager,* a product for the Macintosh that significantly improves the appearance of PostScript screen-fonts.

IBM System Requirements

- 512K of memory.
- A hard disk.
- PostScript printer or typesetter.

Mac System Requirements

- Two 800K disk drives *or* one disk drive and a hard disk.
- PostScript printer or typesetter.

Package # 1

Palatino™
Palatino Italic
Palatino Bold
Palatino Bold Italic

Package # 2

ITC Bookman® Light
ITC Bookman Light Italic
ITC Bookman Demi
ITC Bookman Demi Italic

Package # 3

ITC Zapf Chancery®

Package # 4

ITC Avant Garde Gothic® Book
ITC Avant Garde Book Gothic Oblique
ITC Avant Garde Gothic Demi
ITC Avant Garde Gothic Demi Oblique

Package # 5

New Century Schoolbook
New Century Schoolbook Italic
New Century Schoolbook Bold
New Century Schoolbook Bold Italic

Package # 6

Optima™
Optima Oblique
Optima Bold
Optima Bold Oblique

Package # 7

ITC Souvenir®
ITC Souvenir Light Italic
ITC Souvenir Demi
ITC Souvenir Demi Italic

Package # 8

ITC Lubalin Graph® Book
ITC Lubalin Graph Book Oblique
ITC Lubalin Graph Demi
ITC Lubalin Graph Demi Oblique

Package # 9

ITC Garamond® Light
ITC Garamond Light Italic
ITC Garamond Bold
ITC Garamond Bold Italic

Package # 10

ITC MACHINE®
ITC American Typewriter®
ITC American Typewriter Bold

Package # 11

ITC Benguiat®
ITC Benguiat Bold
ITC Friz Quadrata®
ITC Friz Quadrata Bold

Package # 12

Glypha™
Glypha Oblique
Glypha Bold
Glypha Bold Oblique

Package # 13

Helvetica™ Light
Helvetica Light Oblique
Helvetica Black
Helvetica Black Oblique

Package # 14

Helvetica Condensed Light
Helvetica Condensed Light Oblique
Helvetica Condensed
Helvetica Condensed Oblique
Helvetica Condensed Bold
Helvetica Condensed Bold Oblique
Helvetica Condensed Black
Helvetica Condensed Black Oblique

Package # 15

Trump Mediæval™
Trump Mediæval Italic
Trump Mediæval Bold
Trump Mediæval Bold Italic

Package # 16

Melior™
Melior Italic
Melior Bold
Melior Bold Italic

Package # 17

ITC Galliard® Roman
ITC Galliard Italic
ITC Galliard Bold
ITC Galliard Bold Italic

Package # 18

ITC New Baskerville® Roman
ITC New Baskerville Italic
ITC New Baskerville Bold
ITC New Baskerville Bold Italic

Package # 19

ITC Korinna® Regular
ITC Korinna Kursiv Regular
ITC Korinna Bold
ITC Korinna Kursiv Bold

Package # 20

Goudy Old Style
Goudy Old Style Italic
Goudy Old StyleBold
Goudy Old Style Bold Italic

Package # 22

Century Old Style
Century Old Style Italic
Century Old Style Bold

Package # 23

ITC Franklin Gothic® Book
ITC Franklin Gothic Book Oblique
ITC Franklin Gothic Demi
ITC Franklin Gothic Demi Oblique
ITC Franklin Gothic Heavy
ITC Franklin Gothic Heavy Oblique

Package # 24

ITC Cheltenham® Book
ITC Cheltenham Book Italic
ITC Cheltenham Bold
ITC Cheltenham Bold Italic

Package # 25

Park Avenue®

Package # 26

Bodoni
Bodoni Italic
Bodoni Bold
Bodoni Bold Italic
Bodoni Poster

Package # 27

Letter Gothic
Letter Gothic Slanted
Letter Gothic Bold
Letter Gothic Bold Slanted

Package # 28

Prestige Elite
Prestige Elite Slanted
Prestige Elite Bold
Prestige Elite Bold Slanted

Package # 29

ORATOR
ORATOR SLANTED

Package # 30

News Gothic
News Gothic Oblique
News Gothic Bold
News Gothic Bold Oblique

Package # 31

ITC Tiffany®
ITC Tiffany Italic
ITC Tiffany Demi
ITC Tiffany Demi Italic
ITC Tiffany Heavy
ITC Tiffany Heavy Italic

Package # 32

Cooper Black
Cooper Black Italic

Package # 33

STENCIL
Hobo
Brush Script

Package # 34

Aachen Bold
Revue
University Roman
Freestyle Script

Package # 36

Lucida® Roman
Lucida Italic
Lucida Bold
Lucida Bold Italic

Package # 37

Univers™ 45 Light
Univers 45 Light Oblique
Univers 55
Univers 55 Oblique
Univers 65 Bold
Univers 65 Bold Oblique
Univers 75 Black
Univers 75 Black Oblique

Package # 38

Univers 47 Condensed Light
Univers 47 Condensed Light Oblique
Univers 57 Condensed
Univers 57 Condensed Oblique
Univers 67 Condensed Bold
Univers 67 Condensed Bold Oblique

Package # 39

Futura® Light
Futura Light Oblique
Futura Book
Futura Book Oblique
Futura Bold
Futura Bold Oblique

Package # 40

Stone® Serif
Stone Serif Italic
Stone Serif Semibold
Stone Serif Semibold Italic
Stone Serif Bold
Stone Serif Bold Italic

Package # 41

Stone Sans
Stone Sans Italic
Stone Sans Semibold
Stone Sans Semibold Italic
Stone Sans Bold
Stone Sans Bold Italic

Package # 42

Stone Informal
Stone Informal Italic
Stone Informal Semibold
Stone Informal Semibold Italic
Stone Informal Bold
Stone Informal Bold Italic

Package # 43

Corona™
Corona Italic
Corona Bold

Package # 44

Eurostile®
Eurostile Oblique
Eurostile Demi
Eurostile Demi Oblique
Eurostile Bold
Eurostile Bold Oblique

Package # 45

Excelsior™
Excelsior Italic
Excelsior Bold

Package # 46

Futura
Futura Oblique
Futura Heavy
Futura Heavy Oblique
Futura Extra Bold
Futura Extra Bold Oblique

Package # 47

Futura Condensed Light
Futura Condensed Light Oblique
Futura Condensed
Futura Condensed Oblique
Futura Condensed Bold
Futura Condensed Bold Oblique
Futura Condensed Extra Bold
Futura Condensed Extra Bold Oblique

Package # 48

Lucida Sans Roman
Lucida Sans Italic
Lucida Sans Bold
Lucida Sans Bold Italic

Package # 49

Memphis™ Light
Memphis Light Italic
Memphis Medium
Memphis Medium Italic
Memphis Bold
Memphis Bold Italic
Memphis Extra Bold

Package # 50

Helvetica Compressed
Helvetica Compressed Extra
Helvetica Compressed Ultra

Package #51

Italia Book
Italia Medium
Italia Bold

Package # 52

Belwe Light
Belwe Medium
Belwe Bold
Belwe Condensed

Package # 53

Caslon 540 Roman
Caslon 540 Italic
Caslon 3 Roman
Caslon 3 Italic

Package # 54

Goudy Extra Bold
Goudy Heavyface
Goudy Heavyface Italic

Package # 55

Janson Text™
Janson Text Italic
Janson Text Bold
Janson Text Bold Italic

Package # 56

ITC Eras® Light
ITC Eras Book
ITC Eras Medium
ITC Eras Demi
ITC Eras Bold
ITC Eras Ultra

Package # 57

ITC Kabel® Book
ITC Kabel Medium
ITC Kabel Demi
ITC Kabel Bold
ITC Kabel Ultra

Package # 58

OCRA
OCRB

Package # 59

Helvetica 25 Ultra Light
Helvetica 26 Ultra Light Italic
Helvetica 95 Black
Helvetica 96 Black Italic

Package # 60

Helvetica 35 Thin
Helvetica 36 Thin Italic
Helvetica 55 Roman
Helvetica 56 Italic
Helvetica 75 Bold
Helvetica 76 Bold Italic

Package # 61

Helvetica 45 Light
Helvetica 46 Light Italic
Helvetica 65 Medium
Helvetica 66 Medium Italic
Helvetica 85 Heavy
Helvetica 86 Heavy Italic

Package # 62

Times™ Ten Roman
Times Ten Italic
Times Ten Bold
Times Ten Bold Italic

Package # 63

Kaufmann®
Kaufmann Bold

Package # 64

Clarendon™ Light
Clarendon
Clarendon Bold

Package # 65

PEIGNOT™ LIGHT
PEIGNOT DEMI
PEIGNOT Bold

Package # 66

New Caledonia™
New Caledonia Italic
New Caledonia Semi Bold
New Caledonia Semi Bold Italic
New Caledonia Bold
New Caledonia Bold Italic
New Caledonia Black
New Caledonia Black Italic

Package # 67

ITC Clearface® Regular
ITC Clearface Regular Italic
ITC Clearface Bold
ITC Clearface Bold Italic
ITC Clearface Heavy
ITC Clearface Heavy Italic
ITC Clearface Black
ITC Clearface Black Italic

Package # 68

Americana®
Americana Italic
Americana Bold
Americana Extra Bold

Package # 69

ITC Serif Gothic® Light
ITC Serif Gothic
ITC Serif Gothic Bold
ITC Serif Gothic Extra Bold
ITC Serif Gothic Heavy
ITC Serif Gothic Black

Package # 70

Century Expanded
Century Expanded Italic

Package # 71

Serifa® 45 Light
Serifa 46 Light Italic
Serifa 55
Serifa 56 Italic
Serifa 65 Bold
Serifa 75 Black

Package # 72

Caslon Open Face

Package # 73

Frutiger™ 45 Light
Frutiger 46 Light Italic
Frutiger 55
Frutiger 56 Italic
Frutiger 65 Bold
Frutiger 66 Bold Italic
Frutiger 75 Black
Frutiger 76 Black Italic
Frutiger 95 Ultra Black

Package # 74

Linotype Centennial™ 45 Light
Linotype Centennial 46 Light Italic
Linotype Centennial 55
Linotype Centennial 56 Italic
Linotype Centennial 75 Bold
Linotype Centennial 76 Bold Italic
Linotype Centennial 95 Black
Linotype Centennial 96 Black Italic

Package # 75

Stemple Garamond™ Roman
Stemple Garamond Italic
Stemple Garamond Bold
Stemple Garamond Bold Italic

Package # 76

Weiss®
Weiss Italic
Weiss Bold
Weiss Extra Bold

Package # 77

Garamond 3™
Garamond 3 Italic
Garamond 3 Bold
Garamond 3 Bold Italic

Package # 79

Avenir™ 35 Light
Avenir 35 Light Oblique
Avenir 55 Roman
Avenir 55 Oblique
Avenir 85 Heavy
Avenir 85 Heavy Oblique

Package # 80

Avenir 45 Book
Avenir 45 Book Oblique
Avenir 65 Medium
Avenir 65 Medium Oblique
Avenir 95 Black
Avenir 95 Black Oblique

Package # 81

Walbaum®
Walbaum Italic
Walbaum Bold
Walbaum Bold Italic

Package # 82

Antique Olive™ Light
Antique Olive
Antique Olive Italic
Antique Olive Bold
Antique Olive Black

Package # 83

Life® Roman
Life Italic
Life Bold

Package # 84

Concorde®
Concorde Italic
Concorde Bold
Concorde Bold Italic

Package # 85

Gothic 13
Tempo™ Heavy Condensed
Tempo Heavy Condensed Italic

Package # 86

Cochin™
Cochin Italic
Cochin Bold
Cochin Bold Italic

Package # 87

ITC Bauhaus™ Light
ITC Bauhaus Medium
ITC Bauhaus Demi
ITC Bauhaus Bold
ITC Bauhaus Heavy

Package #88

Sabon™ Roman
Sabon Italic
Sabon Bold
Sabon Bold Italic

Package # 89

Hiroshige™ Book
Hiroshige Book Italic
Hiroshige Medium
Hiroshige Medium Italic
Hiroshige Bold
Hiroshige Bold Italic
Hiroshige Black
Hiroshige Black Italic

Package # 90

Arnold Böcklin
Fette Fraktur
Helvetica Inserat
Present™ Script

Package # 91

Dom Casual
Dom Casual Bold

Package # 92

Post Antiqua™
Post Antiqua Bold

Package # 93

Folio® Light
Folio Medium
Folio Bold
Folio Extra Bold
Folio Bold Condensed

Package # 94

Linoscript™
Linotext™

Package # 95

VAG Rounded Thin
VAG Rounded Light
VAG Rounded Bold
VAG Rounded Black

Package # 96

Akzidenz Grotesk® Light
Akzidenz Grotesk Roman
Akzidenz Grotesk Bold
Akzidenz Grotesk Black

Package # 97

Impressum® Roman
Impressum Italic
Impressum Bold

Package # 98

Bauer Bodoni® Roman
Bauer Bodoni Italic
Bauer Bodoni Bold
Bauer Bodoni Bold Italic

Package # 99

New Aster®
New Aster Italic
New Aster Semi Bold
New Aster Semi Bold Italic
New Aster Bold
New Aster Bold Italic
New Aster Black
New Aster Black Italic

Package # 100

Adobe Garamond™ Regular
Adobe Garamond Italic
Adobe Garamond Semibold
Adobe Garamond Semibold Italic
Adobe Garamond Bold
Adobe Garamond Bold Italic

Package # 101

ADOBE GARAMOND EXPERT COLLECTION
TITLING CAPITALS
ALTERNATE ITALIC

Package # 102

Cándida® Roman
Cándida Italic
Cándida Bold

Package # 103

Franklin Gothic Extra Condensed
Franklin Gothic Condensed
Franklin Gothic No. 2 Roman

Package # 104

Utopia™
Utopia Italic
Utopia Semibold
Utopia Semibold Italic
Utopia Bold
Utopia Bold Italic
Utopia Black

Bitstream

Bitstream®, Inc.
215 First Street
Cambridge, MA 02142
(800) 522-FONT
(617) 497-6222
(617) 868-4732 FAX

IBM

LaserJet
PostScript

Bitstream®, Inc., one of the world's largest font companies, features *Bitstream Fontware™ Typefaces* packages for IBM PCs and compatibles. Each *Fontware* package lets you create either LaserJet fonts in any sizes you wish or PostScript outlines.

Before using Bitstream fonts, you must first obtain a *Bitstream Starter Kit* for your word processing or desktop publishing program. You can get this kit by contacting your local software store or by calling Bitstream. Kits are available for most popular programs.

IBM System Requirements

- Bitstream Starter Kit.

ITC Benguiat®

ITC Benguiat Book

ITC Benguiat Book Italic

ITC Benguiat Bold

ITC Benguiat Bold Italic

Bodoni

Bodoni Book

Bodoni Book Italic

Bodoni Bold

Bodoni Bold Italic

ITC Bookman®

ITC Bookman Light

ITC Bookman Light Italic

ITC Bookman Demi

ITC Bookman Demi Italic

ITC Clearface®

ITC Clearface Regular

ITC Clearface Regular Italic

ITC Clearface Heavy

ITC Clearface Heavy Italic

Dutch

Dutch Roman

Dutch Italic

Dutch Bold

Dutch Bold Italic

Frankin Gothic

Frankin Gothic Roman
Frankin Gothic Italic
Frankin Gothic Extra Condensed

Goudy Old Style®

Goudy Old Style Roman
Goudy Old Style Italic
Goudy Old Style Bold
Goudy Old Style Extra Bold

Hammersmith™

Hammersmith Roman
Hammersmith Italic
Hammersmith Bold
Hammersmith Bold Italic

Provence™

Provence Roman
Provence Italic
Provence Black
Provence Compact

Swiss

Swiss Roman
Swiss Italic
Swiss Bold
Swiss Bold Italic

Swiss Condensed

Swiss Condensed
Swiss Condensed Italic
Swiss Bold Condensed
Swiss Black Condensed

Swiss Light

Swiss Light
Swiss Light Italic
Swiss Black
Swiss Black Italic

Zurich™

Zurich Roman
Zurich Italic
Zurich Black
Zurich Black Italic

Zurich™ Condensed

Zurich Condensed
Zurich Condensed Italic
Zurich Bold Extended
Zurich Black Extended

Zurich™ Light

Zurich Light
Zurich LIght Italic
Zurich Bold
Zurich Bold Italic

Headlines 1

Bitstream Cooper Black®

University Roman

Cloister Black®

Broadway®

Headlines 5

Park Avenue™

Handel Gothic®

Futura® Black

Dom™ Casual

Headlines 6

Mermaid™

ITC Bolt Bold®

P.T. Barnum™

Kaufmann® Bold

Casady & Greene

Casady & Greene, Inc.
P.O. Box 223779
Carmel, CA 93922
(408) 624-8716

IBM
Macintosh

PostScript

Fluent Laser Fonts™ is a unique collection of PostScript fonts from **Casady & Greene, Inc.** *Fluent Laser Fonts* are available for both IBM and Macintosh computers and come complete with four or five screen fonts.

Also included with a font purchase is font management software that helps you download the fonts directly to your printer.

Casady & Greene's English-language fonts are shown on the following pages. A list of the company's foreign-language fonts may be found in the *Appendix*.

IBM System Requirements

- PostScript printer or typesetter.

Mac System Requirements

- PostScript printer or typesetter.

Volume # 1 Bodoni

Bodoni

Bodoni Italic

Bodoni Bold

Bodoni Bold Italic

Volume # 2 Sans Serif

Sans Serif

Sans Serif Italic

Sans Serif Book

Sans Serif Book Italic

Sans Serif Demi Bold

Sans Serif Demi Italic

Volume # 3 Ritz-Right Bank

Ritz

Ritz Italic

Ritz Condensed

RIGHT BANK

Volume # 4 Monterey

MONTEREY MEDIUM

MONTEREY ITALIC

MONTEREY Bold

MONTEREY Bold ITALIC

Volume # 5 Regency Script-Calligraphy

Regency Script

Calligraphy

Volume # 6 Prelude Script

Prelude Script

Prelude Script Light Slant

Prelude Script Bold

Prelude Script Bold Slant

Volume # 7 Coventry Script-Zephyr

Coventry Script

Zephyr Script

Volume # 8 Gregorian-Dorovar

Gregorian

Dorovar

Dorovar Italic

Volume # 10 Bodoni Ultra

Bodoni Ultra

Bodoni Ultra Italic

Bodoni Ultra Condensed

Bodoni Ultra Condensed Italic

Volume # 11 Sans Serif Bold

Sans Serif Bold

Sans Serif Bold Italic

Sans Serif Bold Condensed

Sans Serif Condensed Italic

Volume # 12 Sans Serif Extra Bold

Sans Serif Extra Bold

Sans Serif Extra Bold Italic

Sans Serif Extra Bold Condensed

Sans Serif Extra Bold Condensed Italic

Volume # 13 Gatsby

Gatsby

Gatsby Italic

Gatsby Demi Bold

Gatsby Demi Bold Italic

Volume # 14 Micro

Micro

Micro Italic

Micro Bold

Micro Bold Italic

Volume # 15 Micro Extended

Micro Extended

Micro Extended Italic

Micro Extended Bold

Micro Eteneded Bold Italic

Volume # 16 Galileo Roman

Galileo Roman

Galileo Italic

Galileo Bold

Galileo Bold Italic

Volume # 17 Campanile-Giotto

Campanile

Giotto

Giotto Bold

Volume # 18 Alexandria

Alexandria

Alexandria Italic

Alexandria Bold

Alexandria Bold Italic

Volume # 19 Jott Casual

Jott Casual

Jott Quick

Jott Light

Jott Quick Light

Volume # 20 Gazelle - Kells Meath

Gazelle

Kells

Meath

Volume # 21 Paladin-Abilene

Paladin

ABILENE

DRY GULCH

DESPERADO

Volume # 22 Collegiate

COLLEGIATE

COLLEGIATE BLACK

COLLEGIATE OUTLINE

Good Software

Good Software Corporation
13601 Preston Road
Suite 500W
Dallas, TX 75240
(214) 239-6085 Information
(214) 329-4643 FAX

IBM

LaserJet

Good Software Corporation develops and markets software for IBM PCs and compatibles. The company recently acquired **The Font Factory**, makers of *FontMaker®* font management software and *Office Series Typefaces*, a collection of soft font packages that emulate Hewlett-Packard font cartridges (not shown).

Good Software's primary products that assist desktop publishers is their collection of scalable type styles called *FontMaker Typeface Library*. *FontMaker* font management software is used with the various packages in the *FontMaker Typeface Library* to generate LaserJet fonts in any sizes you wish from 4 to 155 points. The font management software also includes a download utility that sends the generated fonts to your LaserJet or LaserJet compatible printer.

IBM System Requirements

- No special requirements.

Typeface Package #1 - CG Times

CG Times

CG Times Italic

CG Times Bold

CG Times Bold Italic

Typeface Package #2 - CG Triumvirate

CG Triumvirate Medium

CG Triumvirate Italic

CG Triumvirate Bold

CG Triumvirate Bold Italic

Typeface Package #5 - ITC Avant Garde Gothic

ITC Avant Garde Gothic Book

ITC Avant Garde Gothic Book Oblique

ITC Avant Garde Gothic Bold

ITC Avant Garde Gothic Bold Oblique

Typeface Package #7 - Century Schoolbook

Century Schoolbook Medium

Century Schoolbook Italic

Century Schoolbook Bold

Century Schoolbook Bold Italic

Typeface Package #9 - Futura II

Futura II Medium

Futura II Italic

Futura II Bold

Futura II Bold Italic

Typeface Package #10 - Garamond Antiqua

Garamond Antiqua
Garamond Kursiv
Garamond Halbfett
Garamond Kursiv Halbfett

Typeface Package #14 - ITC Souvenir

ITC Souvenir Light
ITC Souvenir Light Italic
ITC Souvenir Demi
ITC Souvenir Demi Italic

Typeface Package #15 - Univers

Univers Medium
Univers Italic
Univers Bold
Univers Bold Italic

Typeface Package #17 - Univers Condensed

Univers Condensed Medium
Univers Condensed Italic
Univers Condensed Bold
Univers Condensed Bold Italic

Typeface Package #18 - ITC Benguiat

ITC Benguiat Medium
ITC Benguiat Italic
ITC Benguiat Bold
ITC Benguiat Bold Italic

Typeface Package #19 - ITC Lubalin Graph

ITC Lubalin Graph

ITC Lubalin Graph Oblique

ITC Lubalin Demi

ITC Lubalin Demi Oblique

Typeface Package #20 - Microstyle

Microstyle Medium

Microstyle Bold

Microstyle Extended

Microstyle Extended Bold

Typeface Package #21 - Decorative 1

Brush

Uncial

Dom Casual

Park Avenue

Hewlett-Packard

Hewlett-Packard Company
P.O. Box 10301
Palo Alto, CA 94303
(800) 752-0900
(415) 857-1501

IBM

LaserJet

Hewlett-Packard Company (HP), maker of the renowned LaserJet laser printers, is one of the industry leaders when setting the standards in desktop publishing. Hewlett-Packard has several font products for desktop publishing including

- *HP Scalable Typefaces,* collections and individual type styles that may be scaled to any size you wish from 4-200 points (in half-point increments).
- *Type Director™*, a font management program that scales type and downloads soft fonts to your LaserJet or LaserJet-compatible printer. *Type Director* was co-developed with Agfa Compugraphic.
- The *LaserJet Printer PostScript Cartridge,* a font cartridge with 35-scalable fonts that turns the HP LaserJet III, IID, or IIP printers into a PostScript printer. (Not compatible with the LaserJet Series II.)

Typically HP font purchases include one or more booklets with information fonts and font terminology and tips on how to create professional documents.

IBM System Requirements

- No special requirements.

Antique Olive®

Antique Olive

Antique Olive Italic

Antique Olive Bold

ITC Avant Garde Gothic®

ITC Avant Garde Gothic

ITC Avant Garde Gothic Oblique

ITC Avant Garde Gothic Bold

ITC Avant Garde Gothic Bold Oblique

ITC Benguiat®

ITC Benguiat

ITC Benguiat Italic

ITC Benguiat Bold

ITC Benguiat Bold Italic

ITC Bookman®

ITC Bookman Light

ITC Bookman Light Italic

ITC Bookman Demi

ITC Bookman Demi Italic

CG Century Schoolbook

CG Century Schoolbook

CG Century Schoolbook Italic

CG Century Schoolbook Bold

CG Century Schoolbook Bold Italic

Decorative 1

Brush
Dom Casual
Park Avenue
Uncial

Futura™ II

Futura Book II
Futura Book Italic II
Futura Bold II
Futura Bold Italic II

ITC Lubalin Graph®

ITC Lubalin Graph Book
ITC Lubalin Graph Book Oblique
ITC Lubalin Graph Demi
ITC Lubalin Graph Demi Oblique

CG Omega

CG Omega
CG Omega Italic
CG Omega Bold
CG Omega Bold Italic

CG Palacio

CG Palacio
CG Palacio Italic
CG Palacio Bold
CG Palacio Bold Italic

ITC Souvenir®

ITC Souvenir Light
ITC Souvenir Light Italic
ITC Souvenir Demi
ITC Souvenir Demi Italic

Stymie

Stymie Medium
Stymie Medium Italic
Stymie Bold
Stymie Bold Italic

CG Times

CG Times
CG Times Italic
CG Times Bold
CG Times Bold Italic

CG Triumvirate™

CG Triumvirate
CG Triumvirate Italic
CG Triumvirate Bold
CG Triumvirate Bold Italic

CG Triumvirate™ Condensed

CG Triumvirate Condensed
CG Triumvirate Condensed Italic
CG Triumvirate Bold Condensed
CG Triumvirate Bold Condensed Italic

Univers®

Univers
Univers Italic
Univers Bold
Univers Bold Italic

SoftCraft

SoftCraft, Inc.
16 North Carroll Street
Suite 500
Madison, WI 53703
(800) 351-0500 Sales
(608) 257-3300 Technical Support
(608) 257-6733 FAX

IBM

LaserJet

SoftCraft, Inc. was founded in 1982 by two computer scientists named Dr. Robert Frenchel and Dr. William Overman. In addition to their own unique (and sometimes whimsical) collection of soft fonts, SoftCraft also carries the complete collection of *Bitstream® Scalable Typefaces.* (See *Bitstream®, Inc.,* earlier in this chapter.)

SoftCraft also offers other desktop publishing products, including

- *Font Solution Pack,* an extensive collection of menu-driven font programs and utilities for installing fonts, making screen fonts from your soft fonts, rotating fonts, creating special fonts, and creating special font effects.
- *Font Special Effects Pack,* a program for creating and installing headlines, logos, and display fonts.
- *FontSpace,* a utility which shrinks the amount of hard-disk space required by your soft fonts.

IBM System Requirements

- No special requirements.

Disk #25-26

Olde English

Disk #27

Olde English Hollow

Disk #28-29

Script
Script Hollow

Disk #38

Tall

Disk #39

Twist
Formal
Calligrapher

Disk #42

Classic Shadow
COMPUTER
Sans Serif Shadow

Disk #47

Overhead Projector Font

Disk #51

Nouveau
Nouveau Bold
Elegant Script
MODERN

Disk #53-57

Block Outline

Disk #66

LCD
LCD ITALIC
Orbit
Optical Style

Disk #77

CARIBBEAN

Disk #86

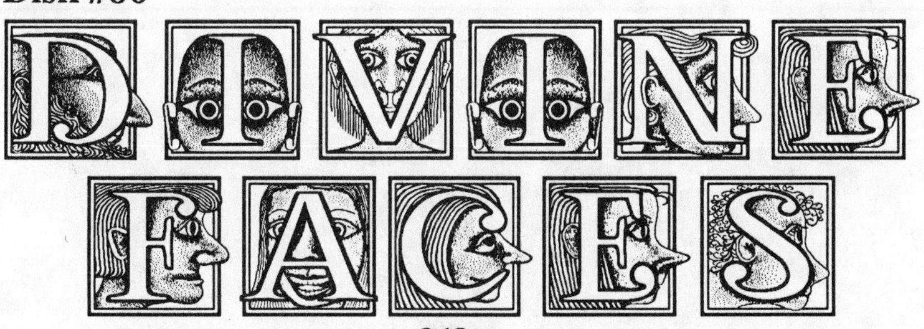

SWFTE

SWFTE International, Ltd.
P.O. Box 219
Rockland, DE 19732
(302) 429-8434
(302) 429-0532 FAX

IBM

LaserJet

SWFTE International, Ltd. is the maker of *Glyphix,* a unique font management program that works between your word processor and your printer.

SWFTE (pronounced *swifty*) offers several font collections for your LaserJet printer. Unlike other soft fonts for the LaserJet, *Glyphix's* soft fonts operate similar to PostScript fonts in that the font sizes you request in your document are generated *on the fly* when you go to print.

Custom versions of *Glyphix* are available for most popular word processors and page layout programs.

IBM System Requirements

- Hard disk required.

Basics

Tymes Roman
Helvenica
Rockland
Exchequer Script

Basics II

Oxford
Eterna
Classic Typewriter
New York Deco

Book

Garamand
Baskerton
Palatine
Century

Sans Serif

Avant Guard
Gibraltar
Bongo Black
Obelisk

Decorative

University Ornate
Manuscript
Buckingham
Copperfield

Fixed

Courier
Prestige
SWFTE Letter Gothic

VS Software

VS Software
2103 South Broadway
Little Rock, AR 72206
(501) 376-2083
(501) 372-7075 FAX

IBM

LaserJet

VS Software, founded in 1982, offers a wide selection of fonts for word processing and desktop publishing. Fonts may be purchased in individual weights, in font families (a few weights of the same type style), or in FontPaks (collections of several popular fonts in one package). Most fonts come packaged with 10-12 sizes ranging from 8 to 30 points.

In addition to their soft font line, VS Software offers custom font services. The company can create a font of your logo, letterhead, or signature or create a unique alphabet based on your logo or other design.

Other products from VS Software include

- Font Cartridges.
- *FontGen V*, a program which lets you to create your own fonts.
- *VS Laser Word Processor Tool Kit*, font utilities which
  (1) Allows you to put LaserJet-style fonts in a form your word processor can use.
  (2) Downloads (sends) fonts to and removes fonts from your laser printer.
- *VS Font Library Manager*, a program which shrinks the size of font files so they take up significantly less disk space.
- *SLED* (*S*ignature *L*ogo *Ed*itor) a program which lets you create a graphic using a logo or signature. Once saved, your graphic can be used in your word processing or page layout program.

IBM System Requirements

- No special requirements.

Family AOV F-A

Antique Olive Medium
Antique Olive Thin
Antique Olive Bold

Family AVG F-A

ITC Avant Garde Gothic Book
ITC Avant Garde Gothic Book Oblique
ITC Avant Garde Gothic Bold
ITC Avant Garde Gothic Bold Oblique

Family BDW F-A

Broadway
Broadway Engraved

Family BHS F-A

VS BHS Medium
VS BHS Bold
VS BHS Extra Bold

Family BKM F-A

VS Bookman Medium
VS Bookman Italic
VS Bookman Bold
VS Bookman Bold Italic

Family BKV F-A

Baskerville II Medium

Baskerville II Italic

Baskerville II Bold

Baskerville II Bold Italic

Family BRS F-A

Brush

Family CEN F-A

Century II Light

Century II Light Italic

Century II Bold

Century II Bold Italic

Family CNT F-D

VS Century Medium

VS Century Italic

VS Century Bold

VS Century Bold Italic

Family CNT F-E

VS CENTURY CAPS

VS Century Slant

VS Century Bold Slant

Family TYP F-A

Courier Medium
Courier Italic
Courier Bold
Courier Bold Italic
Elite Medium
Elite Italic
Elite Bold
Elite Bold Italic
Modern Medium
Modern Gothic Medium
Modern Gothic Bold

Family CTX F-A

Century Textbook Medium
Century Textbook Italic
Century Textbook Bold

Family FTR F-A

Futura II Book
Futura II Book Italic
Futura II Bold
Futura II Bold Italic

Family GIL F-A

Gill Sans Medium
Gill Sans Medium Italic
Gill Sans Bold
Gill Sans Ultra Bold

Family GRM F-A

Garamond Antiqua

Garamond Kursiv

Garamond Halbfett

Garamond Kursiv Halbfett

Family HLV F-A

VS Helv Medium

VS Helv Italic

VS Helv Bold

VS Helv Demi Bold

Family OEC F-A

Old English Cloistered

Family OMG F-A

CG Omega Medium

CG Omega Italic

CG Omega Bold

CG Omega Bold Italic

Family PCF-12

PC Full Medium

PC Full Bold

PC Baby

Family PE F-A

VS Prestige Medium

VS Prestige Italic

VS Prestige Bold

VS Prestige Bold Italic

Family PKA F-A

Park Avenue

Family RKW F-A

Rockwell Medium

Rockwell Italic

Rockwell Bold

Rockwell Bold Italic

Rockwell Extra Bold

Family SVR F-A

ITC Souvenir Light

ITC Souvenir Light Italic

ITC Souvenir Demi

ITC Souvenir Demi Italic

Family TIM F-A

VS Times Medium

VS Times Italic

VS TImes Bold

VS Times Bold Italic

Family TLM F-A

Tall Man

Family TMS F-A

CG Times Medium
CG Times Italic
CG Times Bold
CG Times Bold Italic

Family TRV F-A

CG Triumvirate Medium
CG Triumvirate Italic
CG Triumvirate Bold
CG Triumvirate Bold Italic

Family TRV F-B

CG Triumvirate Light
CG Triumvirate Light Italic
CG Triumvirate Black
CG Triumvirate Black Italic

Family TRV F-C

CG Triumvirate Condensed
CG Triumvirate Condensed Italic
CG Triumvirate Bold Condensed
CG Triumvirate Bold Condensed Italic

Family UNV F-A

Univers Medium
Univers Italic
Univers Bold
Univers Extra Bold

6 Working With Graphics

Images give visual impact to your documents and presentation materials. From computers, to business, to retail, to medical, to sports, to travel, to fitness, to real estate--there are tens of thousands of images to choose from.

Many companies offer collections of clip-art for specific applications or industries (e.g., borders, computers, and business images). Other companies include a potpourri of clip-art that can be used in a variety of situations. See Chapter 7, *Clip-Art Companies*, for samples from over eighty products.

This chapter discusses clip-art basics such as scaling images correctly, working with different graphic formats, and staying within the copyright law.

Clip-Art Basics

What's In A Name?

Clip-Art, Graphics, Images, Electronic Art--these words all refer to electronically-stored pictures, yet each company uses different words to describe the same technology.

It's confusing enough with companies using different words to describe electronic images. To complicate matters, many words that are used to describe electronic images have a different meaning to artists and printers.

For example, *graphics* is often used to describe hand-drawn illustrations; *images* also refers to photographs; and *clip-art* has a meaning all its own.

Clip-art gets is name from art images that are sold on large, printed sheets. The art is clipped-out from the page with a scissors and then pasted (with glue or wax) onto a page layout. This type of clip-art is still used today and is offered by some of the same companies that offer *electronic art*.

What Do You Get?

Most clip-art packages, at minimum, come with a booklet that

- Shows you all of the images in the collection.
- Tells you the name of each image-file on the diskette(s).

Some companies also include an index of the images and/or suggestions for using the graphics effectively.

Subscription Services

Subscription services are another name for clip-art clubs. You pay the company a monthly or quarterly fee and they send you new releases of clip-art on a regular basis.

Copyright

When you purchase a clip-art package, you do not become the owner of the artwork. Whether or not a copyright notice appears next to each image, all the images are either copyrighted individually or as part of the collection.

Your rights to use the clip-art are spelled out in the manufacturer's *License Agreement*. Read the agreement very carefully--it explains how the *owner* of the clip-art (the manufacturer) is letting the *licensee* (you) use the images. Understanding your license now can help you and your company avoid legal trouble later on.

The license will not allow you to make copies of the clip-art to give away or sell, nor will it give you the right to include the clip-art in other collections you intend to sell. It may also place limitations on your use of the art in advertisements.

What you're typically *allowed* to do is make one backup copy of the original diskette(s) and use the art in your own documents without restriction.

Scaling Clip-Art

Many paint, draw, and page layout programs let you resize *(scale)* your clip-art. Keeping your art in correct proportion while scaling can be a little tricky.

For example, enlarging a 2x3-inch image by one inch in both height and width will not keep the image in proportion since 1-inch is a 50% increase to the 2-inch side but only a 33% increase to the 3-inch side. To correctly scale a 2x3-inch image 50% larger, you need to add 1-inch to the 2-inch side and 1.5-inches to the 3-inch side. (Samples of scaling are shown on the following page.)

Graphic Manipulation Programs

Today there are a variety of graphic manipulation programs that let you customize clip-art. Even though many artists are

Scaling Clip-Art

These illustrations were created using *Graphics Composer* from Arts & Letters.

now using electronic methods to produce original artwork, customizing an already-existing clip-art image can save both time and money.

Graphic Formats

There are dozens of graphic file formats that can be used with IBM-compatible computers. However, depending on the capabilities of your printer and desktop publishing program, you may only be able to use a few of them. Before you purchase clip-art, make sure that it is available in a format that you can use.

Bit-Mapped Graphics

A *bit-mapped, raster,* or *paint* graphic is one that is created by turning on or off individual picture elements (pixels) on your screen. This combination of light and dark pixels creates a layout (i.e., *map*) of your screen image.

Bit-mapped graphics are typically stored in the .PCX or .TIF format. They print more quickly (except when stored in the .TIF format) and display shades of gray better than graphics that are created and stored in other formats. Bit-mapped graphics cannot be rotated easily and tend to loose detail when scaled.

PCX and PCC

The *PCX* format is used by *PC Paintbrush* and other paint programs. When the entire screen is saved as an image it is stored in the *.PCX* format. When only a portion of the screen is saved, it is typically saved in the *.PCC* format.

The .PCX format is the most common, graphic-file format for IBM-compatible systems. The .PCX format can be read by most desktop publishing programs and printed by virtually every laser printer.

TIFF

The *TIFF* format (.TIF) is used for scanned images. TIFF is an acronym for *Tagged Image File Format*. TIFF files contain a bit-mapped image for the screen display and a separate set of instructions that describe how the image should be printed.

One problem with TIFF is that there is no standard format. Many companies use their own set of TIFF instructions for the three types of TIFF files.

Bi-level TIFF. This TIFF format is generally used when scanned images contain few or no gray tones. *Bi-level TIFF* file-formats are small and easy to manage.

Halftone TIFF. *Halftone* or *dithered TIFF* has patterns of black and white dots that represent the gray tones. Scaling halftone TIFF images can result in a *moire* pattern, a checkerboard effect that occurs when the printer cannot accommodate the number of dots-per-inch of the image.

Gray-scale TIFF. *Gray-scale TIFF* is used when an image contains many shades of gray.

Object-Oriented Graphics

An *object-oriented, vector,* or *draw* graphic is very different from a *bit-map* image which is comprised of individual dots. As its name implies, object-oriented images are created using a series of objects (e.g., rectangles, ovals, and polygons) rather than individual pixels. Each object in the graphic exists as a whole and can only be manipulated as a whole.

Object-oriented graphics are frequently stored in the .ESP or .CGM formats. Unlike bit-mapped graphics, object-oriented graphics can be scaled and rotated without distortion.

EPS

EPS is an acronym for *Encapsulated PostScript*. EPS graphics are object-oriented graphics written in the PostScript language. The PostScript file includes English-language instructions that you can actually *read* on your screen.

EPS files always include instructions that can be interpreted by a PostScript printer. The file usually (but not always) includes a screen image that allows you to view the image on your monitor.

CGM

CGM is an acronym for *Computer Graphics Metafile.* CGM is an object-oriented graphic file that makes very efficient use of space. You will notice that a graphic stored in the .CGM format typically has a smaller file size than a comparable graphic in another format.

Similar to the TIFF format, the .CGM format has no universal standard. Even though two programs may both claim to read .CGM graphics, a .CGM file from one cannot necessarily be read by the other.

7 Graphic Companies

This chapter is your source for clip-art for IBM-compatible computers. On these pages you'll find several hundred clip-art samples from over eighty different graphic packages.

Each collection was reviewed in its entirety. Unless otherwise noted, the samples on the following pages are representative of the entire clip-art collection.

The individual graphics in each package were counted. That number is displayed on the first page of each layout for each collection (just under the name of the collection).

Some collections received two pages in the *Blue Book* while others received only one. The determining factor was the number of graphics in the clip-art package. When a package includes at least 135 separate images, it receives two pages. When the package includes less than 135 separate images, it receives one page in the *Blue Book*.

In this chapter you'll find clip-art from

3G Graphics
Applied Microsystems, Inc.
Archive Arts
ARKEO™ Graphics
Computer Support Corporation
Dream Maker Software™
Dynamic Graphics, Inc.
Eykon Computer Graphics
Logitech, Inc.
MGI (Marketing Graphics, Inc.)
Metro ImageBase™, Inc.

MicroMaps Software, Inc.
Migraph, Inc.
Multi-Ad Services, Inc.™
One Mile Up, Inc.
PC Globe, Inc.
Studio Advertising Art
T/Maker Company

In addition to clip-art samples, you'll find

- Each company's address and phone numbers.
- A brief company profile.
- A description of the product line.
- A legend that lets you know whether the graphics are only available for IBM-compatible computers, or are also available for the Mac.
- A legend that lists the graphic formats available and the printer output (dpi) for each format.

3G

3G Graphics
11410 N.E. 124th Street
Suite 6155
Kirkland, WA 98034
(800) 456-0234 Orders
(206) 823-8198 Information
(206) 823-6204 FAX

IBM
Macintosh

EPS: Variable

We at 3G Graphics make every effort to bring a fresh, unique approach to our clip-art because we care about improving the quality of your printed piece, says Gail Giaimo (President) and Glenn Giaimo (Vice President) of **3G Graphics**. 3G offers two contemporary clip-art collections called ***Images With Impact!***

- Graphics and Symbols 1
- Business 1

Both collections are available for IBM and Mac computers and include ideas for using the art in a variety of applications.

Many of 3G's images were created by layering different graphic elements. These individual graphic elements can be separated (ungrouped) by using either Aldus Freehand™ or Adobe Illustrator®. Separating the elements significantly increases the size of the clip-art collection.

The image count that we give for the clip-art packages does not include separating the images.

IBM System Requirements

- PostScript printer or typesetter.
- 640K RAM (1.2 megs recommended).
- One high density 5.25-inch (3.5 disks available upon request).
- Program that can read *.EPS* files.

Macintosh System Requirements

- PostScript printer or typesetter.
- 1 Meg RAM (2 megs recommended).
- One 800K Disk Drive.
- Program that can read *.EPS* files.

Images With Impact! Graphics and Symbols 1

(80 images)

Images with Impact!
Business 1
(142 images)

Applied Microsystems

Applied Microsystems, Inc.
510 W. Tudor Rd. Suite 3
Anchorage, AK 99503
(903) 563-1313
(800) 327-2588 Orders
(903) 561-1543 Fax

IBM

dpi varies

Applied Microsystems, Inc., began as a producer of 35mm slides for local businesses and has now extended their services to include the production of custom-designed electronic clip-art. The company prides itself on giving its customers personal attention.

Applied Microsystems' clip-art library is called *ImageFile*™. The images are available in two versions. One that is compatible with *Freelance Plus* (Lotus) and *Picture It* (General Parametrics); another that is compatible with *VideoShow* (General Parametrics). To use the images in other popular word processing and desktop publishing programs, you must first import the image into *Freelance Plus*, then save the image in .CGM format. Samples from the *People* section of *ImageFile* are shown on the following pages.

IBM System Requirements

- 640K RAM.
- Hard disk.
- *Freelance Plus* or *Picture It*.

ImageFile™
(303 images)

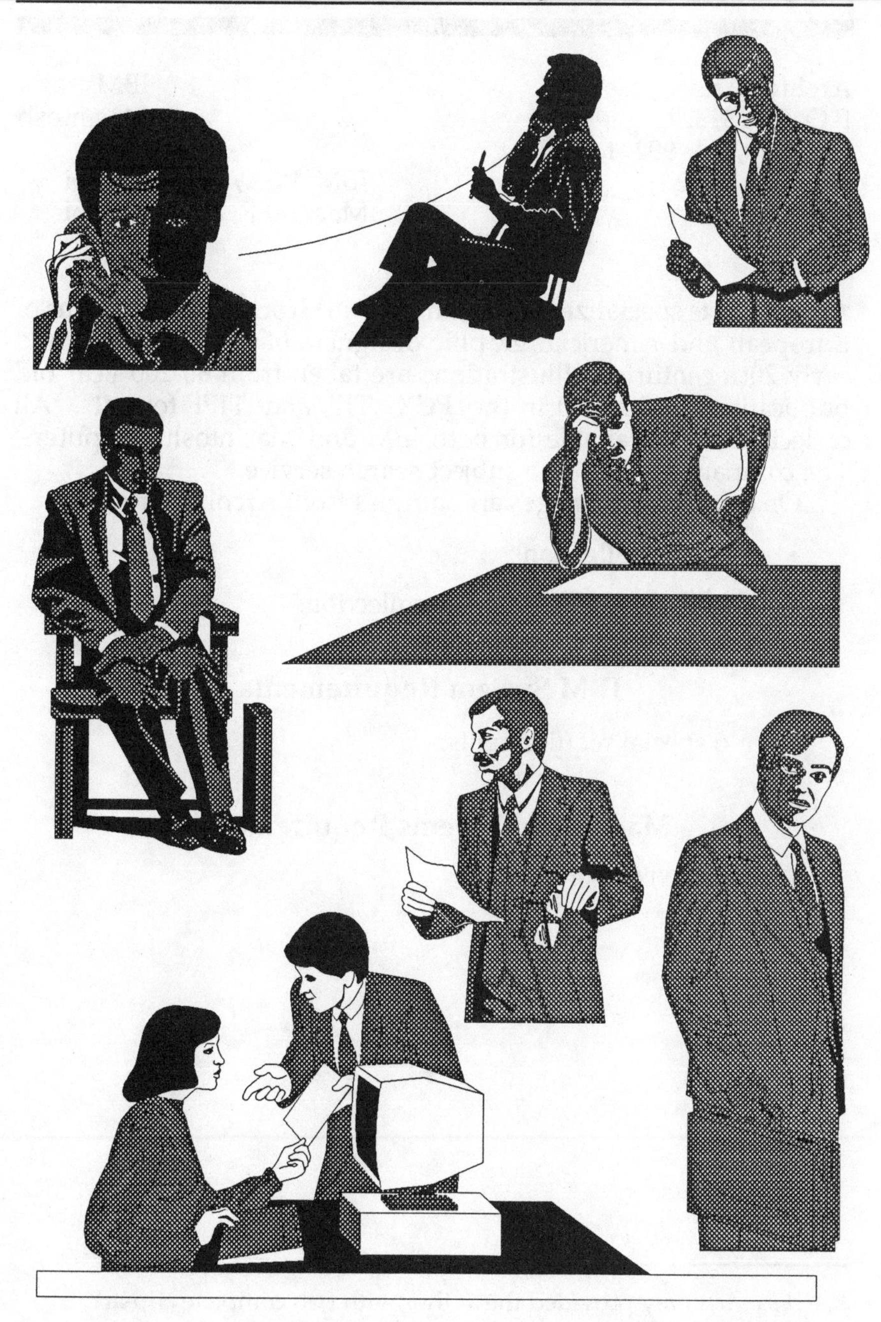

Archive Arts

Archive Arts
P.O. Box 39522
Downey, CA 90241
(213) 861-7562

IBM
Macintosh

IBM: PCX/TIF 300dpi
Mac: TIFF 300dpi

Archive Arts specializes in creating clip-art from the illustrations of European and American graphic designers of the 18th, 19th, and early 20th centuries. Illustrations are taken from 60-200 year old publications and saved in the .PCX, .TIF, and .TIFF formats. All collections are available for both IBM and Macintosh computers. The company also offers a subject-search service.

On the following pages are samples from Archive Arts[1]

- Sampler collection.
- Old Fashioned Christmas collection.

IBM System Requirements

- No special requirements.

Macintosh Systems Requirements

- One 800K disk drive.

---

[1] *Archive Arts* only provided the author with two complete clip-art packages. For this reason, only two of their collections are shown.

Archive Arts
Old Fashioned Christmas Edition
(49 images)

MERRY CHRISTMAS

Archive Arts Sampler Disk
(15 images)

ARKEO Graphics

ARKEO™ Graphics
5225 Canyon Crest Drive
Riverside, CA 92507
(714) 788-8081

IBM

dpi varies

ARKEO™ Graphics is the maker of *Perfect Art™*, a collection of map packages including

- USA
- State Counties (USA)
- World
- Regions
  - Canada-Polar
  - Central America-Caribbean
  - Western Europe
  - Eastern Europe-USSR
  - South America
  - Asia
  - Middle East
  - Africa
- Map Symbols

Additionally, ARKEO offers a service which creates custom map and symbol graphics. Sample maps and selections from the *Symbols* package are shown on the following pages. All *Perfect Art* is available in a variety of formats, including

- CGM
- DRW
- DXF
- EPS
- GEM
- HPGL
- IGES
- PCL
- PCX
- TIFF
- TXT

ARKEO will answer general questions about computer graphics. Anyone with a question may call ARKEO's customer service number (shown above).

IBM System Requirements

- No special requirements.

Perfect Art™ Map Samples

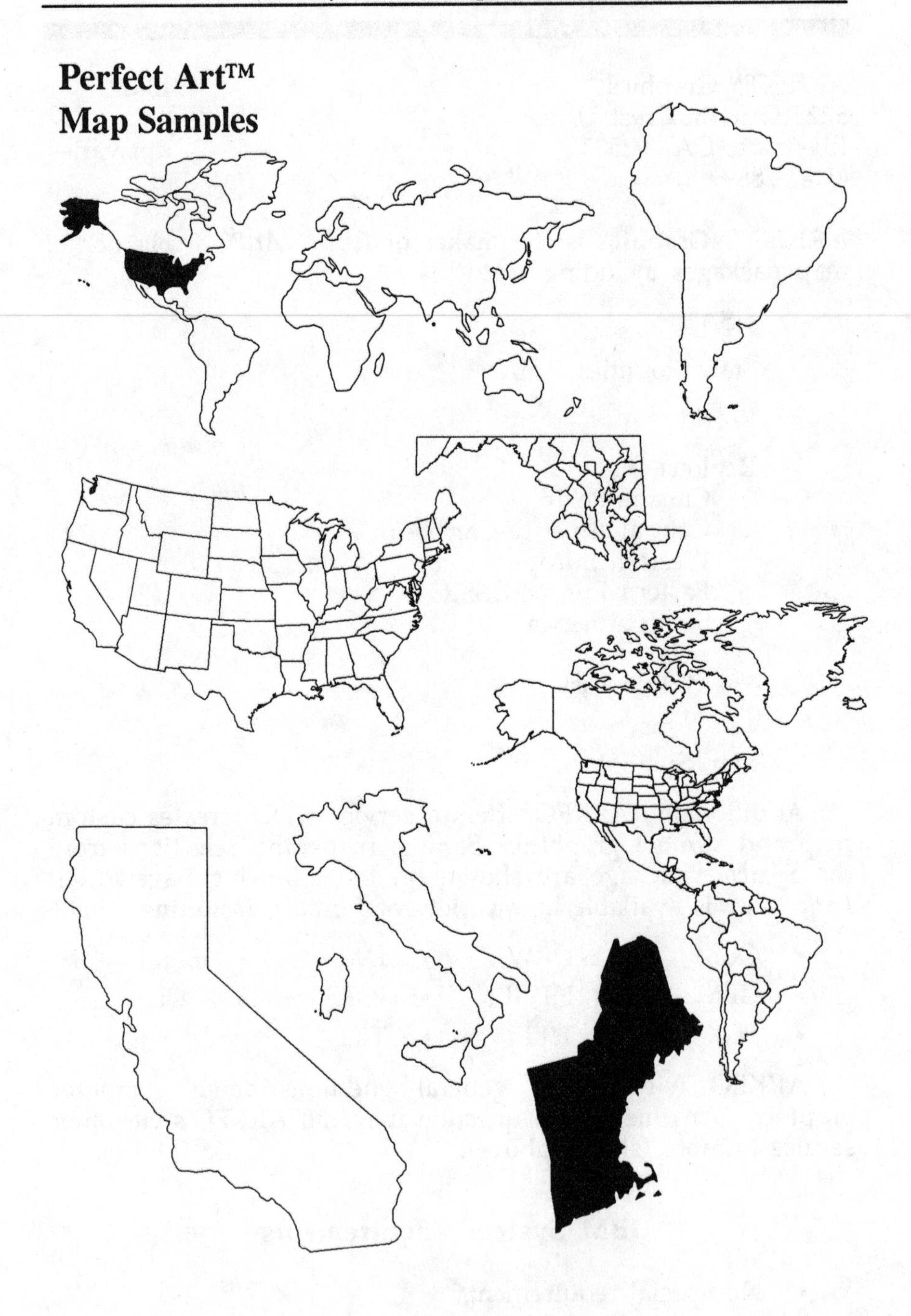

Perfect Art™
Map Symbols
(154 images)

Computer Support

Computer Support Corporation
15926 Midway Road
Dallas, Texas 75244
(214)661-8960
(214)661-5429

IBM

EPS: Variable

Computer Support Corporation (CSC) is a leading developer of innovative, application software for desktop publishers. Founded in New York City in 1970, CSC now markets their products in 47 countries around the world.

CSC's clip-art is included in the company's *Arts and Letters®* *Graphics Composer™* package. Over 4,000 clip-art images and 15 typefaces are included with *Graphics Composer*. Additional clip-art libraries may be purchased separately. (You must have *Graphics Composer* to use the other clip-art packages.)

Graphics Composer runs under *Microsoft Windows*. It is a mouse-driven program with an assortment of tools that allow you to flip, rotate, stretch, size, color, and slant the clip-art images and typefaces. Images can be printed on any Windows-supported printer or saved as a .EPS, .CGM, or Windows Metafile file for use with other programs. Other programs from Computer Support Corporation include

- *Diagraph™*, a DOS-based program that lets you manipulate typefaces and clip-art.
- *Picture Perfect™*, a DOS-based program that turns facts and figures in into bar charts, line charts, and pie charts.
- *Arts and Letters® Graphics Editor™*, a program that enhances the features of *Art and Letters Graphics Composer* by adding an assortment of drawing tools.
- *PC Emcee™*, a program for creating electronic presentations.

In addition to computer-graphic software, Computer Support Corporation markets *On-Que™*. *On-Que* is a remote control device that lets you run an electronic presentation without touching the keyboard. *On-Que* is available for both IBM-compatible and Macintosh computers.

IBM System Requirements

- 640K RAM.
- Microsoft *Windows* 1.0 or higher.
- *Windows*-supported mouse device.

Arts & Letters® Graphics Composer
(over 4000 images)

R
R
-3σ
-2σ
-1σ
0
1σ
2σ
3σ

Dream Maker

Dream Maker Software™
7217 Foothill Boulevard
Tujunga, CA 91402
(800)876-5665 Orders
(818)353-2297 Business
(818)353-6988 Fax

IBM
Macintosh

EPS: Variable
Paint: 72 dpi

Dream Maker Software™ has two clip-art lines: *Clipture*s™ and *MacGallery*™ (not shown).

Cliptures

Cliptures is a collection of business graphics in the encapsulated PostScript (EPS) format. Each package includes a booklet which has several pages of ideas and layouts. Cliptures is available for both the IBM and Macintosh computers. *Cliptures* consists of two volumes.

- Business Images 1
- Business Images 2

MacGallery

MacGallery is only available for the Macintosh. The collection includes a selection of general purpose clip-art. MacGallery is available in both the MacPaint and HyperCard formats.

IBM System Requirements

Cliptures

- Postscript printer or typesetter.
- IBM-compatible computer (286 or 386 recommended).
- One 5.25-inch disk drive.[1]

[1] If your original order specifies 3.5-inch diskettes, they are provided without additional charge. If you exchange your 5.25-inch disks for 3.5-inch disks after receiving the clip-art, there is a $20 handling fee.

Macintosh System Requirements

Cliptures

- Postscript printer or typesetter.
- Program that can read *.EPS* files.

MacGallery, MacPaint version

- No special requirements.

MacGallery, Hypercard version

- Postscript printer or typesetter.
- Mac Plus or higher.
- Two 800K disk drives (hard disk recommended).
- *HyperCard* or *HyperDA*™.

Cliptures™
Business Images Volume 1
(139 images)

SOLD

Clipturesᵀᴹ
Business Images Volume 2
(206 images)

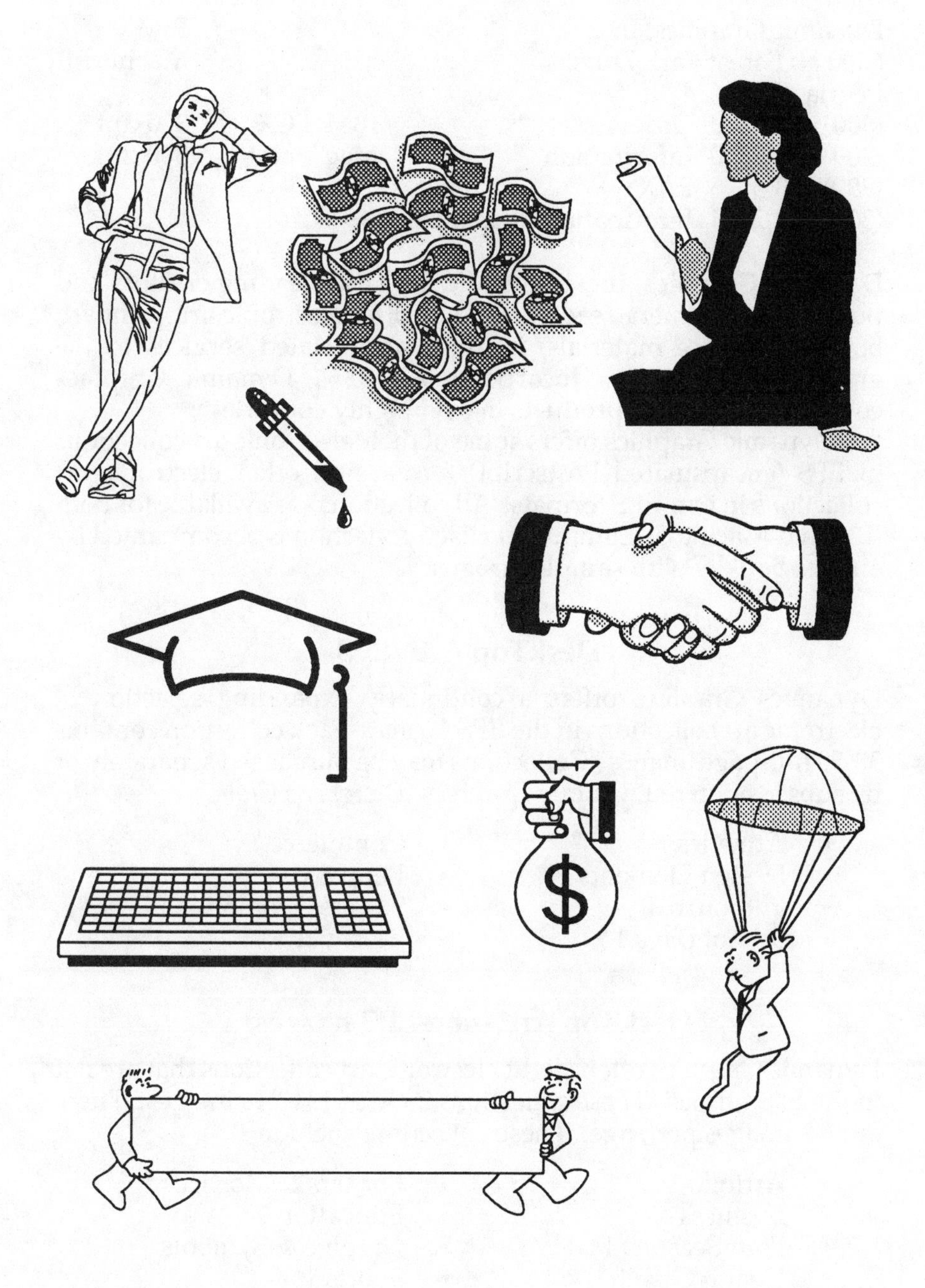

Dynamic Graphics

Dynamic Graphics, Inc.
6000 N. Forest Park Drive
Peoria, IL 61614
(800) 255-8800 Orders
(309) 688-8800 Information
(309) 688-3075 FAX
(309) 688-2244 Information in Spanish

IBM
Macintosh

IBM: PCX 300 dpi
Mac: Paint 300 dpi

Dynamic Graphics, Inc. is one of the world's leading creators and publishers of camera-ready art. They offer electronic art, print art, books, reference materials, training, and related services to the graphic arts industry. Incorporated in 1964, Dynamic Graphics currently distributes products in over eighty countries.

Dynamic Graphics offers some of their electronic art collections in EPS (encapsulated Postscript) format and other electronic art collections in non-EPS formats. All collections are available for both IBM and Macintosh computers. Each collection is accompanied by an idea booklet with sample designs.

DeskTop Art® /EPS

Dynamics Graphics offers a continually expanding selection of electronic art collections in the EPS format. Each collection contains 38-50 full-page images. Collections may be purchased separately or by subscription to Dynamic Graphics' *Designer's Club*.

- Athletics 1
- Design Elements 1
- Potpourri 1
- School Days 1
- Commerce 1
- People 1
- Sales & Promotions 1
- Seasonal 1

DeskTop Art® (non-EPS images)

Dynamic Graphics offers eight electronic art collections that are not in the EPS format. These collections include 131-216 images. There are 3-9 images per page. These collections include

- Artfolio 1
- Business 1
- Four Seasons 1
- Health Care 1
- Borders & Mortices 1
- Education 1
- Graphic & Symbols 1
- Sports 1

IBM System Requirements

EPS Collections

- PostScript printer or typesetter.
- 640K RAM (1.2 megs expanded memory recommended).
- One high-density Disk Drive.
- Program that can read *.EPS* files.

Non-EPS Collections

- 640K RAM (1.2 megs expanded memory recommended).

Macintosh System Requirements

EPS Collections

- PostScript printer or typesetter.
- 1 Meg RAM (2 megs recommended with *Adobe Illustrator 88*).
- One 800K Disk Drive.
- Program that can read *.EPS* files.

Paint Collections

- No special requirements.

DeskTop Art® Athletics 1
(40 images)

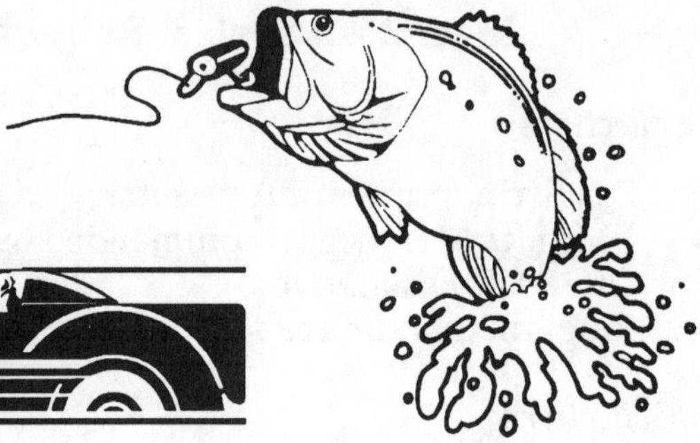

DeskTop Art®
Commerce 1
(46 images)

DeskTop Art®
Design Elements 1
(46 images)

DeskTop Art®
People 1
(38 images)

DeskTop Art®
Potpourri 1
(46 images)

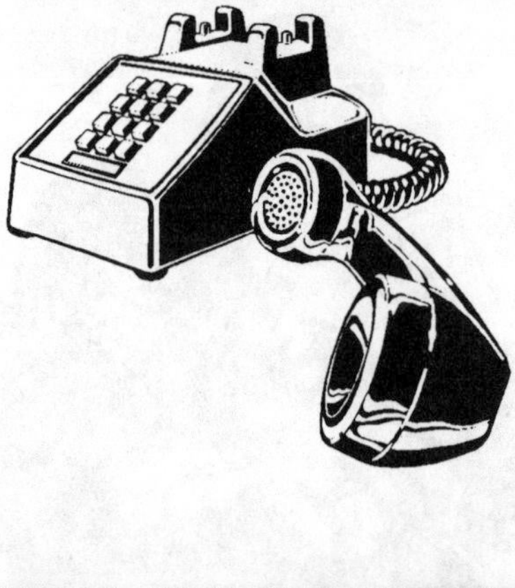

DeskTop Art®
Sales & Promotions 1
(46 images)

DeskTop Art®
School Days 1
(44 images)

DeskTop Art®
Seasonal 1
(44 images)

DeskTop Art®
Artfolio 1
(191 images)

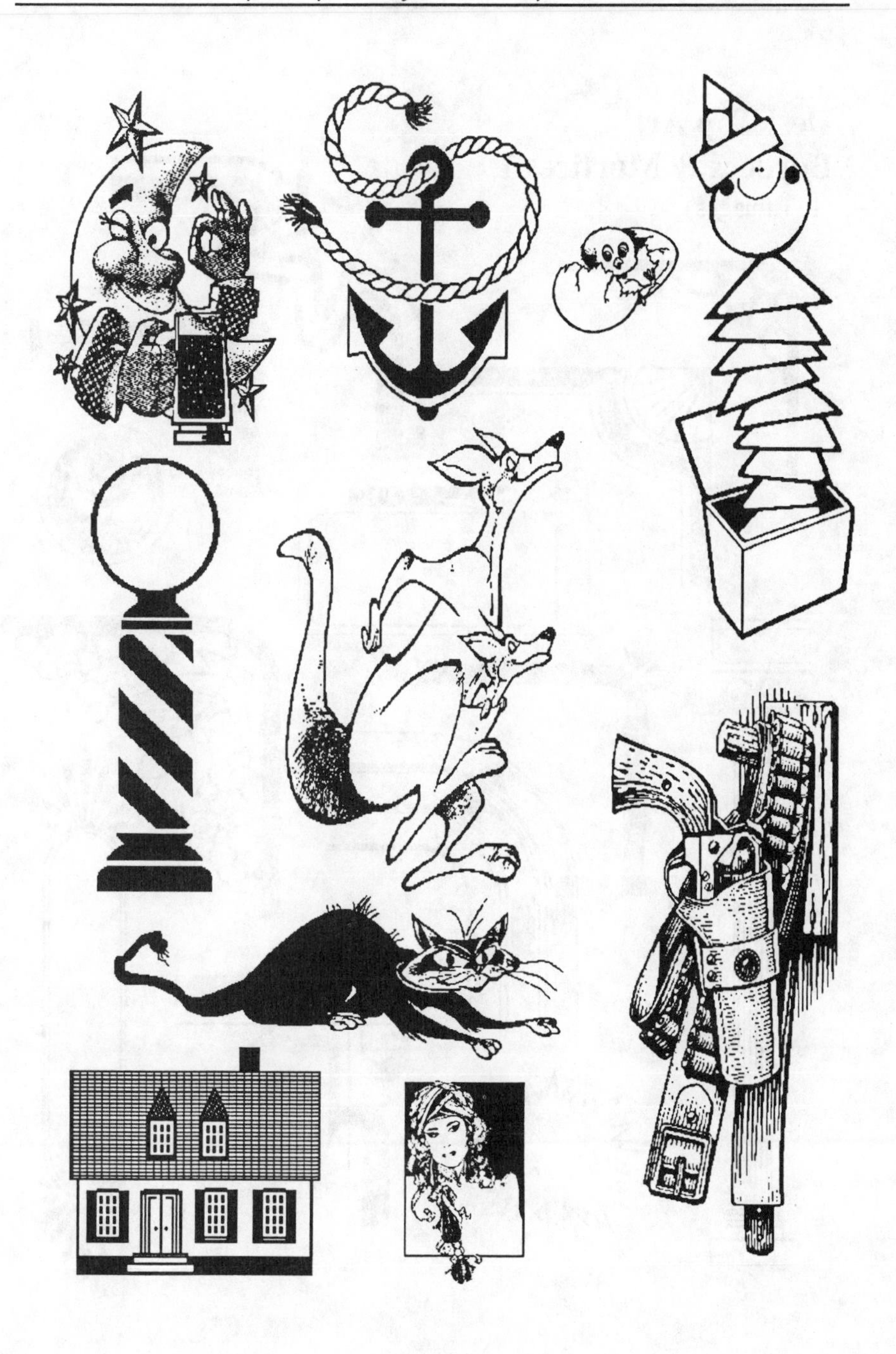

DeskTop Art®
Borders & Mortices 1
(131 images)

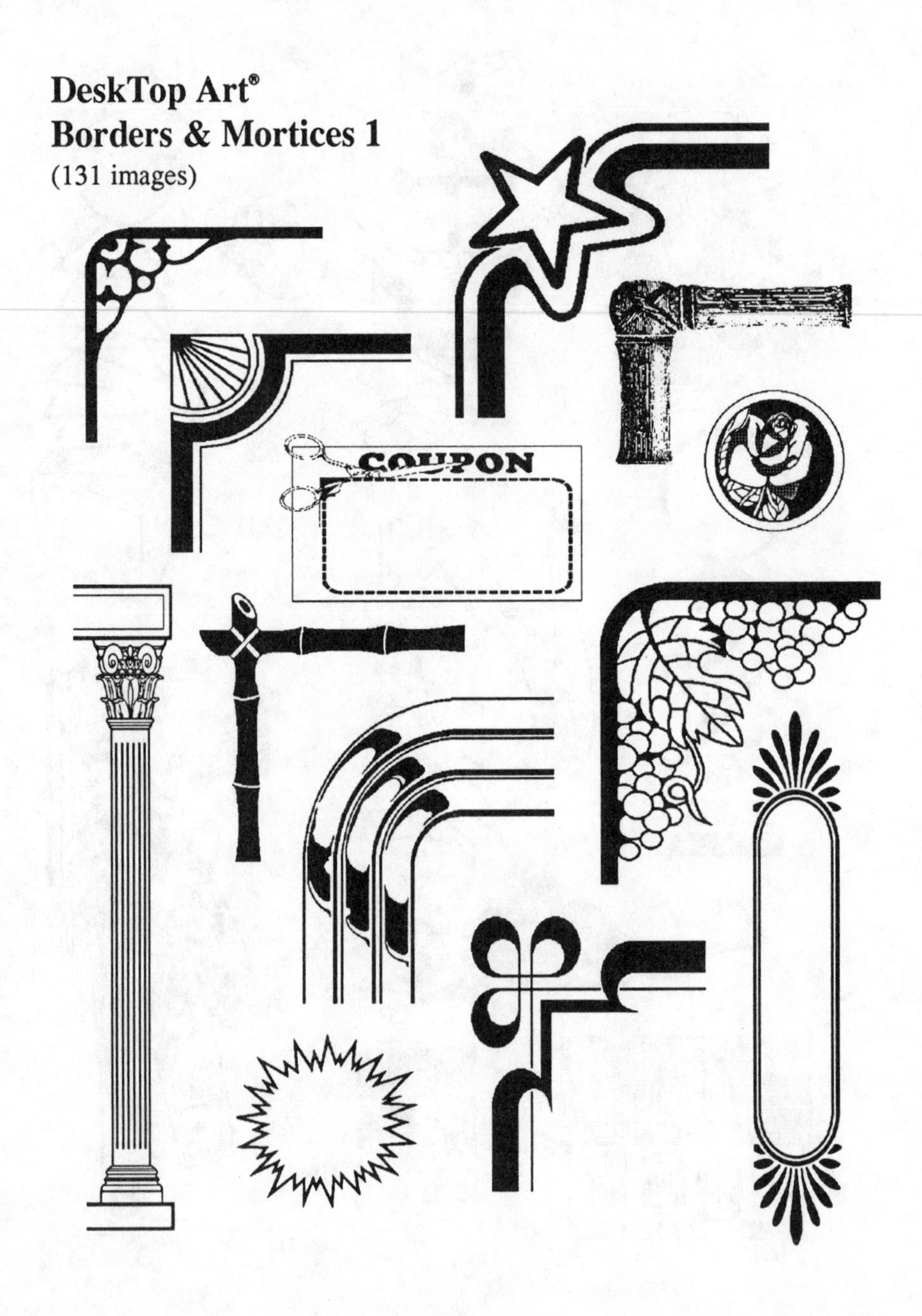

DeskTop Art®
Business 1
(201 images)

DeskTop Art®
Education 1
(201 images)

BACK TO SCHOOL

DeskTop Art®
Four Seasons 1
(201 images)

WASHINGTON

DeskTop Art® Graphics & Symbols 1
(216 images)

ADMIT ONE
ADMIT ONE

DeskTop Art®
Health Care 1
(201 images)

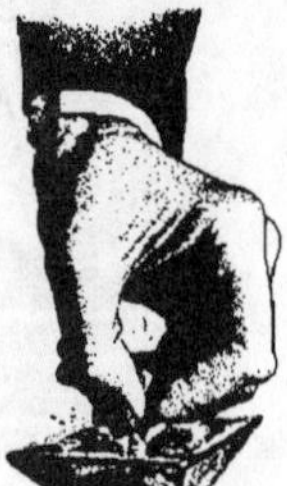

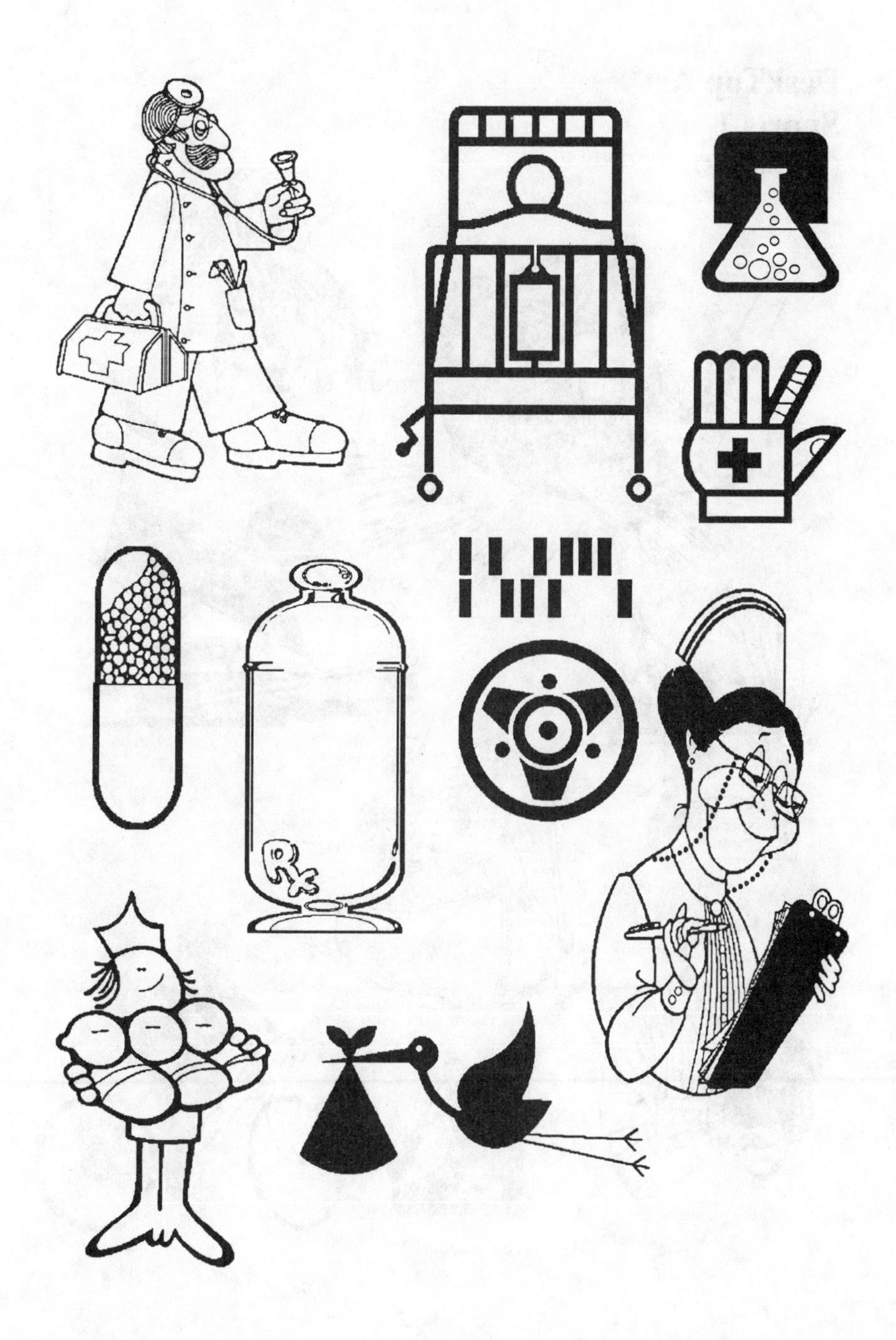

DeskTop Art®
Sports 1
(199 images)

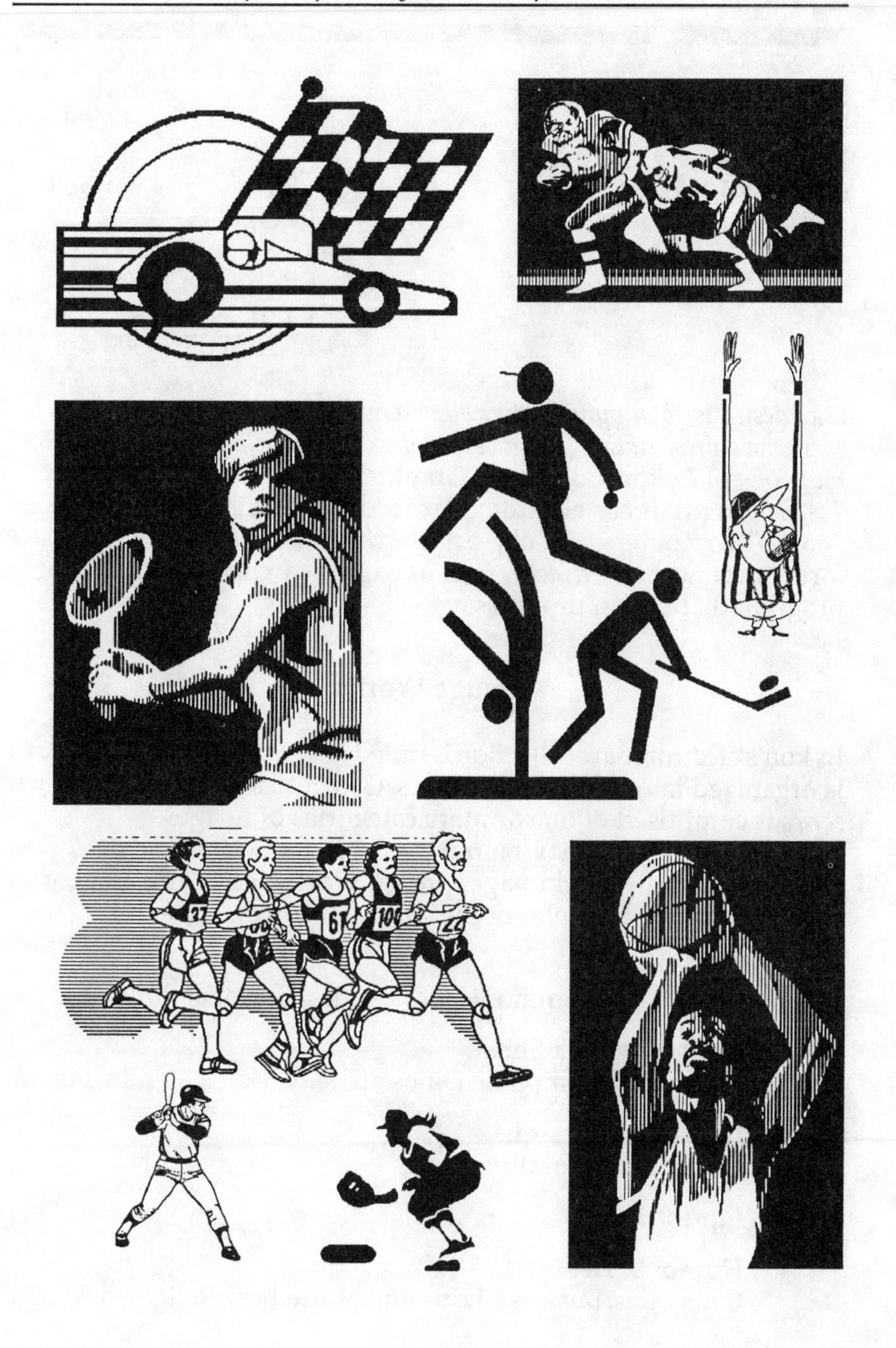

Eykon

Eykon Computer Graphics
P.O. Box 2142
Round Rock, Texas 78680
(512) 388-7099

IBM
Macintosh

IBM:	EPS	Variable
	IMG/PCX/ TIF	300 dpi
Mac:	EPS	Variable
	Paint	72 dpi
	PICT/TIFF	300 dpi

Our desire is to supply quality electronic art at a competitive price for everyone's presentation graphics and desktop publishing needs, says Jeff Hancock of **Eykon Computer Graphics**.

Eykon produces electronic art for IBM, Macintosh, Apple, and Atari ST computers. All clip-art is *archived* (saved in a compressed form) and must be *extracted* (removed from archived form) using a program that Eykon provides.

Image Works

Eykon's electronic art collection is called *Images Works*. Image Works is organized into three levels: Series, Categories, and Images. Each *series* is comprised of one or more categories of images.

Eykon's clip-art may be purchased in its entirety or by series, category, or individual image. Image Works series and categories are listed below. Samples of the clip-art begin on page 314.

- **Antics Series.**
  Categories: Communication Antics, Seasonal Silhouettes.
- **Cartoon Mania Series.**
  Categories: Computer, Dinosaur, Jelly Bean, Penguin, Potato.
- **Decorative Designs.**
  Category: Decorative Flora.
- **Equestrian.**
- **Humor Series.**
  Categories: Business, Educational, Medical, Religious, Sports.

- **Precision Portfolio.**
  Categories: Education, Greeting Cards, Hands, People Silhouettes, Special Occasions.
- **Studio Editions.**
  Category: Business graphics.

IBM System Requirements

- No special requirements.

Macintosh System Requirements

- No special requirements.

Image Works
Antics Series
(54 images)

Image Works
Cartoon Mania Series
(66 images)

Image Works
Decorative Designs
(27 images)

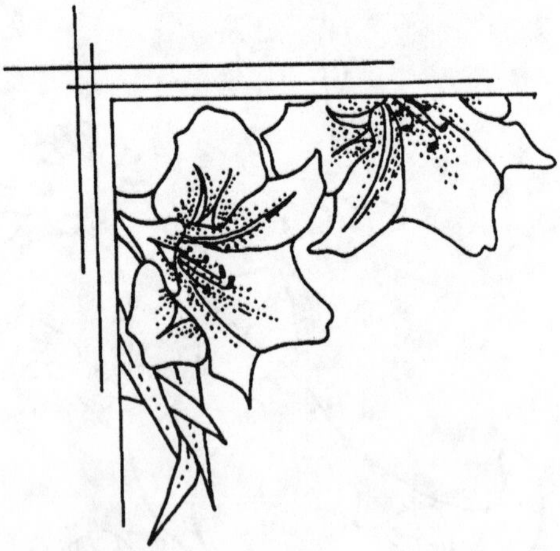

Image Works
Equestrian
(26 images)

Image Works
Humor Series
(126 images)

Image Works
Precision Portfolio
(101 images)

Image Works
Studio Editions
(30 images)

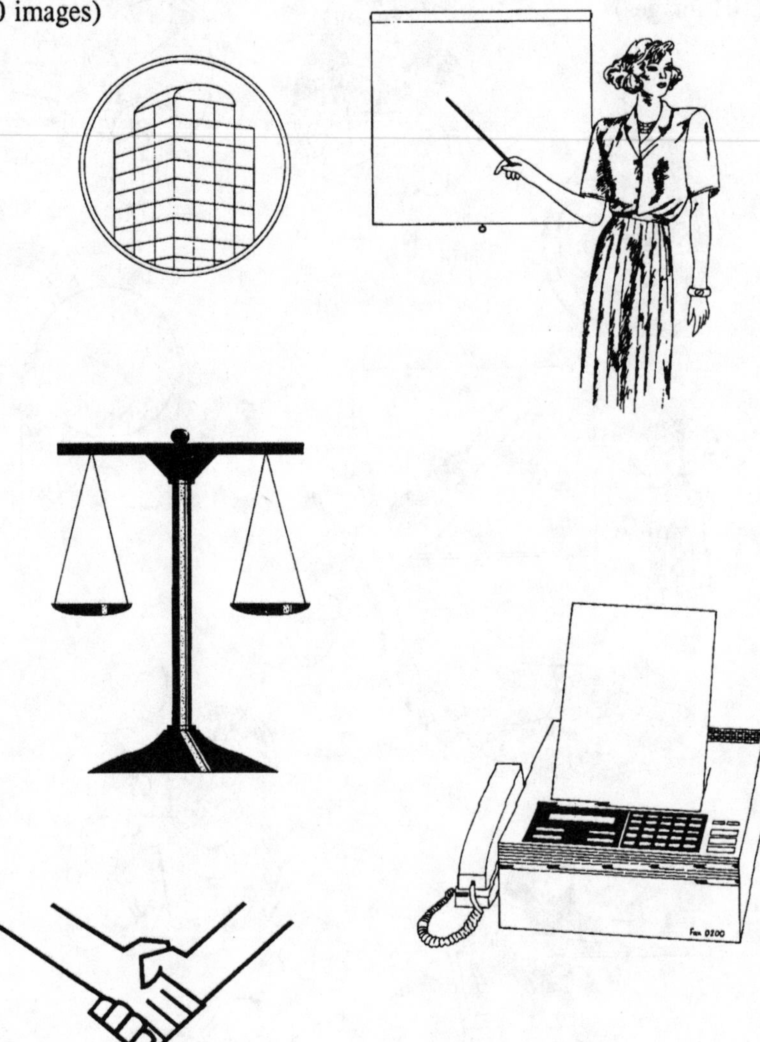

Logitech

Logitech, Inc.
6505 Kaiser Drive
Fremont, CA 94555
(415) 795-8500

IBM

TIF: 200 dpi

Logitech, Inc. was founded by Pierluigi Zappacosta, Giacomo Marini, and Daniel Borel. The company is best known for the *Logitech Mouse,* a popular mouse device for IBM and IBM-compatible computers and *ScanMan*™, the company's hand-held scanning device.

Logitech provides a collection of general-interest clip-art images with its *Finesse*™ software. *Finesse* is a mouse-driven, page-layout program used for desktop publishing. Logitech's clip-art collection is called the *Logitech Image Library.*

The *Logitech Image Library* comes in a compressed format and must be expanded prior to use. The images themselves are stored in the .TIF format and may be used independently of the *Finesse* software program.

Also included with *Finesse* software is the *Bitstream Fontware Installation Kit,* a program which lets you use Bitstream fonts within your *Finesse* documents.

IBM System Requirements

- 640K RAM.
- Hard disk.
- Graphic card (e.g., CGA, EGA, MCGA, VGA, or Hercules).
- Logitech or compatible mouse.
- DOS 2.1 or later (3.1 or later when using *Bitstream's Fontware*).

Finesse™
Clip Art
(70 images)

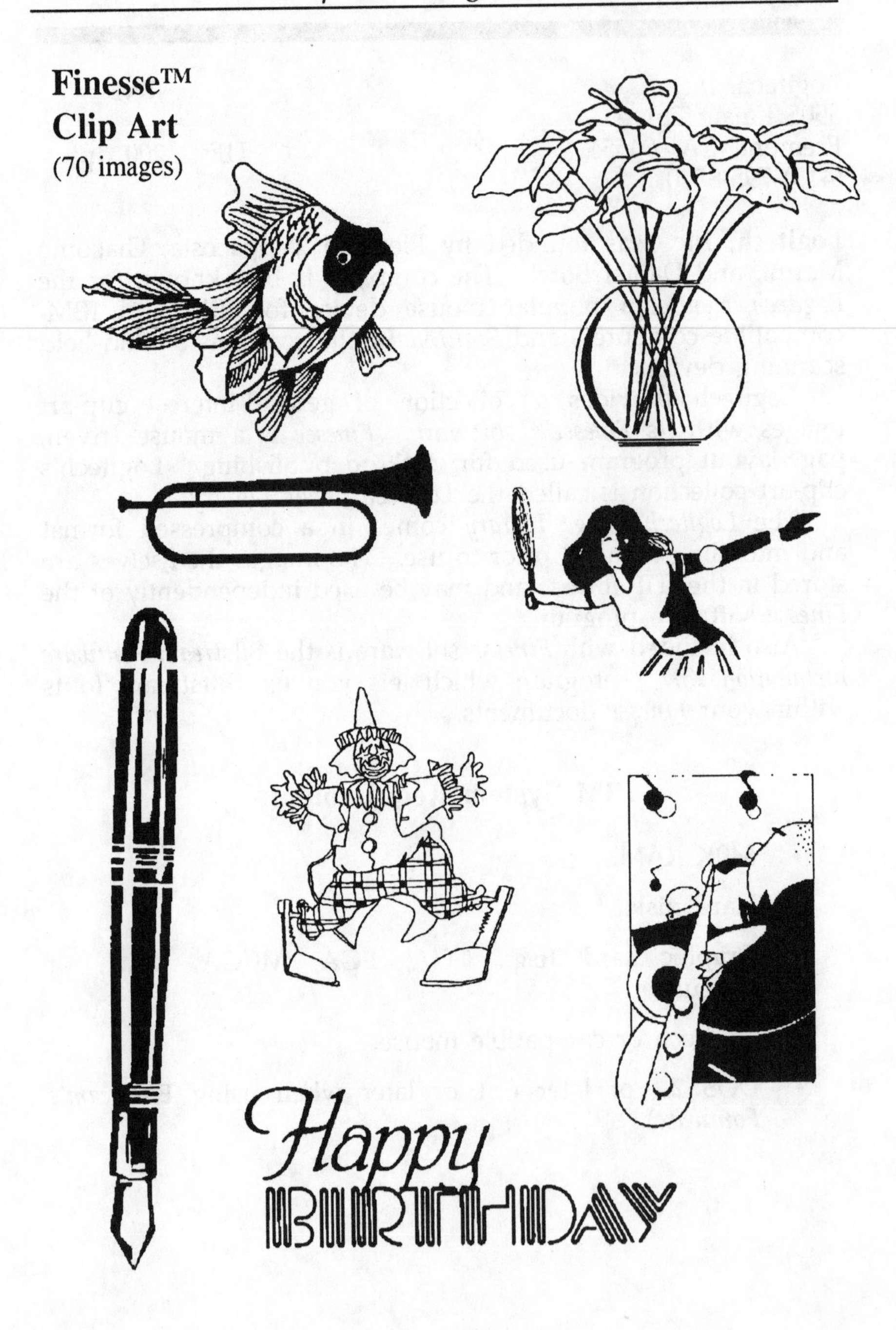

MGI

Marketing Graphics, Inc.
4401 Dominion Boulevard
Suite 210
Glen Allen, VA 23060
(804) 747-6991

IBM
Macintosh

IBM: PCX/CGM	300 dpi
Mac: Paint	72 dpi
PICT	300 dpi

Marketing Graphics, Inc. (MGI) specializes in computer-generated graphic products. MGI was established in 1985 and now markets its products worldwide.

MGI's electronic-art libraries are called *PicturePaks™* and are designed primarily for business publications and presentations. All *PicturePak* editions are available for both IBM and Macintosh computers.

PicturePak editions for IBM computers include clip-art in both the *CGM* and *PCC* (PCX) formats. *PicturePak* editions for the Mac include clip-art in both the *Paint* and *PICT* formats. Each *PicturePak* edition has a reference manual with tips on using the clip-art with several popular software programs. The *PicturePak* line is divided into two series.

- **Eye Openers Series.**

  Editions: Finance and Administration, Executive and Management, Sales and Marketing.

- **USA Series.**

  Edition: Federal Government.

Several *PicturePak* editions are also available for demonstration software packages such as *Storyboard*, *Show Partner*, and *VideoShow*.

IBM System Requirements

- No special requirements.

Macintosh System Requirements

- No special requirements.

PicturePak™
Executive & Management Edition
(180 images)

and

PicturePak™
Finance & Administration Edition
(180 images)

Message
Report
Card
A+

PicturePak™
Sales & Meetings Edition
(180 images)

LUNCHTIME

PicturePak™
Federal Government Edition
(169 images)

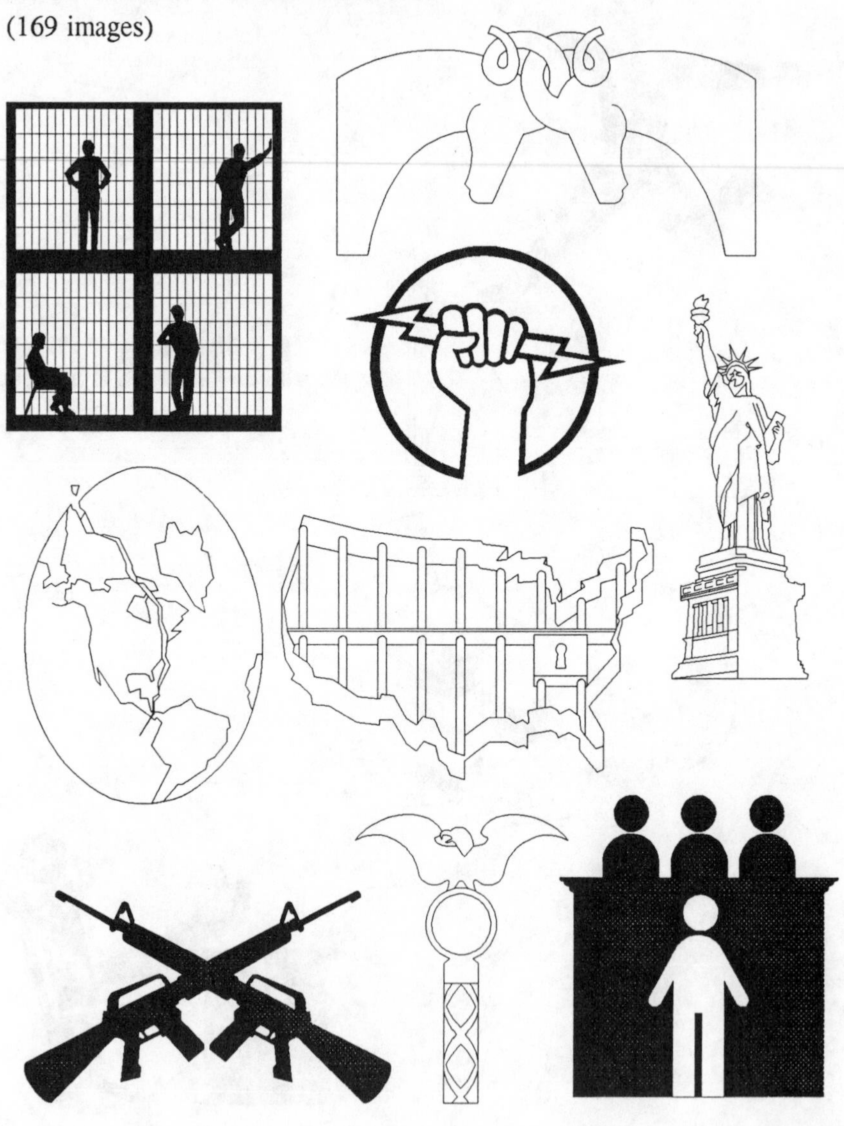

VETO

Metro ImageBase

Metro ImageBase™, Inc.
18623 Ventura Boulevard, Suite 210
Tarzana, CA 91356
(800) 843-3438 Orders
(800) 525-1552 Information/Service

IBM
Macintosh

IBM: PCX/TIF 300 dpi
Mac: TIFF 300 dpi

Metro ImageBase™, Inc. is a division of Metro Creative Graphics, a leading supplier of advertising art for newspapers since 1910. Metro ImageBase has selected images from its extensive clip-art library and made them available in electronic form for both IBM and Macintosh computers.

All of Metro ImageBase's electronic-art is *archived* (saved in a compressed form) and must be *extracted* (removed from archived form) using a program that Metro ImageBase provides. Detailed instructions for using the program are provided in the user manual that comes with each of Metro ImageBase's fourteen collections.

- Art Deco
- Borders and Boxes
- Business Graphics
- Computers & Technology
- Exercise and Fitness
- Food
- The Four Seasons
- Newsletter Maker
- Nine to Five
- People
- ReportMaker
- Team Sports
- Travel
- Weekend Sports

IBM System Requirements

- Hard disk.
- DOS 3.1 or higher.

Macintosh System Requirements

- Hard disk.

Electronic Art
Art Deco
(101 images)

Electronic Art
Borders and Boxes
(100 images)

Electronic Art
Business Graphics
(100 images)

Electronic Art
Computers and Technology
(100 images)

Electronic Art
Exercise and Fitness
(100 images)

Electronic Art
Food
(100 images)

Electronic Art
The Four Seasons
(100 images)

Electronic Art NewsLetter Maker
(100 images)

Electronic Art
Nine to Five
(100 images)

Electronic Art People

(100 images)

Electronic Art ReportMaker
(100 images)

Electronic Art
Team Sports
(100 images)

Electronic Art
Travel
(100 images)

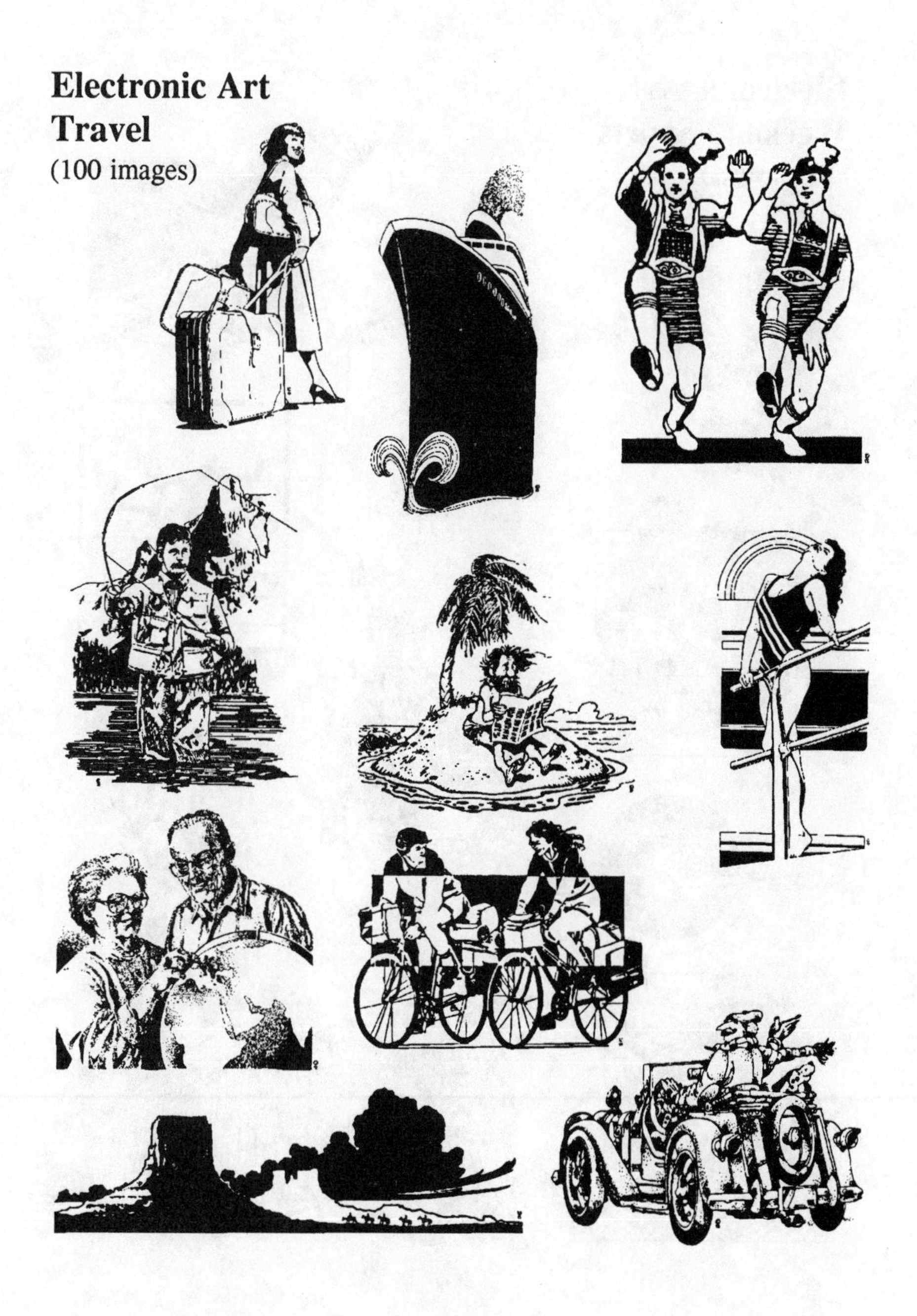

Electronic Art
Weekend Sports
(100 images)

MicroMaps

MicroMaps Software, Inc.
P.O. Box 757
Lambertville, NJ 08530
(609) 397-1611
(800) 334-4291 Orders

IBM
Macintosh

IBM:	EPS	Variable
	PCX	72 dpi
Mac:	EPS	Variable
	Paint	72 dpi
	PICT	300 dpi

Micro Maps Software, Inc., offers collections of maps drawn by a professional cartographer. The clip-art map collections are available in several formats for both IBM-compatible and Macintosh computers. Each package includes a collection of world, region, country, United States, and U.S. state maps.

- *AtlasPC™* is available for IBM-compatible systems in both the .PCX and .EPS formats.
- *MacAtlas™* is available for Macintosh systems in the EPS, PICT, and Paint formats.

IBM System Requirements

AtlasPC, EPS Version
- Postscript-compatible printer.
- 5.25-inch high-density disk drive.

AtlasPC, PCX (Paint) Version
- No special requirements.

Macintosh System Requirements

MacAtlas, EPS Version
- Postscript-compatible printer.
- 1-Meg RAM.

MacAtlas, Paint Version
- No special requirements.

MacAtlas, PICT Version
- 300 dpi printer.
- 512K memory.

Atlas PC™

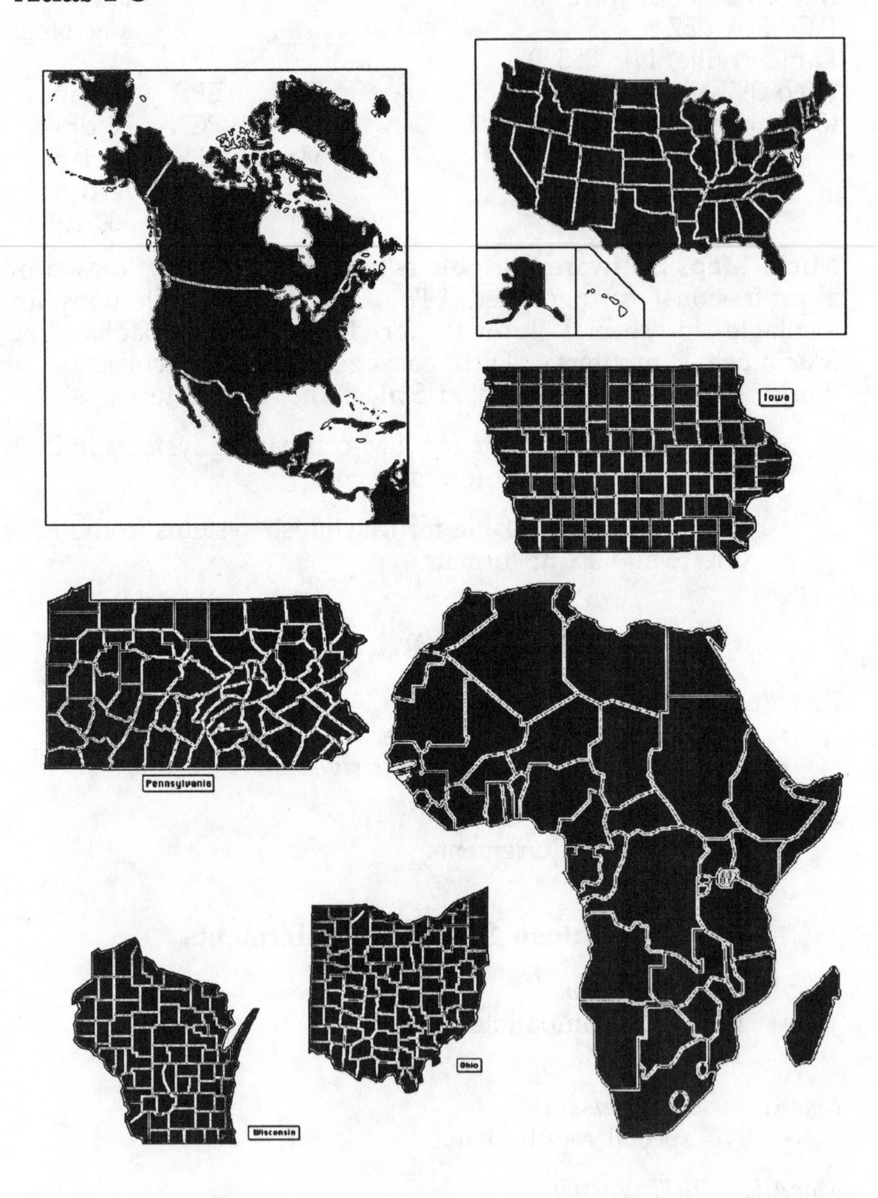

Migraph

Migraph, Inc.
200 South 333rd Street
Suite 220
Federal Way, WA 98003
(206) 838-4677
(206) 838-4702 Fax

IBM	
GEM	Variable
IMG	150/300

Migraph, Inc., has two clip-art libraries. One library is in the .GEM format and the other is in the .IMG format. Each library has a different collection of clip-art images.

- *ScanArt*™ is a collection of general-interest images stored in the .IMG format. *ScanArt* images may be printed on either a laser printer or a dot matrix printer.
- *DrawArt*™ *Professional* is a collection of general-interest images stored in the .GEM format.

In addition to their clip-art collections, Migraph offers a graphic-editing tool called *Touch•Up*™. *Touch•Up* can import and export graphics in a variety of formats.

Migraph publishes a desktop publishing newsletter several times a year. A complimentary copy of the newsletter is sent to all registered users of Migraph products.

IBM System Requirements

- No special requirements.

ScanArt™
(103 images)

DrawArt™
(112 images)

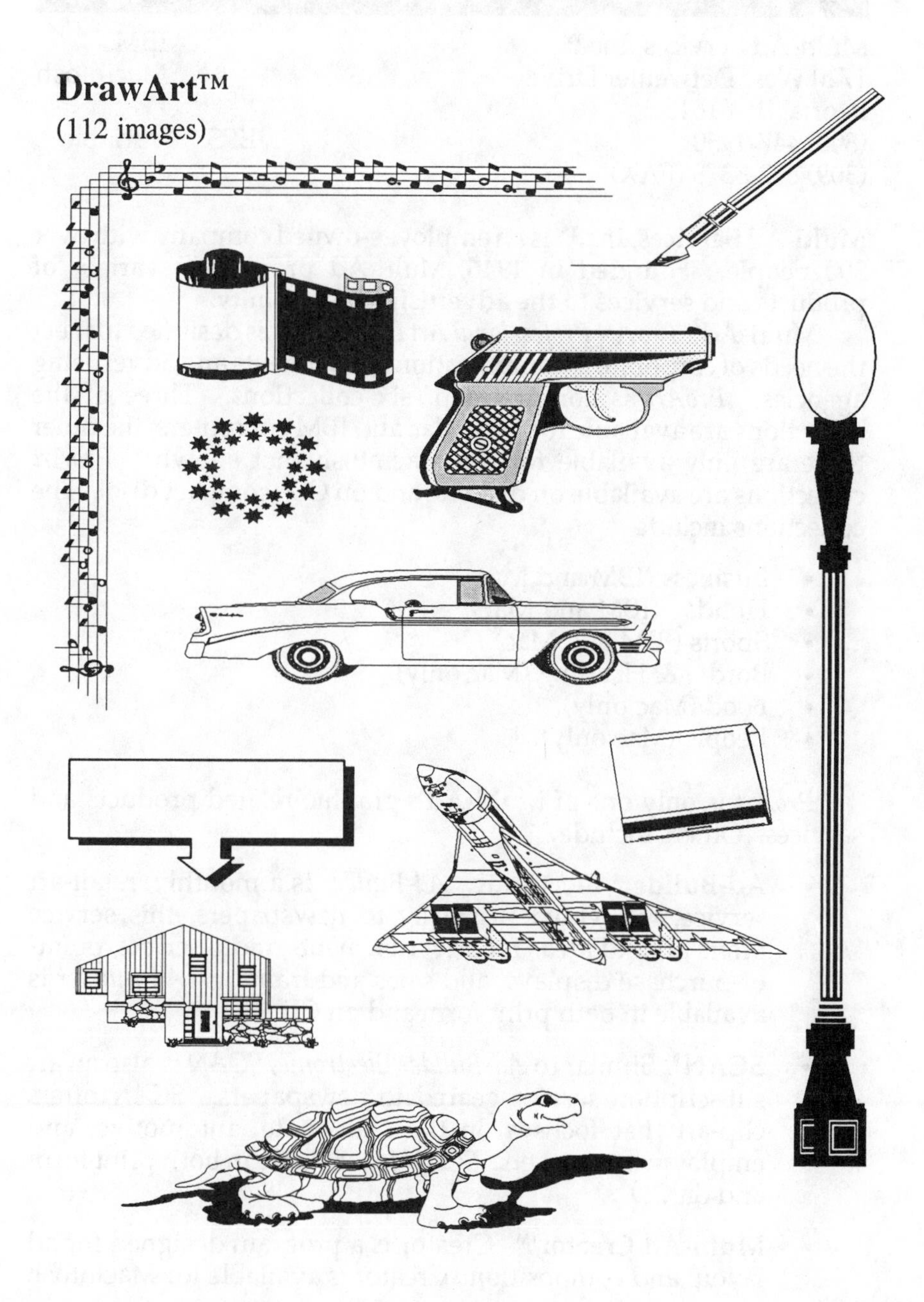

Multi-Ad

Multi-Ad Services, Inc.™
1720 West Detweiller Drive
Peoria, IL 61615
(800) 447-1950
(309) 692-8378 (FAX)

IBM
Macintosh

EPS: Variable

Multi-Ad Services, Inc.™ is an employee-owned company with over 300 people. Founded in 1946, Multi-Ad provides a variety of products and services to the advertising community.

Multi-Ad's *ProArt Professional Art Library™* was designed to meet the needs of corporate communication departments and advertising agencies. *ProArt* is comprised of six collections. Three of the collections are available for both Mac and IBM computers; the other three are only available for the Macintosh (not shown). *ProArt* collections are available on diskette and on CD (compact disc). The collections include

- Business (IBM and Mac).
- Holiday (IBM and Mac).
- Sports (IBM and Mac).
- Border & Heading (Mac only).
- Food (Mac only).
- People (Mac only).

ProArt is only one of Multi-Ad's graphic-related products and services. Others include

- **Ad-Builder® Electronic**. *Ad-Builder* is a monthly, retail-art service. Provided primarily to newspapers, this service offers art and ideas for advertisements, radio scripts, point-of-purchase displays, and sales and training. *Ad-Builder* is available in both print form and on CD.

- **SCAN®**. Similar to *Ad-Builder Electronic, SCAN* is also an art subscription service geared to newspapers. *SCAN* offers clip-art that focuses on the real estate, automotive, and employment markets. *SCAN* is available in both print form and on CD.

- **Multi-Ad Creator™**. Creator is a program designed for ad layout and composition. Creator is available for Macintosh computers.

- **Kwikee® Illustration System.** Kwikee is a collection of print clip-art of products from major US food manufacturers. Kwikee is distributed free of charge to advertising chains and supermarkets. Other Kwikee systems exist for other markets including Mass Merchandising, Automotive, and Toy & Games.

IBM System Requirements

- PostScript printer or typesetter.
- Program that can read *.EPS* files.

Macintosh System Requirements

- PostScript printer or typesetter.
- Program that can read *.EPS* files.

ProArt
The Business Collection
(132 images)

ProArt
The Holiday Collection
(118 images)

ProArt
The Sports Collection
(108 images)

One Mile Up

One Mile Up, Inc.
7011 Evergreen Court
Annandale, VA 22003
(703) 642-1177

IBM
Macintosh

EPS: Variable

Founded in 1987, **One Mile Up, Inc.** specializes in clip-art images for the United States government, the Department of Defense, and contractors doing business with the Federal government.

One Mile Up's collection of clip-art is called *Federal Clip Art*. Federal Clip Art is available for IBM (MS-DOS), Macintosh, and UNIX-based computers.

In addition the clip-art provided in the package, the purchaser is invited to select and send away for five additional images which are provided without charge. The purchaser may select from a variety of illustrations such as government leaders, computers, and the emblems and seals of various United States government agencies and departments.[1]

IBM System Requirements

- Postscript printer or typesetter.
- Program that can read *.EPS* files.

Macintosh System Requirements

- Postscript printer or typesetter.
- 800K disk drive (hard disk recommended).
- 1 Meg RAM (more memory recommended).
- Program that can read *.EPS* files.

---

[1] Although One Mile Up offers clip-art of the seals and emblems of the United States government, the use of some these seals and emblems is regulated by Federal law. Misuse of official seals and emblems may be punishable by fine and/or imprisonment.

Federal Clip Art™
(159 images)

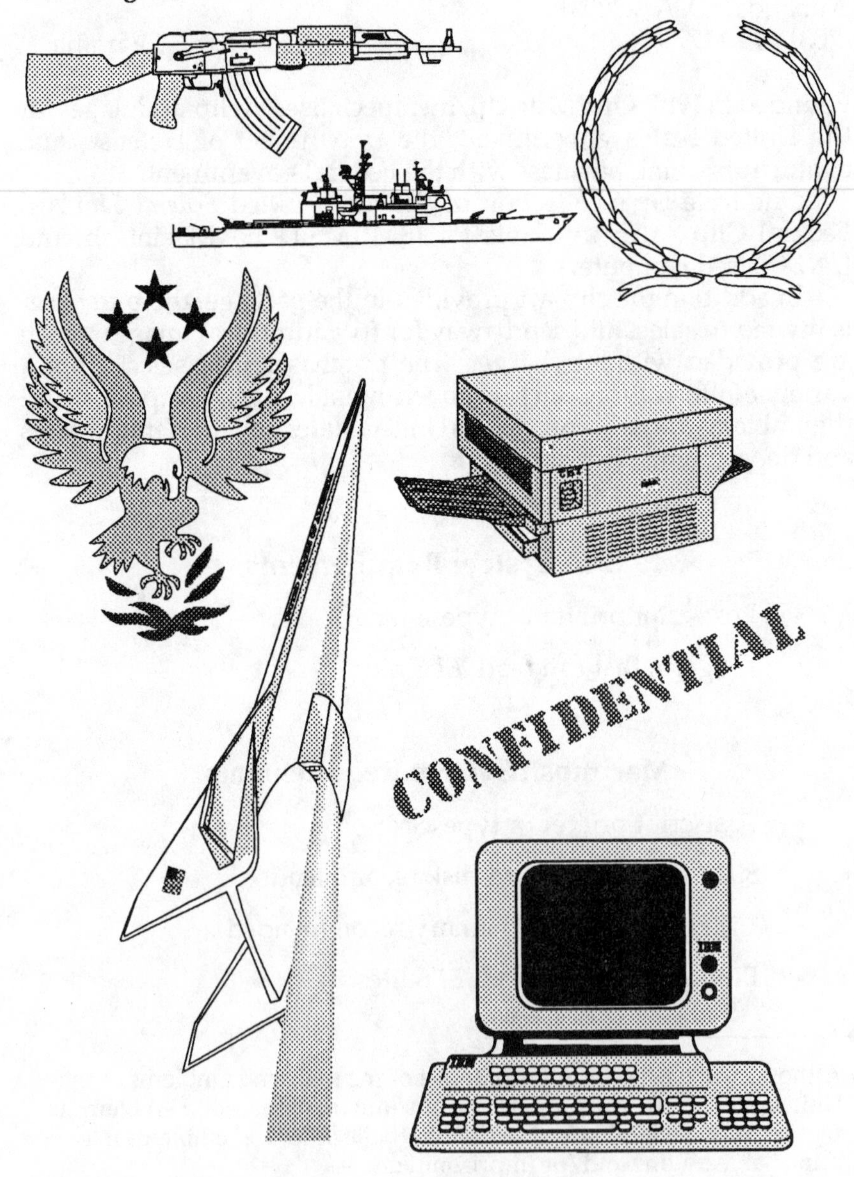

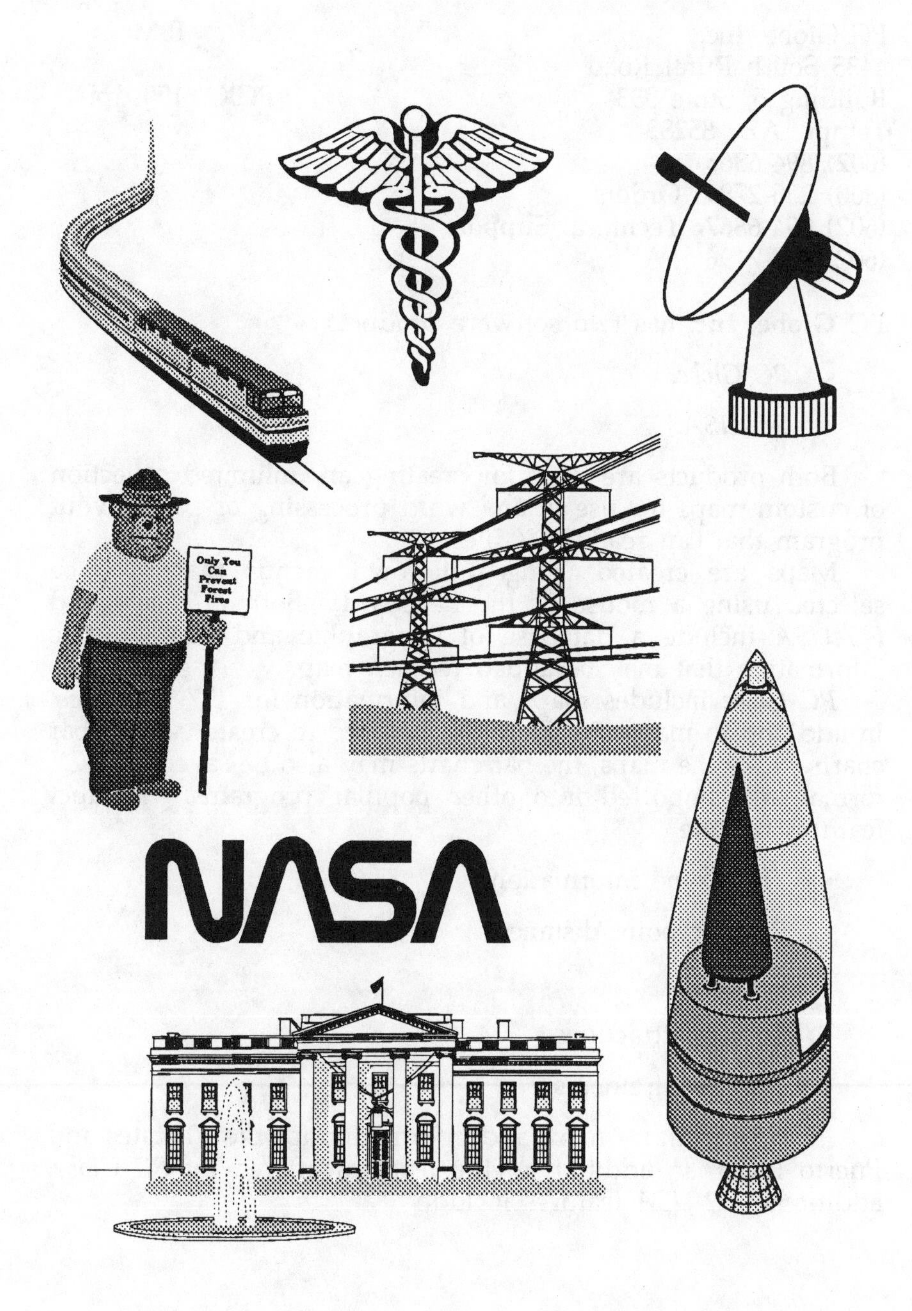
Only You
Can
Prevent
Forest
Fires
NASA

PC Globe

PC Globe, Inc.
4435 South Rural Road
Building 5, Suite 333
Tempe, AZ 85282
(602) 894-6866
(800) 255-2789 Orders
(602) 894-6867 Technical Support
(602) 968-7196 FAX

IBM

PCX 150 dpi

PC Globe, Inc. has two software products.

- *PC Globe.*
- *PC USA.*

Both products are used for creating an unlimited collection of custom maps for use in any word processing or page layout program that can read .PCX files.

Maps are created using pull-down menus that may be selected using a mouse or the keyboard. Both *PC Globe* and *PC USA* include a database of geographic and demographic information that may be added to each map.

PC Globe includes maps and information for 177 countries. In addition to maps, *PC Globe* can be used to create custom bar charts. Like the maps, the bar charts may also be saved in .PCX format and imported into other popular programs. Product features include

- Time zone information.
- Point-to-point distances.
- Climates.
- Tourist attractions.
- Visa requirements.

PC USA includes maps and information for the 50 states and Puerto Rico. In addition to the features offered by *PC Globe*, additional *PC USA* features include

- Population information.
- Average retail sales.
- Per capita income.
- Private housing construction.
- Economic trends.
- Tax rates.
- Area codes and zip codes.

A Demo disk is available for a nominal fee.

IBM System Requirements

- 512K RAM.
- DOS 2.0+ or higher.

PC Globe Sample Maps

(Unlimited images)

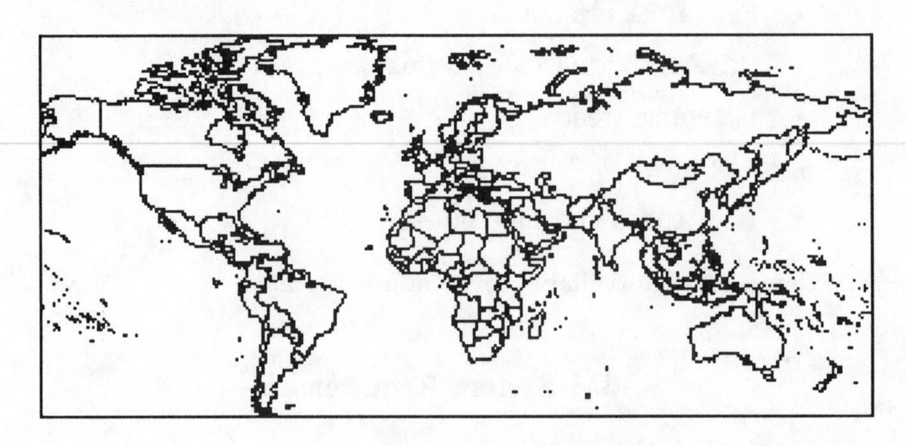

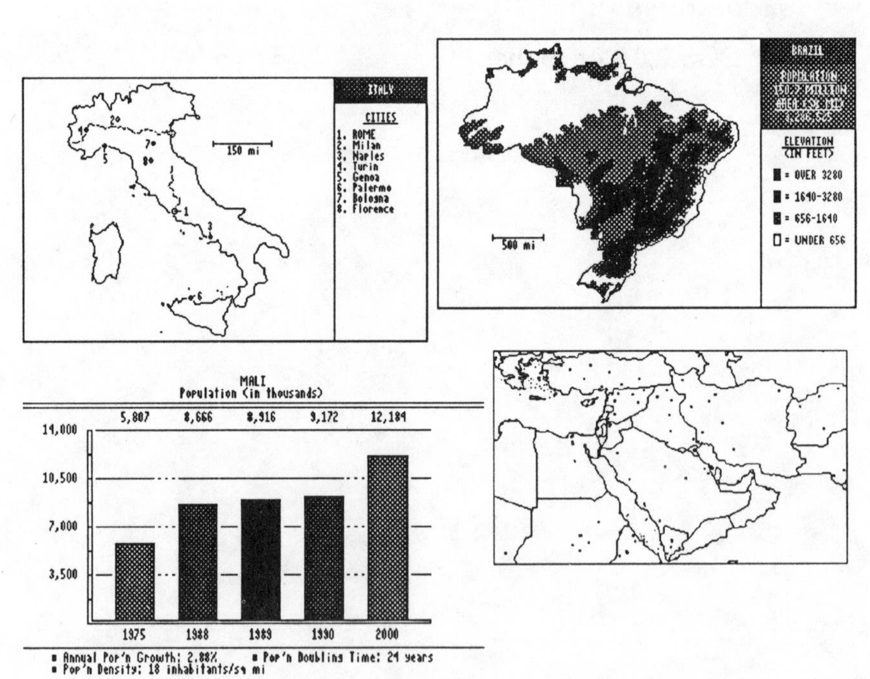

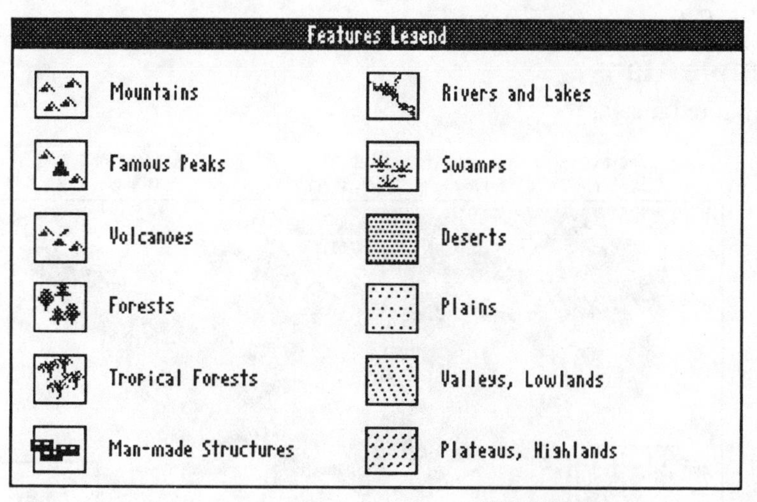
Features Legend
Mountains
Rivers and Lakes
Famous Peaks
Swamps
Volcanoes
Deserts
Forests
Plains
Tropical Forests
Valleys, Lowlands
Man-made Structures
Plateaus, Highlands

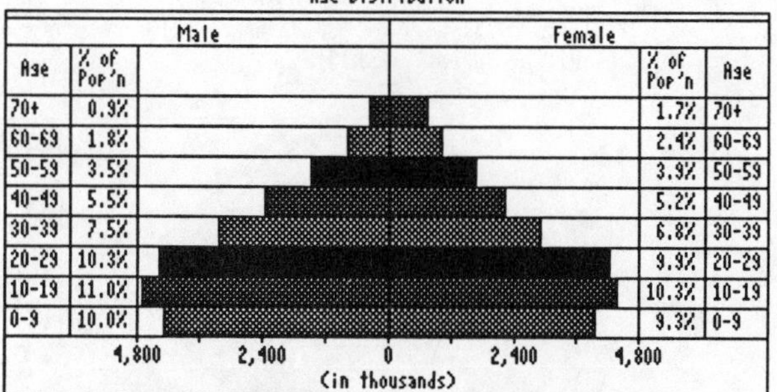
SOUTH KOREA
Age Distribution
Male
Female
Age
% of Pop'n
70+ 0.9% 1.7% 70+
60-69 1.8% 2.4% 60-69
50-59 3.5% 3.9% 50-59
40-49 5.5% 5.2% 40-49
30-39 7.5% 6.8% 30-39
20-29 10.3% 9.9% 20-29
10-19 11.0% 10.3% 10-19
0-9 10.0% 9.3% 0-9
4,800 2,400 0 2,400 4,800
(in thousands)
Total Population: 42,773,000
Total Male Pop'n: 21,600,000
Total Female Pop'n: 21,173,000
Literacy Rate: 90%
Urbanization: 65.4%

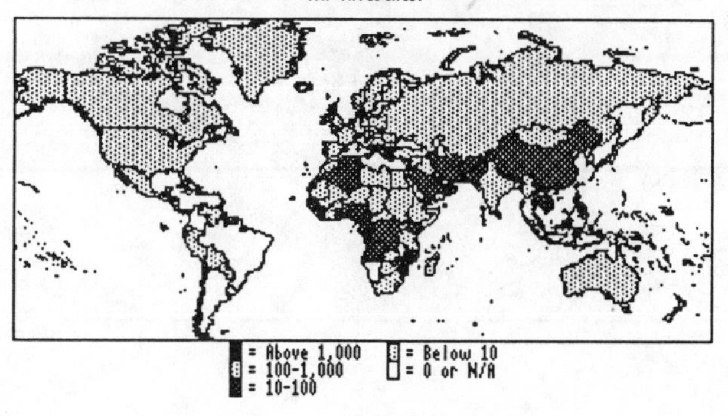
POPULATION PER PHARMACIST
(in thousands)
= Above 1,000
= 100-1,000
= 10-100
= Below 10
= 0 or N/A

PC USA
Sample Maps

(Unlimited images)

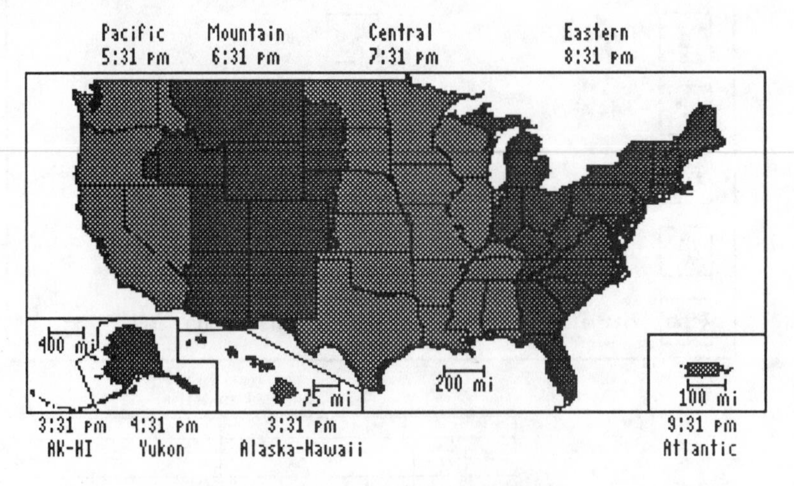

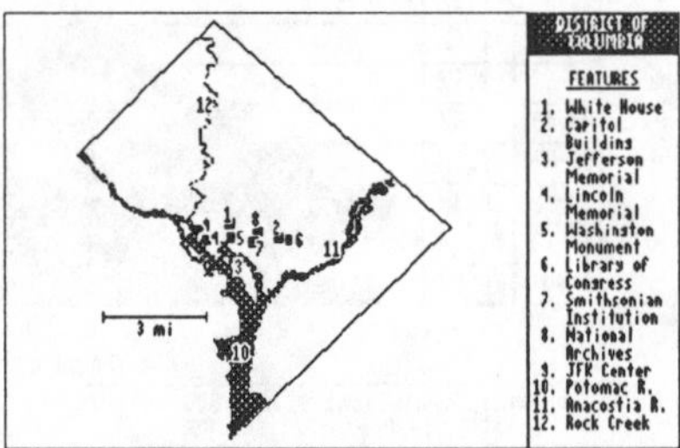

Distance = 1,961 miles   Bearing = 269.3 degrees

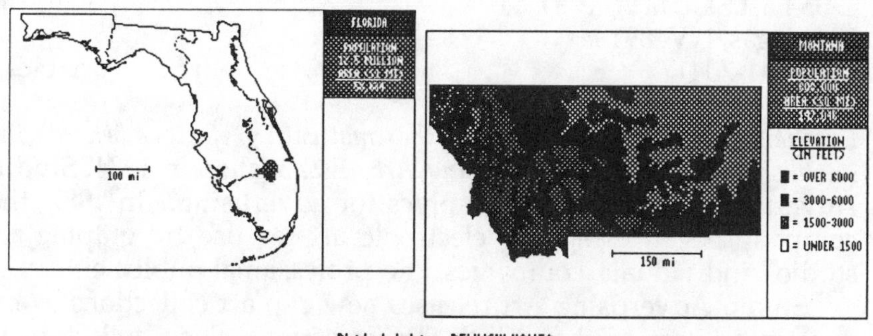

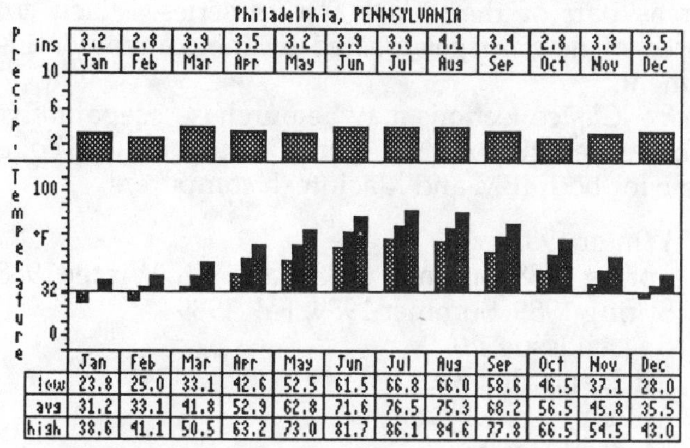

ins	Jan	Feb	Mar	Apr	May	Jun	Jul	Aug	Sep	Oct	Nov	Dec
	3.2	2.8	3.9	3.5	3.2	3.9	3.9	4.1	3.4	2.8	3.3	3.5

	Jan	Feb	Mar	Apr	May	Jun	Jul	Aug	Sep	Oct	Nov	Dec
low	23.8	25.0	33.1	42.6	52.5	61.5	66.8	66.0	58.6	46.5	37.1	28.0
avg	31.2	33.1	41.8	52.9	62.8	71.6	76.5	75.3	68.2	56.5	45.8	35.5
high	38.6	41.1	50.5	63.2	73.0	81.7	86.1	84.6	77.8	66.5	54.5	43.0

1803 Louisiana Purchase - France

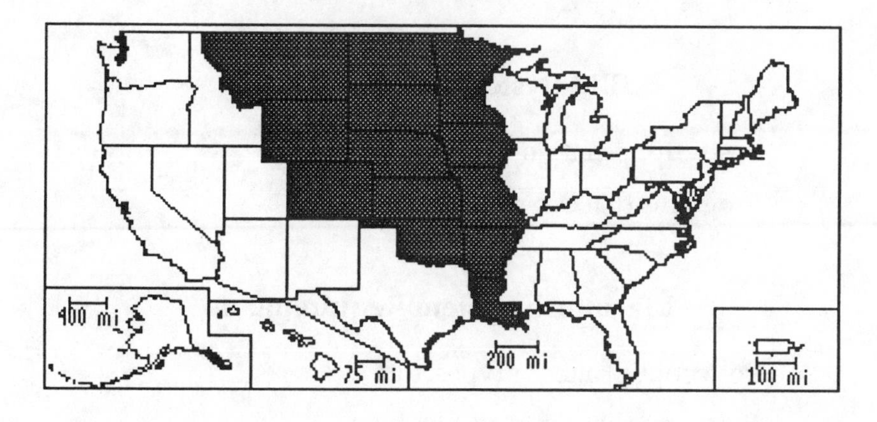

Studio Advertising Art

Studio Advertising Art
4305 East Sahara Ave. #1
Las Vegas, NV 89104
(702) 641-7041

IBM
Macintosh

EPS: Variable

Excellence in advertising was the motivating factor behind the establishment of Studio Advertising Art. Established in 1984, **Studio Advertising Art** designed graphics for advertising. In 1987, the company began designing electronic art for use by graphic art studios, individuals, companies, and professional publishers.

Studio Advertising Art releases new clip-art collections every quarter as part of their *Click & Clip* series. Each collection is composed of new images created by the company's in-house art department.

Click & Clip collections may be purchased separately or as part of Studio Advertising Art's subscription service. All collections are available for both IBM and Macintosh computers.

- Winter 1987
- Spring 1988, Summer 1988, Fall 1988, Winter 1988
- Spring 1989, Summer 1989, Fall 1989
- Special Issue 1.0
- Click and Clip 500
- Military Art 1.1
- Medical Health
- Road & Warning Signs

IBM System Requirements

- Postscript printer or typesetter.
- Programs that can read EPS files.

Macintosh System Requirements

- Postscript printer or typesetter.
- Programs that can read EPS files.

Click & Clip
Winter Issue 1987
(50 images)

Click & Clip
Spring Issue 1988
(50 images)

Click & Clip
Summer Issue 1988
(49 images)

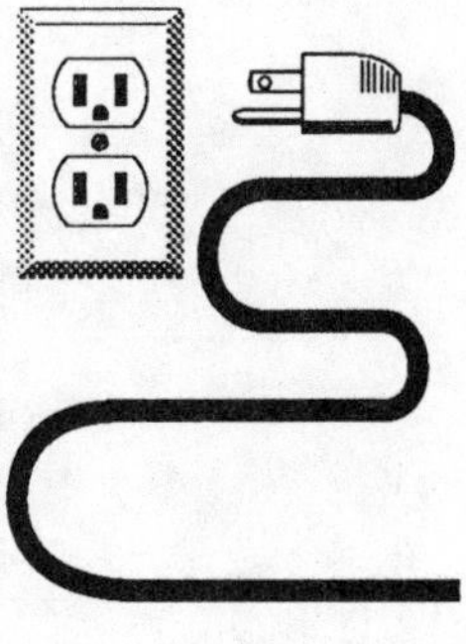

Click & Clip
Fall Issue 1988
(50 images)

Click & Clip
Winter Issue 1988
(50 images)

Click & Clip
Spring Issue 1989
(50 images)

Click & Clip
Summer Issue 1989
(50 images)

Click & Clip
Fall 1989
(51 images)

Click & Clip
Special Issue 1.0
(20 images)

Click & Clip
500 Illustrations
(503 images)

NEWS

Click & Clip
Military Art 1.1
(147 images)

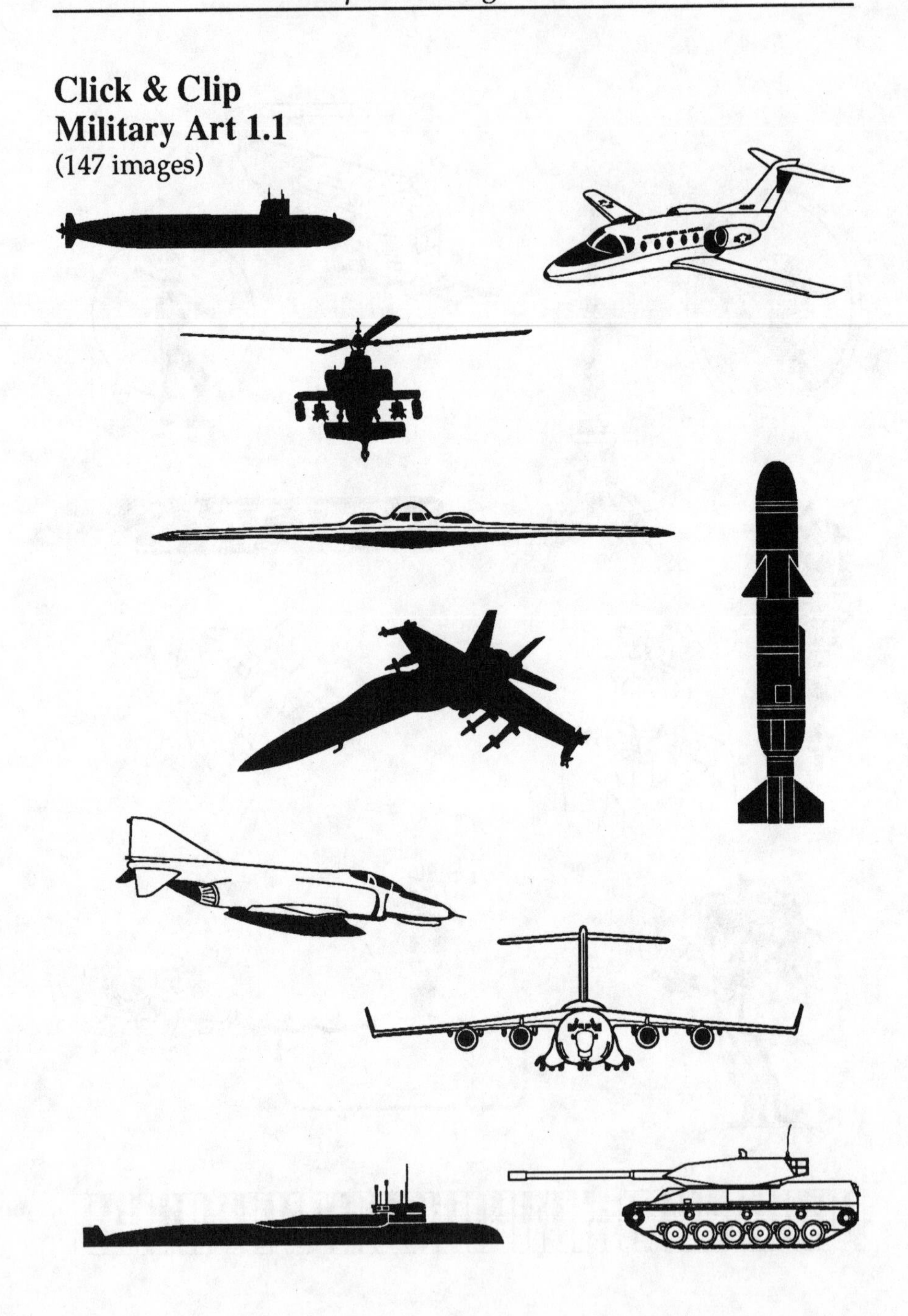

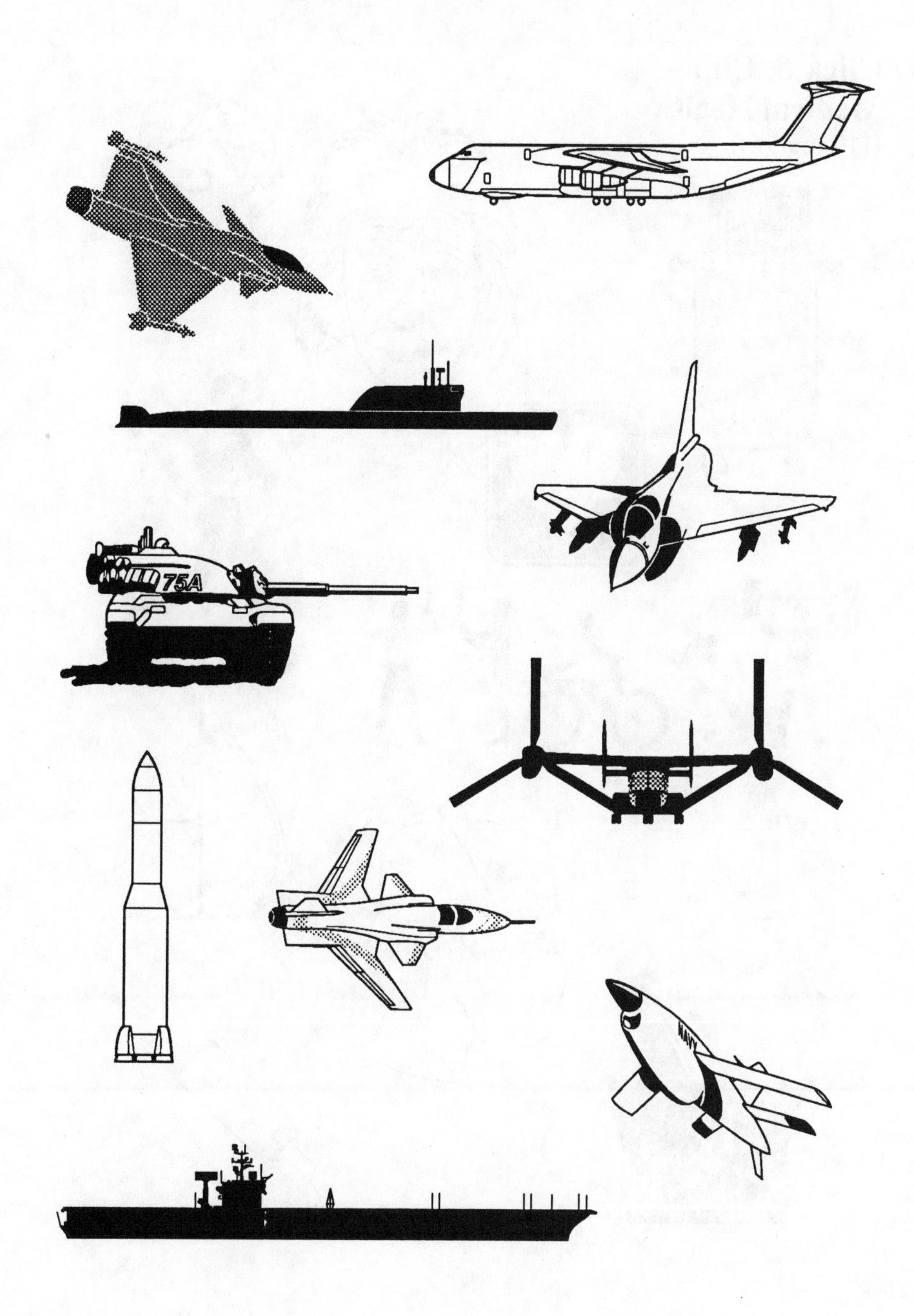
75A

Click & Clip
Medical Health
(110 images)

Click & Clip
Road & Warning Signs
(105 images)

T/Maker

T/Maker Company
1390 Villa Street
Mountain View, CA 94041
(415) 962-0195 Orders/Information
(415) 962-0201 FAX

IBM
Macintosh

IBM:	EPS	Variable
	GEM/PCX	72 dpi
	MSP/PCX	72 dpi
Mac:	EPS	Variable
	Paint	72 dpi

Founded in 1979, **T/Maker Company** is dedicated to developing and shipping graphic-oriented products. T/Maker has seven clip-art collections which the company refers to as *ClickArt*®. Each collection is available for both IBM and Macintosh computers. Different collections are offered in various formats for each of the two systems. A detailed user manual and index is included with each collection.

EPS Collections

Two of T/Maker's collections are offered in the *.EPS* format. Each collection includes over 180 images. Some are a full-page in size.

- Business Art.
- EPS Illustrations.

Non-EPS Collections

T/Maker offers five *ClickArt* collections in non-EPS formats.

- Business Images.
- Christian Images.
- Holidays.
- Personal Graphics.
- Publications.

Collections for the IBM are available in either the GEM/PCX or MSP/PCX (Windows) formats. *Note: In some collections, the GEM format contains fewer images.*

Collections for the Macintosh are supplied in both the MacPaint and HyperCard Stackware formats.

In addition to *ClickArt*, T/Maker offers other graphic-oriented products, including

- *Scrapbook+*, a program which lets you store, organize, view, retrieve, and manipulate graphic images. (IBM only)
- *ClipOut*, a painting and organization tool that lets you access MacPaint files without leaving your current program. *ClipOut* is included free with all non-EPS art collections. (Macintosh only)
- *Effects*, a tool which lets you rotate, slant, distort, or change the perspective of graphic images. (Macintosh only)

IBM System Requirements

EPS Collections

- Postscript-compatible printer.

Other Collections

- No special requirements.

Macintosh System Requirements

EPS Collections

- Postscript-compatible printer.
- One 800K Disk Drive.

Other Collections

- No special requirements.

ClickArt® /EPS Business Art
(220 images)

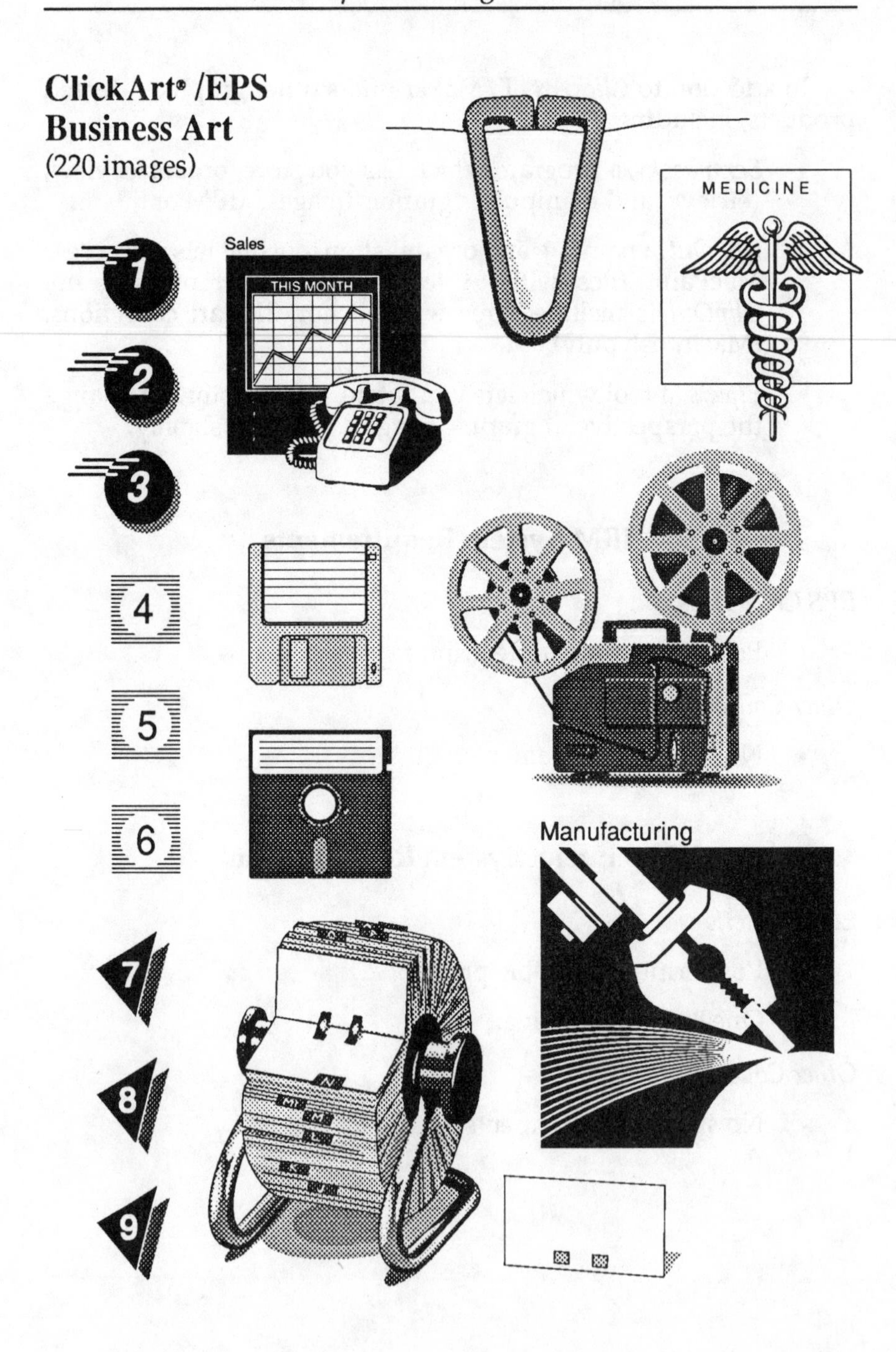

VISA
AMERICAN EXPRESS

ClickArt®/EPS Illustrations
(177 images)

ANNOUNCEMENTS

ClickArt® Business Images

(1,246 images)

ClickArt®
Christian Images
(602 images)

WELCOME
IHS
Announcing
Bulletin Board
BAZAAR
CARNIVAL
FESTIVAL

ClickArt®
Holidays
(251 images)

BOO!
Happy
Mother's Day
Happy
Hanukkah

ClickArt®
Personal Graphics
(139 images)

ASAP!

8 Appendix

Foreign Language Fonts

Many foreign language fonts are available for IBM-compatible computers. Some foreign language fonts are available in the PostScript format and others are available in the LaserJet format.

Two lists of foreign language fonts appear on the following pages: one for PostScript fonts and the other for LaserJet fonts. Each list is in alphabetical order by foreign language (left-most column). A complete list of font company addresses and phone numbers appears at the end of the *Appendix*.

PostScript

Language	Font Name	Font Company
Albanian	Albanian	VN Labs
Arabic	Arabic	VN Labs
Armenian	Armenian	VN Labs
Bulgarian	Bulgarian	VN Labs
Bulgarian	Cyrillic	Casady & Greene
Bulgarian	Glasnost	Casady & Greene
Bulgarian	Murmansk	Casady & Greene
Bulgarian	Odessa Script	Casady & Greene
Croatian	Croatian	VN Labs
Czechoslovak	Czechoslovak	VN Labs

Language	Font Name	Font Company
Danish	Danish	VN Labs
Dutch	Dutch	VN Labs
Esperanto	Esperanto	VN Labs
Estonian	Estonian	VN Labs
Farsi	Farsi	VN Labs
Finnish	Finnish	VN Labs
French	French	VN Labs
German	German	VN Labs
Greek	Greek	VN Labs
Hebrew	Hebrew	VN Labs
Hungarian	Hungarian	VN Labs
Icelandic	Icelandic	VN Labs
Italian	Italian	VN Labs
Latvian	Latvian	VN Labs
Lithuanian	Lithuanian	VN Labs
Macedonian	Macedonian	VN Labs
Maltese	Maltese	VN Labs
Norwegian	Norwegian	VN Labs
Polish	Polish	VN Labs
Portuguese	Portuguese	VN Labs
Romanian	Romanian	VN Labs
Russian	Cyrillic	Casady & Greene
Russian	Glasnost	Casady & Greene
Russian	Murmansk	Casady & Greene
Russian	Odessa Script	Casady & Greene
Russian	Russian	VN Labs
Serbian	Cyrillic	Casady & Greene
Serbian	Glasnost	Casady & Greene
Serbian	Murmansk	Casady & Greene
Serbian	Odessa Script	Casady & Greene
Serbian	Serbian	VN Labs
Spanish	Spanish	VN Labs
Swedish	Swedish	VN Labs
Turkish	Turkish	VN Labs
Ukrainian	Cyrillic	Casady & Greene
Ukrainian	Glasnost	Casady & Greene
Ukrainian	Murmansk	Casady & Greene
Ukrainian	Odessa Script	Casady & Greene
Ukrainian	Ukrainian	VN Labs

Language	Font Name	Font Company
Urdu	Urdu	VN Labs
Vietnamese	Vietnamese	VN Labs

LaserJet

Language	Font Name	Font Company
Albanian	Albanian	VN Labs
Arabic	Arabic	VN Labs
Armenian	Armenian	VN Labs
Bulgarian	Bulgarian	VN Labs
Croatian	Croatian	VN Labs
Czechoslovak	Czechoslovak	VN Labs
Danish	Danish	VN Labs
Dutch	Dutch	VN Labs
Esperanto	Esperanto	VN Labs
Estonian	Estonian	VN Labs
Farsi	Farsi	VN Labs
Finnish	Finnish	VN Labs
French	French	VN Labs
French	French Classic*	SoftCraft
French	French San Serif**	SoftCraft
German	German	SoftCraft
German	German Italic	SoftCraft
German	German	VN Labs
Greek	Greek	SoftCraft
Greek	Greek	VN Labs
Greek	Greek	VS Software
Hebrew	Hebrew	SoftCraft
Hebrew	Hebrew	VN Labs
Hungarian	Hungarian	VN Labs
Icelandic	Icelandic	VN Labs
Indic	Indic***	SoftCraft
Indic	Indic Italic	SoftCraft
Italian	Italian	VN Labs
Japanese	Japanese (Hiragana and Katakana)	SoftCraft
Latvian	Latvian	VN Labs

Language	Font Name	Font Company
Lithuanian	Lithuanian	VN Labs
Macedonian	Macedonian	VN Labs
Maltese	Maltese	VN Labs
Norwegian	Norwegian	VN Labs
Polish	Polish	VN Labs
Portuguese	Portuguese	VN Labs
Proto-Indoeuropean	Proto-Indoeuropean	SoftCraft
Romanian	Romanian	VN Labs
Russian	Cyrillic	SoftCraft
Russian	Russian	VN Labs
Serbian	Serbian	VN Labs
Spanish	Spanish	VN Labs
Spanish	Spanish Classic*	SoftCraft
Spanish	Spanish San Serif**	SoftCraft
Swedish	Swedish	VN Labs
Turkish	Turkish	VN Labs
Ukrainian	Ukrainian	VN Labs
Urdu	Urdu	VN Labs
Vietnamese	Vietnamese	VN Labs

* Weights are Regular, Italic, Bold, Fixed Width, Fixed Bold

** Weights are Regular, Italic, Bold, Compressed

*** Transliterated

Symbol Fonts

Several companies offer a variety of symbol fonts for the IBM PCs and compatibles. Some symbol fonts are available in the PostScript format while others are designed for the LaserJet.

Two lists of symbol language fonts appear on the following pages: one for PostScript fonts and the other for LaserJet fonts. Each list is in alphabetical order by subject matter (left-most column). The middle column show you the name of the font. The right column give you the name of the company which offers the font. A complete list of font company addresses and phone numbers appears at the end of the *Appendix*.

PostScript

Symbol Subject	Font Name	Font Company
Commercial Symbols	Universal News & Commercial Pi	Adobe
Commercial Symbols	Symbol A Monospaced Sanserif	Bitstream
Commercial Symbols	Symbol A Proportional Serif	Bitstream
Dingbats	Carta	Adobe
Dingbats	ITC Zapf Dingbats	Adobe
Dingbats	ITC Zapf Dingbats	Bitstream
Dingbats (decorative)	Ornaments	Adobe
Greek	Universal Greek & Math Pi	Adobe
IBM Keys/Components	KeyCaps	Paperback
Macintosh Keys	KeyCaps	Paperback
Math Symbols	Universal Greek & Math Pi	Adobe
MICR Characters[1]	MICR	Adobe
Music Notation	Sonata	Adobe

LaserJet

Symbol Subject	Font Name	Font Company
Accents and Ligatures	Accents & Ligatures	SoftCraft
Bar Code	Barcode 3-of-9	Good
Bar Code	Barcode EAN/UPC	Good

---

[1] Magnetic Ink Character Recognition.

Symbol Subject	Font Name	Font Company
Bar Code/OCR	Bar Code/OCR Fonts	SoftCraft
Borders	Borders	SoftCraft
Borders (ornate)	Divine Borders I	SoftCraft
Borders (ornate)	Divine Borders II	SoftCraft
Chess pieces	Chess	SoftCraft
Commercial Symbols	Copyright & Symbols	SoftCraft
Commercial Symbols	Special Font 1	VS Software
Commercial Symbols	Special Font 2	VS Software
Commercial Symbols	Symbol A Monospaced Sanserif	Bitstream
Commercial Symbols	Symbol A Proportional Serif	Bitstream
Commercial Symbols	Symbols Mono	SoftCraft
Commercial Symbols	Symbols Proportional	SoftCraft
Dingbats	Dingbats	SoftCraft
Dingbats	ITC Zapf Dingbats	Bitstream
Dingbats	ITC Zapf Dingbats	Good
Dingbats	ITC Zapf Dingbats	HP
Dingbats	Zapf Dingbats	SoftCraft
Dingbats	Zingbats	SWFTE
Dots/border patterns	Dots/Vertical Borders	SoftCraft
Keys	Keys	SoftCraft
Key Tops	Key Tops	SoftCraft
Manual alphabet	Manual Alphabet	SoftCraft
Math Symbols	Math Symbols	SoftCraft
Math Symbols	Math Symbols	VS Software
Math & Greek Symbols	Classic Special Symbols	SoftCraft
Music notation	Music	SoftCraft
Phonetic alphabet	International Phonetic Alphabet	SoftCraft

Foreign Language & Symbol Font Companies

Adobe® Systems, Inc.
1585 Charleston Road
Mountain View, CA 94039
(800) 83-FONTS / (415) 962-2100

Bitstream, Inc.
215 First Street
Cambridge, MA 02142
(800) 522-FONT / (617) 497-6222
(617) 868-4732 FAX

Casady & Green, Inc.
P.O. Box 223779
Carmel, CA 93922
(408) 624-8716

Good Software, Inc.
13601 Preston Road
Suite 500W
Dallas, TX 75240
(214) 239-6085 Information
(214) 329-4643 FAX

Hewlett-Packard Company
P.O. Box 10301
Palo Alto, CA 94303
(415) 857-1501

Paperback Software
2830 Ninth Street
Berkeley, CA 94710
(415) 644-2166

SoftCraft, Inc.
16 North Carroll Street
Suite 500
Madison, WI 53703
(800) 351-0500 Sales
(608) 257-3300 Technical Support
(608) 257-6733 FAX

SWFTE International
P.O. Box 219
Rockland, DE 19732
(302) 429-8434
(302) 429-0532 FAX

VS Software
2103 South Broadway
Little Rock, AR 72206
(501) 376-2083
(501) 372-7075 FAX

VN Labs
P.O. Box 9878
Newport Beach, CA 92658
(714) 474-6968
(714) 250-8117 FAX

9 Index

Note: Font prefixes such as Adobe, Bitstream, CG, HP, ITC, SWFTE, and VS were not taken into consideration for alphabetization.